THE HIDDEN POWER OF DREAMS

ALSO BY DENISE LINN

Books/Oracle Cards

Altars: *Bringing Sacred Shrines into Your Everyday Life*

Dream Lover: *Using Your Dreams to Enhance Love in Your Life*

Feng Shui for the Soul: *How to Create a Harmonious Environment That Will Nurture and Sustain You**

Four Acts of Personal Power: *How to Heal Your Past and Create a Positive Future**

If I Can Forgive, So Can You: *My Autobiography of How I Overcame My Past and Healed My Life**

Past Lives, Present Miracles: *The Most Empowering Book on Reincarnation You'll Ever Read . . . in This Lifetime!**

Quest: *A Guide for Creating Your Own Vision Quest*

Sacred Space: *Clearing and Enhancing the Energy of Your Home*

The Secret Language of Signs: *How to Interpret the Coincidences and Symbols in Your Life*

Secrets & Mysteries: *The Glory and Pleasure of Being a Woman**

Soul Coaching: *28 Days to Discover Your Authentic Self**

Soul Coaching Oracle Cards: *What Your Soul Wants You to Know* (a 52-card deck)*

The Soul Loves the Truth: *Lessons Learned on My Path to Joy**

Space Clearing: *How to Purify and Create Harmony in Your Home*

Space Clearing A–Z: *How to Use Feng Shui to Purify and Bless Your Home**

Audio Programs

Angels! Angels! Angels!
Cellular Regeneration
Complete Relaxation*
Dreams
Journeys into Past Lives*
Life Force
Past Lives and Beyond
Phoenix Rising
The Way of the Drum

Video

Instinctive Feng Shui for Creating Sacred Space*

*Available from Hay House

Please visit Hay House USA: **www.hayhouse.com**®
Hay House Australia: **www.hayhouse.com.au**
Hay House UK: **www.hayhouse.co.uk**
Hay House South Africa: **www.hayhouse.co.za**
Hay House India: **www.hayhouse.co.in**

THE HIDDEN POWER OF DREAMS

The Mysterious World of Dreams Revealed

Denise Linn

HAY HOUSE, INC.
Carlsbad, California • New York City
London • Sydney • Johannesburg
Vancouver • Hong Kong • New Delhi

Copyright © 1988 by Denise Linn
Revised copyright © 2009

Published and distributed in the United States by: Hay House, Inc.: www.hayhouse.com • *Published and distributed in Australia by:* Hay House Australia Pty. Ltd.: www.hayhouse.com.au • *Published and distributed in the United Kingdom by:* Hay House UK, Ltd.: www.hayhouse.co.uk • *Published and distributed in the Republic of South Africa by:* Hay House SA (Pty), Ltd.: www.hayhouse.co.za • *Distributed in Canada by:* Raincoast: www.raincoast.com • *Published in India by:* Hay House Publishers India: www.hayhouse.co.in

Editorial supervision: Jill Kramer • *Design:* Jen Kennedy
Indexer: Richard Comfort: **http://comfortindexing.com**

The poems by M. Anne Sweet and Karl Bettinger are used by permission of the authors.

Originally published in 1988 in Australia by Nacson & Sons under the title *Pocketful of Dreams.*

Library of Congress Cataloging-in-Publication Data

Linn, Denise.
  The hidden power of dreams : the mysterious world of dreams revealed / Denise Linn.
    p. cm.
  Includes index.
  ISBN 978-1-4019-1791-3 (tradepaper : alk. paper) 1. Dreams. 2. Dream interpretation. I. Title.
  BF1091.L55 2009
  135'.3--dc22

                              2008012646

ISBN: 978-1-4019-1791-3

14 13 12 11   6 5 4 3
1st Hay House edition, March 2009
3rd edition, April 2011

This book is dedicated to David, the man of my dreams;
and to Meadow, my dream child.

❦ CONTENTS ❦

As I travel through this lifetime
swimming down the stream,
I pick up many baubles,
people, places, things.

The one thing I'll take with me
when it's time to leave the stream,
isn't any bauble,
it's the power of my dreams.

— **Karl Bettinger**

༄ ༄ ༄

INTENT

Each of us is on a quest, a journey that carries us through time and space. Your quest has led you to this book, and it will continue to lead you through your personal evolution. The purpose of this book is to show you how your dreams can help you penetrate the realm beyond your physical senses to gain answers to your deepest questions and help you reach self-knowledge. My intent is to provide information that will allow you to discover your own internal answers, which aren't found in anyone's teaching but are woven within your feelings, within the patterns of your life, and within your dreams.

𝕯 𝕯 𝕯 𝕯 𝕯 𝕯

THE BEGINNING

Dreams are the mysterious language of the night. Each evening after the setting sun has beckoned the moon, a golden harvest is woven into our slumbering consciousness. Visions from the enigmatic, nocturnal realm have been described as messages from the gods and have helped shape the destiny of individuals as well as nations. Since the dawn of time, dream weavers have slipped through the crack between the two worlds to touch the reaches of inner space and reap the bounty of the night.

These secret messages can foretell your future, reveal your past, and warn you of danger. They can contain creative inspiration or assist in releasing the barriers in your life. Dreams can serve as a doorway to a mystic arena for inner-dimensional travel and communication with loved ones who have passed on. They can be a springboard for night healing, astral travel, and soul searching.

But we have forgotten.

Dreams are now but relics of the mind. We no longer call on the Muses of the Night, as people in the far past did. In those ancient times, when the cycles of nature and man were closely intertwined, dreams directed the course of the tribe or culture. They were a natural outflow originating from a deep alignment with the forces of nature. In those night hours, the emissaries of nighttime wisdom were called upon to send forth inner truths, and they answered by providing invaluable information.

But we have forgotten.

It has become commonplace to consider sleep as a time when we don't do anything productive. We acknowledge the reality of dreams; however, even if we can recall them, they're rarely considered valuable or imperative to our well-being, as are the *real* events of the day.

When our children have nightmares, we comfort them by saying, "It's only a dream," casually tossing aside a remarkable communication from the depths of their being. At best, dreams are viewed as an inner data processing of the mind.

But the time has come to remember. We're passing through a crucial period on our planet. It will become increasingly important to awaken the dreamer within each of us and listen to the oracle of the heart so that we may step lightly through the times ahead.

My Dream Journey

My journey into the realm of dreams began on an early summer afternoon more than 40 years ago in the Midwest. It was a glorious day, with golden summer haze dusting the fields. Amber swirls of wheat and honey-colored corn tassels sailed by on either side of me as I joyously drove my motorbike down the back roads of our rural farming community. I was 17 years old. Suddenly, the serenity of that summer day was shattered by a gunman's bullet. I was left for dead by an unknown assailant. In that one piercing instant, my life and all that was familiar to me spun crazily; when it settled, I was no longer the same person.

Someone driving by summoned an ambulance, and I was taken to a nearby hospital. As I lay in the emergency room, struggling with searing pain, abruptly the pain subsided and I was enveloped in a quiet stillness. And then a velvet-soft, gentle blackness descended. Was I dead? I felt as if I were encased in a black bubble. Then suddenly the orb burst, and I was bathed in brilliant light. It was a most peculiar experience—because I *was* the light. I was an all-pervading, luminescent light. I then became aware of sweet, pure music that ebbed and flowed like waves of liquid light wafting through the universe. It was more exquisite than any symphony I'd ever heard. This undulating harmony pervaded me until I *became* the music. In that moment, I was made only of light and sound.

There was nothing that wasn't me. I had no sense of time—no past or future. Everything just *was* . . . and at the same time, I felt so loved and so very loving. Something about the place that I'd traveled to—when I left my body—felt familiar. *I knew that I'd been there before.*

In each of us resides an intuitive sense of love that's as natural as breathing, which goes beyond all boundaries, beyond form, like an unlimited ocean penetrating every cell and molecule of our being. I felt a deep inner awareness of this kind of love. It wasn't the type that you can fall "into" or "out of." There was no separation, no "me-ness" or "you-ness," in this love. It just was.

I knew I'd come home. Then, unexpectedly, a deep and powerful voice declared, "You may not stay here. There's something you still need to do."

I shouted, "Nooo!" as I was pulled back into my body.

I later discovered that my experience was very similar to what many individuals describe as a *near-death experience.* These individuals often report seeing a bright light, feeling an extraordinary peacefulness, and experiencing a vague sense of familiarity. Regardless of how you define what happened to me, it changed my perception of reality forever.

My near-death experience was completely foreign to me. I was the eldest of four children, and both my parents had spent time in the scientific community. My father was an engineer, and my mother, who was of Native American descent, had worked as a chemist. Growing up, I thought the only things that were real were those that were tangible and provable by the laws of science. After being shot, I struggled to find a way to fit my near-death experience into my beliefs about the nature of reality. Instead, everything in which I'd believed began to slowly disintegrate, and in its place, a new understanding started to emerge. It seemed that my life was to take an entirely new direction.

As I recovered from my injuries, I began to hear music that no one else could hear, and I was often aware of very loving spirit beings surrounding me. Another astonishing revelation was the awareness that "I" was separate from my body; "I" wasn't my body. As a result of the shooting, my physical being was damaged—my body lost a spleen, adrenal gland, and a kidney; had damage to my stomach, intestines, lung, and diaphragm; and also had a plastic tube inserted to replace my aorta—but "I" was whole. To me, this was an amazing realization, and it greatly assisted me in the healing of my body. It was a subtle shift, but simply beginning to identify with my spiritual essence—instead of my physical presence—allowed me to recover more quickly. I became extraordinarily healthy in spite of my injuries.

In addition, my dreams began to take on a particular vividness and significance. Somehow, my brush with death allowed me to stumble into dreamscapes of inner dimensions long forgotten. This was all very strange to me because of my previous rational, linear approach to life. Even though my dreams took on an intensity and were often prophetic, they weren't always idyllic. Somehow, when those nocturnal portals opened for me, images that had been held back surged forward *en masse*. Often the visions were terrifying; at other times, they were profoundly soothing and reassuring. In my dreams, I'd occasionally catch a fleeting glimpse of the beautiful, golden place to which I'd traveled when I was thought to have died. When I clutched at these cloudy images, they vanished like mist. I longed to return, but I wasn't willing to die to get there.

During this time, I frequently dreamed of a shadowy figure chasing me, and I'd often wake too terrified to return to sleep. This foreboding, formless creature of the night continued to haunt my dreams through the next few years.

I began a career in journalism, and in the summer of 1969, I was in Eastern Europe attending a journalism conference. Upon its culmination, I decided to camp on one of the numerous islands off the coast of what was then Yugoslavia. I persuaded a very reluctant fisherman to take me to a beautiful deserted island. As I lay in my sleeping bag that first night, I looked up at the stars and lost myself in the loneliness of the galaxy. God seemed so close, yet so very far away.

The next morning, the sun-dappled stillness was invaded by a plane flying low overhead—too low, I thought. Without warning, I was showered with a rain of gunfire! Bullets were everywhere, ricocheting off rocks and trees. I scrambled for cover, crawling under some bushes for safety while the shooting continued. And then, just as suddenly as it started, it stopped. As I crept out from beneath the bushes, a black terror filled me.

Why was I being shot at again? I didn't understand.

Within a short time, I was able to flag down a passing fisherman, who in broken English explained that no one should have taken me to that area in the first place. It was off-limits because it was sometimes used for aerial target practice for the Yugoslavian military.

In my dreams, my shadowy pursuer increased his nightly rampage.

Later that year, I returned to the United States. The newspaper I worked for sent me to cover anti–Vietnam War riots in the cities of Chicago, New York, and Washington, D.C. I was on the front line of a march in D.C. when policemen with gas masks and billy clubs exploded onto the street from every direction and shot tear gas and pepper gas into the front line of the protesters. These exceedingly painful and noxious gases feel as if they're searing your eyes and skin. Canisters of gas exploded at my feet. Added to the din were the screams of the panicked crowd. I watched as people near me, unable to match the force of the crowd, were swept under the feet of those desperately trying to flee from the gas.

As tumultuous as my daylight hours were, my nights were even more terrifying. My vigilant assailant of the night continued to hound me like a wolf on the scent of an impending kill. To hold the tenacious grip of my midnight pursuer at bay, I used my daylight hours to enhance my willingness to face danger. To compensate for my fear, I tested my mettle with karate lessons and skydiving. At the same time, my work was filled with the violence associated with reporting riots and confrontations. I even had to fend off the attack of a knife-wielding rapist.

Shortly after that attack, a book on Zen Buddhism found me. I was impressed with the remarkable similarity between my near-death experience and the content of the book. It talked of enlightenment, of going beyond linear time, and how a *satori* experience allowed a person to see the great light and feel a oneness with all things. Reading this book, I wondered if it was possible to reach that place again without dying. I knew that it was time for a change in my life: the time had come for me to search for the land beyond the living that I'd encountered when I was shot.

Expecting to stay only a short while, I moved into a Zen monastery in the early 1970s, but my brief visit stretched into more than two years. During much of this time, I gazed at a wall from 4 to 16 hours a day, sitting in full- or half-lotus position. In a Zen monastery, it's easy to be distracted by pain or tiredness, so as an act of compassion, the Zen master would hit my shoulder with a *kyosaku* stick to ensure attentiveness in his disciple. A *kyosaku* stick is similar to a flat baseball bat. The sound of the excruciating blow landing on my shoulder would reverberate off the monastery walls. The catch-22 of this practice was that if the Zen master deemed that I was doing really well, he'd smack me as hard as he could with the *kyosaku* to encourage me!

Visions would come to me and the Zen master would say, "They are only illusions . . . go deeper." Great insights would surface and the Zen master would say, "Only illusions. Keep going. Go for the underlying reality . . . the true reality. See yourself as you really are." These words eventually became a recurring theme in my life.

As I stayed on in the Zen monastery, my dreams began to change and even spilled into my waking hours. One morning a radiant, three-dimensional mandala spontaneously appeared before me . . . *in the daytime, when I was wide awake.* (A mandala is a symbolic pattern divided into four sections, usually found within a circle or square and thought to represent the universe.) When I inquired into the unprompted appearance, I was told that Swiss psychologist Carl Jung believed that mandalas were symbols heralding wholeness, and when they mystically appeared, it was a powerful symbol of integration. Jung indicated that the universal occurrence of the number four (four directions, a square with four sides, a mandala with four sides) also promoted wholeness.

While I was living in the monastery, I made a discovery concerning the nightly antagonist of my dreams. One night as I was once again chased down a labyrinth of shadowy corridors, I stopped abruptly and thought, *This is only a dream. I'm going to face whoever is chasing me.* As I did so, my nemesis became a nebulous form, slinking away into the shadows. Although the nightly appearances continued, each time as I turned and faced my pursuer, it would disappear without revealing its face.

My Zen training made me aware that there were ways to heal my body from within. It was during this time that I met a Hawaiian kahuna (shaman) who was a renowned healer. She agreed to train me only after she learned of my Native American heritage and then showed me how to consciously enter the inner realms that I'd been exploring randomly in my dreams. This wise woman opened the doors of my understanding so that I could see how Spirit resides in everything, and how one can call on Spirit for healing. I recall an occasion when I took her to Jackass Ginger, a tropical forest in Hawaii, so that she might present fruit to the menehune king. (Menehunes are Hawaiian elves.) As I stood lingering at the forest's edge, I was struck by how incredible it was that I was with someone who was talking with *elves*. For the kahuna, the boundaries between the dream state and the waking state are blurred, and one can step lightly between the two worlds.

During my training with the kahuna, I began to recognize an entirely new dimension of dreaming. I discovered that I could leave my body, astral-travel around my cottage, and even turn to look at my sleeping body (see Chapter 13). The visits of my nightly tormentor became fewer and fewer during this time; and even though they weren't as terrifying, I was still unable to view the face, and the lingering shadow continued to haunt me.

During this time in my life, I wanted to understand as much as I could about my inner potential, so I began to study with various spiritual teachers. Among those who touched me deeply was a diminutive Japanese woman named Hawayo Takata. When we met, she said that she'd been waiting for me for several years and asked what had taken me so long. (She was the Reiki Grand Master who brought the healing system of Reiki from the Japanese monasteries to the West.) Takata Sensei (*sensei* is a term of respect for a teacher) taught me to access the life-force energy so that it would surge down my arms in my healing work. I eventually organized her first courses for Westerners.

Another teacher—an eccentric shiatsu master—taught me how to balance the body through pressure points, and I eventually taught shiatsu all over the world. As I further explored healing modalities, I was asked to teach massage through the University of Hawaii Continuing Education Program. Thus began my vocation as a teacher.

During this time, an elusive, serene, yet strong man began to drift into my dreams. Who was this pleasant intruder? I jotted down a list of his characteristics, and they seemed to be all that I'd ever wanted in a lover and companion.

Two weeks after I made the list, I attended a self-growth communication course. I was dissatisfied with the course and raised my hand to share this with the instructor. Rather than deal with my questions, he apparently thought that what I really needed was something to keep me busy. His response was, "So why don't you marry that guy sitting next to you?" Feeling very irritated, I blurted offhandedly to the tranquil man next to me, "Will you marry me?" To my utter amazement, he calmly said *yes*. (I knew this individual, but I wasn't dating him.)

I felt shaky, as I'd just asked someone—whom I barely knew—to marry me. The instructor began to goad me as to when the momentous event would take place. "Okay, I'll get married tomorrow!" I said petulantly but never really imagined that I'd actually get married the next day. My logical, conscious mind thought, *This is completely absurd!* But a gentle tugging welled up from deep within me, and as I turned to face the man sitting beside me, the vague, benevolent being who'd recently been appearing in my dreams seemed to metamorphose into this man—the one who would become my husband, the man of my dreams.

After our marriage (which *did* happen the next day), the most remarkable thing happened: I dreamed that my tormentor was chasing me again! This time, however, when I turned to face my fear, I was shocked. It was *me!* It had always been me.

In my dream, I hugged and embraced this lonely waif who'd been pursuing me for so long. She just wanted to be loved and appreciated. I felt as if I were coming home. Shortly after this, a child was conceived and born to my husband, David, and me. As a result of my injuries, the doctors had told me that I could never have children, so this was miraculous. I had a healthy, easy home birth. Our daughter, Meadow, has grown into a lovely woman. Being a mother has been perhaps my greatest teacher of all.

ⅅ ⅅ ⅅ

This book is a culmination of years of self-exploration. Through many dramatic and often painful experiences, I've been beckoned to come closer to understanding myself through my dreams. May this book help *you* gain self-knowledge through *your* dreams, in safety and joy. Thank you for allowing me to participate in your life.

ⅅ ⅅ ⅅ   ⅅ ⅅ ⅅ

PART I

Dream Gates

Come into my dream garden,
Across the bridge of sleep . . .

Chapter 1

What Scientists Say about Dreams

Imagine a resplendent garden surrounded by a wall with many gates. As you enter from the eastern gate, you see rich, black soil. A pungent smell permeates the warm air. You might think that this garden is the place where seeds are planted and new beginnings occur. It's the fertile ground for regeneration and renewal.

Entering from the southern gate reveals a magic carpet of dahlias, cosmos, sunflowers, daisies, and marigolds. A wild symphony of color envelops you in a blanket of fragrance. This exquisite flower garden is certainly a creative place of beauty and vitality.

The western gate swings open to reveal tall, golden-tasseled corn gently undulating in the warm breeze. Ripe, full grapes hang on the vines; and giant tomatoes radiate their sweet fragrance. You might imagine that this is surely a garden of nourishment and sustenance.

Advancing through the northern gate, you see tall evergreens surrounding statues that are carved in marble and stone. Certainly this must be an elegant, refined, and stately garden. This must be a place for reflection and meditation.

The same garden . . . yet such different gates—each one offers a new and varied perception.

There are various "gates" through which you can enter your garden of dreams. Stepping through the well-worn gate of science, the verdant rows of new growth are neat and orderly, each carefully tended and numbered. Scientists know that dreaming is an activity in which we all participate. Moreover, research indicates that *everyone* dreams, including people who are blind. Individuals with an extremely low IQ have no fewer dreams than those possessing a high IQ. Dreaming is as natural a process as breathing. There's no way, with the exception of drug use or overindulgence in alcohol, that dreaming can be prevented.

Although we can experience as few as three or as many as nine, we average four to five dreams per night. Those who claim they don't dream actually have difficulty *remembering* their dreams. In fact, each of us spends approximately 20 percent of our total sleep time dreaming. On average, we dream for about an hour and a half each night. Over a lifetime, we spend as much time dreaming as it takes to get an advanced university education. Yet researchers really know very little about dreams.[1]

What researchers do know is that during the dream state, our heartbeat speeds up or slows down for no discernible reason. Blood pressure climbs and dives unpredictably, and our pulse rate becomes irregular, as does our breathing pattern. Metabolism is raised; and kidneys produce less, but more concentrated, urine. Spontaneous firing of brain cells is sometimes increased beyond normal waking levels. In addition, blood flow to the brain increases 40 percent. Smaller muscles, such as those in the fingers, tend to twitch, while larger muscles go limp.

REM Sleep

Dreams usually occur during REM sleep (REM refers to *rapid eye movement*), which is a state of sleep identified by scientists in the early 1950s. Until that time, most scientists even remotely interested in the sleep state agreed with the renowned Russian physiologist Ivan Pavlov, who believed that the brain sort of "tuned down" during sleep. Then Dr. Nathan Kleitman, a professor of physiology at the University of Chicago and considered the father of modern sleep research, requested that one of his graduate students, Eugene Aserinsky, help him investigate the relationship between eye movement and sleep. Aserinsky and Kleitman discovered that if they woke someone while his eyes were still moving rapidly from side to side and asked what was being experienced, the person would almost always say that he was in the middle of a dream. This discovery had an amazing impact on the scientific community, which could now begin the research and study of dream phenomena.[2]

During REM sleep, vivid images in the brain can issue commands to the body, such as jump, run, or kick. Movement of the eyes in various directions corresponds with the type of actions reported by the dreamer. These action-oriented messages are countermanded by neurons in the brain stem that disconnect much of our muscular apparatus so that our large muscle groups are effectively paralyzed during the dream state. When this area of the brain stem has been damaged, people have been known to act out their dreams dramatically, sometimes to the extent that they may need to be restrained in their beds in order to prevent them from injuring themselves or others.[3]

REM states generally repeat in 90-minute cycles. A 90-minute cycle of non-REM sleep usually occurs when we first drift off to sleep. Our brain waves then begin to put on a remarkable display as the sleeper begins the first REM period of the night. When awakened during the night, a person may not be able to go back to sleep until one complete 90-minute sleep session has been missed. The average sleeper has four or five REM periods per night. These spans each begin with a very short REM period of 10 minutes and end in the early morning with a dream period of 30 to 45 minutes. Some scientists say that dreaming refreshes the cortex (the outer layer of the brain) by clearing overloaded circuits. This means that dreams are considered an electrochemical process to clear away unusable data collected during the day.[4]

Dreams and Twins

Experiments in France suggest that genetics plays some role in the phenomenon of dreaming. Research using identical twins reflects an unusual similarity in REM patterns, one far greater than that between ordinary siblings. In fact, identical twins share the same timing and duration of their REM periods. These French scientists believe that the portion of the brain that controls the dream state is governed by heredity. They go on to note instances where twins have had the same dream on the same night. However, perceiving the dream garden from a different gate, a metaphysician would explain that twins have the same dream because they're psychically connected. Current scientific investigation into clairvoyant and precognitive dreams proposes that the experiences and emotions of our ancestors are contained in our DNA and RNA through genetic coding.[5]

Necessity of Dreams

Even if we don't recall our dreams, they're necessary to our emotional and physical balance. Deprived of our dream states, we have difficulty concentrating and become nervous and edgy. Without REM sleep, in many instances, people will experience psychotic symptoms and hallucinations.[6]

It used to be thought that insomnia was harmful because it deprived us of the activity of sleep, but it's now realized that insomnia is harmful because it deprives us of *dreams* as well. Great personality disturbances result from dream deprivation. Even if they're getting plenty of sleep, few people can endure more than

72 hours without dreaming. Subjects who persevere finally begin to experience hallucinations. The mind appears to create its own stimulation in the form of fantasy when the normal channels of stimulation are cut off. One of the dangers of alcohol use is that it's been proven to shorten dream time. When an alcoholic withdraws from addiction, almost 100 percent of his or her sleep time is spent dreaming. This is because the person who doesn't dream recovers REM sleep on subsequent nights in the exact amount of time as that lost during previous nights' deprivation. Interestingly, deprivation of non-REM sleep doesn't appear to create a need to make up for lost sleep. Perhaps the body, in its wisdom, knows something that the mind has not yet begun to comprehend.[7]

Hypnagogic Dreams

Not technically defined as a REM dream, the hypnagogic dream belongs to the mysterious realm between wakefulness and dreaming. It's characterized by quick, random images that often take the form of faces or country scenes. You might have experienced this just as you were falling asleep. Each can continue for a significant period of time.[8]

Scientists don't consider these "true dreams" because you remain semiconscious of all that's going on around you. The scientific view is that these are simply memory pictures clearing from the brain. However, a metaphysical perspective would be that during hypnagogic dreaming, the mind acts much like a radio flipping randomly among stations. The various stations are thoughts, feelings, and images that other people have had in the past, present, and future. From a mystical perspective, this type of dreaming reflects a random tuning in to different realities.

Children and Dreams

Research indicates that REM sleep may be related to brain development. Premature newborns spend as much as 75 percent of their sleep time in REM, while in normal newborns that rate is around 50 percent. Five-year-olds typically spend 25 to 30 percent of their sleep time in REM. By adolescence, the rate is about 20 percent, which is typical for most adults as well. In older adults—aged 60 and older—the rate drops to about 15 percent. The content of dreams also changes with increasing age. Young children often dream of animals, such as tigers, lions, snakes, and spiders. As they age, they dream less and less about animals, until adulthood, when such dreams occur less than 8 percent of the time.[9]

Animals and Dreams

You might have noticed your cat or dog showing signs of REM when their eyes twitch or their breathing becomes irregular during sleep. This has led researchers to hypothesize that most animals do, in fact, dream. Reptiles and snakes, however, have never been shown to dream, even though they spend some 60 percent of their time asleep. Interestingly enough, if you separate mammals into two groups—the hunted (rabbits, sheep, deer, elk, and so forth) and the hunter (such as dogs, cats, and man)—the hunters usually spend 20 to 35 percent of their sleep time dreaming. The hunted sleep less with only 6 to 8 percent of their sleep time spent in dreaming.[10]

Research with animals suggests that dreaming must have an essential evolutionary value. There's no single mammal that doesn't dream, with the exception of the dolphin, which possesses an unusual sleep pattern. Instead of REM sleep, dolphins sleep with only half of their brain at a time. I believe that the dolphin may be the keeper of a secret of sleep. To the advanced yogi, there's very little difference between the dream state and the wakeful state. Perhaps the dolphin has unwittingly dissolved the dream boundaries at the cellular level.[11]

Dream-Inspired Scientific Discoveries

While scientific dream research and investigation continue, many scientific discoveries have been dream inspired. Descartes, the man who first postulated Rational Empiricism, came upon this as a result of a vivid dream (Rational Empiricism is the theory underlying the development of modern science).[12] The man who understood the molecular structure of benzine made his discovery after dreaming of a snake biting its tail. This resulted in the ringlike shape of molecular structure. He once counseled his fellow colleagues, "Gentlemen, learn to dream!"

Einstein, when asked about the inspiration for his theory of relativity, replied that it came from a dream during his youth. In this dream, he was riding on a sled; and as the sled sped faster and faster, it seemed to approach the speed of light. The stars were distorted and transformed into astonishing colors and patterns. In that moment, Einstein was profoundly aware of the immense power of this transformation. He related that not only did this dream inspire his theory of relativity, but that his entire scientific career could be seen as an extended meditation on that particular dream.[13]

Niels Bohr, the man who developed the theory of the structure of the atom, also based his discovery on a dream. He dreamed that he was at the races. As he observed the marked lanes on the track within which the horses were running, he constructed the analogy of fixed and specific orbits of electrons circulating around the atomic nuclei. This led to the formulation of his quantum theory, for which he later won the Nobel Prize.[14]

In the middle of the 19th century, a man named Elias Howe had been working for some time to invent a machine that could sew. He tried one design after another, but none was successful in stitching layers of fabric together. One day, in complete despair, he fell asleep at his work. He was rapidly plunged into a nightmare in which he was pursued and captured by a savage group of African warriors. They tied him up and poked at him with their spears. Howe awoke feeling very upset and was unable to get back to work or dispel the vivid images of the dream from his mind. He could still clearly see the warriors' odd spears. Strange blades were tied to the ends of the long sticks—the ends of the points were perforated by a hole. *That was it!* A needle with a hole in the end of it! Howe immediately set to work and came up with the basic design for the first successful sewing machine. Mass production of clothing became possible for the first time in history, and his original design is still used for all sewing machines. Howe solved the impasse in his invention through creative dreaming.[15]

🜲 🜲 🜲　🜲 🜲 🜲

Chapter 2

What Psychologists Say about Dreams

To a psychologist, dreams are more than an electrochemical process. Each one is a precious seed that can be nurtured and fertilized so that it will sprout, grow, and bloom to give fullness and understanding to our waking hours.

Therapists feel that dreams are the secret portal through which the psyche pours vital information into consciousness as a way to keep emotional balance during waking life. Dreams are a way for us to work out the difficulties that are suppressed rather than experienced during the day.

In my private healing practice, I've discovered that it isn't always the traumas that we have fully experienced that block us. It's often the traumas or difficulties that we did not allow ourselves to experience fully, or that we have suppressed, that create barriers in our lives. Dreams can be one way to release those repressed emotional barriers.

One time in Hawaii when I'd hurt my foot running into a large stump, my mentor, the kahuna, told me to place my foot against the stump and put the pain back into it. As I put my foot against the base of the tree, I was astonished to feel a release of pain and a soothing wave of relaxation fill my foot. I thought it was kahuna magic. In a primordial way, it made sense: the tree stump had given me the pain, so I gave it back.

When I mentioned this incident to a psychologist friend, he said, "You're so dumb! You can't put pain back into a tree stump. What you were doing was allowing yourself to experience the pain that you were suppressing. By reenacting the situation that caused you the pain in the first place—by putting your foot to the stump—you felt and released what you didn't allow yourself to feel when it first happened. By suppressing physical or emotional pain, you often sustain it. When you allow yourself to feel it totally and completely or become 'one' with your pain, there's no separation between you and it. It disappears."

To relive is to relieve, and dreams are a safe way to relive and relieve the feelings and sensations that you don't process or experience during the day.

Dream Analysts

Psychological study of dreams has its roots in the late 1800s. In 1861, a therapist named Karl Scherner brought forth the idea that daytime objects or emotions could be objectified in a dream. For example, lungs could be seen as balloons, and anger could become a raging fire.[1]

In 1877, Ludwig Strümpell, another dream explorer, stated that dreams were escape mechanisms, a way to avoid experiencing the world. He formulated the law of association, and from this, Sigmund Freud's theory of association of ideas evolved. Another theory explored during this time was that the function of dreams was similar to that of our eliminative processes. Their purpose was to rid us of useless thoughts. Dreams were also theorized as being signs of wish fulfillment. Other analysts believed that dreams were memories from childhood, complexes, or sexual desires, but it was Freud who united the different theories into a viable therapy.[2]

Sigmund Freud (1856–1939)

Freud encouraged his patients to talk at length about their dreams and suggested that they notice the thoughts that the dreams evoked. His technique of free association of ideas evolved from working with his patients in this way. Freud felt that dreams were a form of repression or wish fulfillment or both. He asserted that a person could reach walled-up emotions only through free association. Even dreams with painful content were analyzed as fulfillment dreams. He divided the psyche into three parts: the ego, the id, and the superego. The ego reflects our conscious self, the id is associated with our primitive instincts, and the superego represents our social conditioning.[3]

Freud thought that during sleep, the ego is absent and the id—our basic primordial need for sex and survival—comes forth. To protect the ego and the superego from these sexual desires, the id camouflages them by producing symbolic dreams to hopefully avoid shocking the dreamer. The function of a dream, in Freud's theory, is to preserve sleep. Therefore, our irrational wishes are disguised as other things to deceive our self-censoring superego. Freud viewed dreams as a compromise between the suppressing forces of the id and the repressing forces of the superego. Thus, they are a code to be figured out. Freudian symbolic language was very narrow, for it mostly concerned our primitive desires. The vast majority of Freudian symbols were disguises for the various forms of the sexual drive. Freud felt that even if the experiences during the day triggered dreams, their primary energy came from a childhood experience usually regarding sexual frustration.[4]

Carl Jung (1875–1961)

Swiss psychologist Carl Jung, an associate of Freud, found the Freudian approach rather limiting. Jung felt that the sexual drive was important, but it wasn't the determining factor in dreams. In

Jung's approach, a dream object could be exactly what it was. A snake could be just a snake; it wasn't always a phallic symbol. Jung focused on the actual form of a dream rather than branch off into free association. He felt that there was no censor at work in the mind and that dreams were revelations of the unconscious wisdom of the individual.[5]

Jung also felt that dreams were a way to delve into the collective unconscious. To test his theory that there was a collective unconscious common to all cultures and societies, he used mythology. Traveling to Africa and the United States, he studied African blacks and Native Americans. In his research, he became convinced that there were two layers of consciousness: the *collective unconscious* and the *personal unconscious*. He believed that the collective unconscious contained archetypal symbols that represented the wisdom of all humanity. He called these primordial images "ancestral memory archetypes" and felt that an individual inherits these just as he or she inherits physical characteristics. To Jung, our personal unconscious was recognizable material from our past that had been forgotten or repressed.[6]

Jung noted that archetypal images appeared in the dreams of people who were in life-threatening or life-transforming situations. He observed that these images would be present when a person was experiencing illness, enduring specific types of stress, or releasing an attitude or belief system. When a new orientation was needed, it was as if the individual were connected with life-force energy in the form of symbols. Jung felt that the archetype was a primordial image that met a need of the moment. He stated that true archetypal symbols were never invented; they were already in the collective unconscious of all people.[7]

Jung liked to work with a series of dreams, associating one with the next and so on to unravel his patients' difficulties. Freud, however, concentrated on one dream at a time, viewing them as isolated incidents. Both had success with their patients, and their theories were appropriate for the time.[8]

Alfred Adler (1870–1937)

Another associate of Freud, Alfred Adler, also disagreed with his techniques. Adler felt that the major influence on a person's character development was the struggle for power. He introduced into our language terms such as *sibling rivalry, inferiority complex,* and *superiority complex.* He felt that people were looking for meaning in life and that values and purposes were as necessary for life as sex and power drives. Adler didn't focus on the concepts of the unconscious as Jung and Freud had. Instead, he saw dreams more in terms of wishful thinking and wish fulfillment. Unlike Freud, he didn't see sex as an underlying cause; rather, he felt that dreams were influenced by our urge for power.[9]

Erich Fromm (1900–1980)

Psychoanalyst Erich Fromm said that there was one universal language from which all languages developed—the symbolic language that appeared in dreams.[10] He divided symbols in dreams into three categories: conventional, accidental, and universal symbols. He believed that conventional symbols held only one actual meaning, such as a stop sign, or a plus or minus sign. Accidental symbols were personal to the individual in the dream, or personal to a group of people, but not real to people in general. Universal symbols were those found to be common throughout the world, such as water representing emotion and intuition and fire representing energy, power, purification, and transformation.[11]

࿐ ࿐ ࿐ ࿐ ࿐ ࿐

Chapter 3

What Metaphysicians Say about Dreams

I stood at the tip of the long, rocky jetty that extended far into the tranquil sea. Low-lying clouds hugged the horizon, merging the boundary between the blue sky and ocean. Without warning, a huge wave roared up from the sea, cascaded over the jetty, and knocked me into the water. I tried to cling to the jagged rocks but was ripped from my hold and thrown into the churning sea. All my strength drained from me as a riptide pulled at my waterlogged clothes, and I struggled to stay afloat. Searing pain filled my lungs as I inhaled salt water and was sucked down into the dark, cold sea. I knew that I was drowning and there was nothing I could do to prevent it.

I sat up in bed and fearfully fumbled for the light. I let out a long sigh of relief: it was only a dream. I nestled back into the cool comfort of my sheets, and the images slowly faded from my consciousness as I snapped off the light and returned to a deep sleep.

The morning disclosed no hint of the night's terror. In fact, I had no conscious memory of the dream. As I was getting up, a friend telephoned with an invitation to go to the beach. (I lived in Hawaii at the time.) It was a clear, perfect day; and my friend and I drove to an unfamiliar beach. There was a long jetty stretching into the sea. As we climbed and explored along the rocks, not even the smallest hint of my dream came to mind. I perched at the end of the jetty, gazing at the horizon where a lazy cloud melded the sea and sky into one endless universe of blue. Suddenly, my mind was flooded with memories from the night before. With a desperate sense of urgency, I grabbed my friend. Puzzled by my panic, yet compliant, she scrambled with me as we made our way back over the rocks to the security of the beach. After we got to the shore, I explained to her, in detail, about my dream. Shortly after that, we watched in disbelief as the sea began to churn, sending a powerful, single wave crashing over the jetty where we'd stood only moments before. We were frightened by the thought of what might have happened if we'd been standing on the end of the jetty when the wave hit.

I credit that dream for saving both of us from a very uncomfortable experience, and maybe even saving our lives.

Before I had that dream, I had no knowledge that I was going to the beach the next day. And I'd never been to that particular beach, nor had I ever seen any pictures of it. In the realm of science, my dream would probably be considered a coincidence. A scientist might rationalize that given the vast number of dreams an individual has, statistically there's a chance that one would come true at some point. The metaphysician, however, would consider this a dream of true prophecy.

In times long past, dreamers attributed their nightly prophetic visions to external forces. They believed that God, angels, nature spirits, gods and goddesses, various entities, and the spirits of their ancestors would visit them in the night hours, presenting themselves through dreams. Ancient dreamers deliberately invoked these influences by incubating their dreams (a process by which you select a dream topic and then program yourself for it). Spiritual truths and information gleaned during these programmed dreams were used for telepathic purposes and prophecy, as well as astral travel and communication with the dead.

Metaphysicians believe that dreams are not only neurons firing in the brain (as scientists believe) or psychological release of unresolved daytime difficulties, but that dreams are a way to touch the inner realms. The popularity of Carlos Castaneda's books regarding the Mexican mystic Don Juan exemplifies the interest in this belief system. Don Juan stated that dreams were aids to the development of psychic and mental powers. To increase these abilities, he affirmed that a person need only remain conscious while dreaming, learning how to control the dream itself. Maintaining consciousness during the dream state has been referred to as "lucid dreaming." (See Chapter 9.)

Edgar Cayce, the Sleeping Prophet

Edgar Cayce, aptly referred to as the "sleeping prophet," has often been considered the grandfather of metaphysical and psychic interpretation of dreams. The waking Edgar Cayce was known as a talented professional photographer and was admired as an amicable Sunday-school teacher. The sleeping Edgar Cayce, however, possessed a far broader and more colorful reputation. He was a gifted psychic, able to give valuable information that had a profound effect on thousands of people.[1]

The sleeping Edgar Cayce was a medical diagnostician and a visionary. The fascination with his life and work was reflected in 1954, when the University of Chicago awarded a Ph.D. based on a study of his work. In the thesis, Cayce was referred to as a religious seer.[2]

When Cayce was a young boy, he'd fall asleep with his head resting on his schoolbooks; and by the following morning, he'd absorb information that he had never consciously studied. As a result, Cayce was able to advance rapidly in school. This gift faded, however, and he completed only seven grades.

When Cayce reached the age of 21, he developed a gradual paralysis of the throat muscles, which threatened the loss of his voice. Although several doctors were consulted, none was successful in discovering the cause of Cayce's condition. As a last resort, he asked a friend to assist him in moving into the same level of sleep that had enabled him to memorize his schoolbooks as a child. His friend gave him the appropriate suggestion, and at once, Cayce entered a sleeplike state. From this level of consciousness, he recommended medication and manipulative therapy for his own condition, and taking his own advice, he was able to heal the paralysis and restore his voice.[3]

As news traveled of Cayce's gift, many doctors in Kentucky began to use Cayce's unique talent to diagnose their patients. They learned that he needed only the name and address of a patient in order to disclose—in a dream state—valuable information regarding the individual. By the time Cayce died in 1945, in Virginia Beach, Virginia, he'd given thousands of people information over a period of 43 years. *One in 20 of his readings refer to dreams.* Cayce regarded dreams as a kind of problem-solving exercise. He referred to dream incubation (see Chapter 8) as a way to present solutions to daytime problems.[4]

Cayce continually illustrated how various dream symbols attempt to develop awareness within the dreamer. He felt that symbols could signify that it's time to develop new beliefs, take more responsibility for life, be more accepting, or expand horizons. Cayce explained that all dreams weren't necessarily problem solving in nature, but often assisted in the self-transformation process of the dreamer. He advocated that certain series of dreams were devoted to developing new qualities within the dreamer, such as humility, nonjudgment, self-acceptance, love, and courage.[5]

Cayce believed that some dreams represented a new energy or change in a person's life and that certain dreams could even prophesy the future. For example, one woman wrote to Cayce relating a dream in which she saw five chrysanthemums resting on the grave of her husband's father. Cayce responded that within five weeks, her husband would have an experience of being taught by his deceased father through the medium of dreams. He also affirmed that the experience would be a joyful one. Within five weeks, the dreams did, in fact, come to her husband. Perhaps Cayce's greatest gift was his intuition with regard to health and dreams. He believed that people could not only receive signals of impending physical imbalances while in the dream state, but also receive the cures within dreams.[6]

When a woman sorrowfully said that she'd dreamed she'd never be able to conceive a child, Cayce reassured her that she most definitely _would_ give birth. He advised her to release any literal interpretation of the dream and counseled that the dream was simply encouraging her to take careful preparation for motherhood, especially with regard to her diet and her belief patterns. These were areas in which she required a rebirth within herself in order to conceive the child she so desperately wanted. Shortly thereafter, she became the joyful mother of a healthy baby.[7]

Cayce consistently urged his clients to solve their problems through their own interpretation of their dreams. His work made such an impact that it remains the foundation of a great portion of modern metaphysics.

Connecting Through Your Dreams with Those Who've Died

Another aspect of dreams and metaphysics is connecting with those who have passed over, both from this life and from shared past incarnations. Doing so affirms that our true essence is Spirit, not a mere body. There have been many reports of dreams in which someone who has died reassures the dreamer that the deceased is alive and well and that there's no further need to grieve. Occasionally, the deceased will instruct the dreamer in some basic concern of daily life. Let me share a powerful example of this from my experience.

I was working on Union Street in San Francisco at a healing center during a very rewarding time in my life. My shiatsu practice (pressure-point therapy similar to acupressure) was at a peak. In addition, my Zen training, with its disciplined commitment to focus, enhanced my ability to achieve a tremendous sense of clarity and healing with each point I pushed.

One evening, as the San Francisco fog was settling in and the foghorns were sounding, the phone rang. The call was from a friend who said hesitantly, with a voice full of emotion, "David's dead." David was a healer and a medical doctor who also worked at the center. He had a youthful exuberance and passion for life that permeated the entire clinic. My first thought was one of disbelief: *not David!* He had so much to live for. His practice was thriving, he and his wife had just purchased a beautiful home in Mill Valley, and they were joyfully anticipating the birth of their child. Why David?

That night in my dreams, a beckoning presence seemed to flutter at the edges of my consciousness. As I stumbled through the next few days feeling numb, I began to experience strange phenomena. When walking through various rooms in our apartment, the lights would flicker on and off. Vaguely, I thought about calling an electrician. My dreams were filled with an elusive sense of urgency. I didn't, however, connect any of this with David. I merely assumed it was part of my grieving process.

Just before Christmas, my shiatsu group gathered in my living room for a class. Our valiant little Christmas tree was radiant with miniature lights, and as the class began, the nonblinking lights on the tree started to blink. I explained to the group that we'd been having trouble with our electrical system and that we should ignore it. However, the lights continued to blink in a definite, steady sequence. Turning our attention back to the tree, an individual in the class asked it, "Are you trying to tell us something?" The tree lights responded with a pattern of blinks. It finally dawned on me that David had been attempting to make contact with me through my dreams in order to provide comfort and information to his grieving wife. With unfailing determination, he was now trying to contact me through our electrical system. We continued to ask yes-and-no questions, which he initially responded to via the Christmas tree lights, blinking once for *yes* and twice for *no*. Eventually we were able to garner information that he wished us to pass on to his wife. As soon as I gave his wife the necessary message, the dreams ceased and our electrical system returned to normal.

A psychologist would probably analyze my dreams during this time as a way to process and release my grief. The metaphysician, however, would perceive that David was indeed attempting to communicate with me in order to give me information. For me, the metaphysical interpretation is validated by the occurrence of the blinking lights and by the fact that the information I relayed to his wife was valuable to her. Communication with deceased friends or family members is a skill that can be learned through dream incubation. (See Chapter 8.)

Other Mystical Dreams

The flying dream is another type of metaphysical dreaming. A psychologist might identify this as a psychological sense of freedom expressed by the symbol of flying. To a metaphysician, however, dream flying is *astral projection*. Simply defined, astral projection occurs when one's soul actually leaves the body—connected only by a single cord of energy called an *astral cord*—to explore other realms and dimensions. Later on in this book is more information about astral traveling. (See Chapter 13.)

Another common spiritual belief is that while you're dreaming, guides come to give you valuable messages and insight. It's believed that when the conscious mind shuts down during sleep, these guides have easier access to your inner self. A guide is generally a discarnate being with whom you were connected in a previous lifetime. This being continues to be interested in you, working with you to provide guidance that benefits the evolution of your soul.

🖙 🖙 🖙　🖙 🖙 🖙

PART II

Dream Weavers

Ancestors, you have crossed over,
epic journey of the night,
to weave the fabric of our dreams
reflections of our innermost realms.

Deft masters of the dream loom
ever mindful of the texture and dye
of one thread against another,
we follow the footsteps of your crossing.

— M. Anne Sweet

Chapter 4

Ancient Dreamers

Somewhere beyond the window of your consciousness, elusive secret messages hover just out of reach. You may sense them waiting there, yet when you reach out to touch them, you find that they quickly slip away. These divinely inspired communications are beyond the world of form and illusion. They dwell in the mysterious realm of dreams.

Throughout history, in every culture, there have been rare individuals who have stepped through the sleepers' veil to listen to messages of the night. From silent spaces of the night, these dream weavers have carried back precious gifts into wakeful reality that have changed the destiny of individuals and nations alike.

Even though the histories of most of the countless nocturnal mystics have been lost forever, a few tales have survived. One such story concerns an emperor of the Shang Dynasty, Wu Ting (1324–1266 B.C.). When one of his most trusted counselors died, Wu Ting was devastated by the loss. He presented ritual offerings to the ruler of the gods, Shang-ti, and asked this god to show him who should be the successor to his beloved counselor. He then had a dream in which he clearly saw the face of the new counselor. This dream was so vivid that he was able to have a portrait made of the dream man's face. Unable to find this person, he had the painting shown throughout the empire. One man was found whose face matched the portrait, yet he was only a common worker. However, Wu Ting's faith in his dream was so complete that he elevated this man to the position of prime minister of his empire.[1]

Researchers believe that 300 to 400 temples were erected in ancient Greece for the purpose of practicing dream control. These temples, thought to be in existence for more than a thousand years, were used as facilities for physical and emotional healing.[2] Within these temples, help was evoked from the gods. Hypnos, the god of sleep, was said to fan mortals with his wings to induce slumber. Then Zeus would give Morpheus, the god of dreams, warnings, prophecies, and inspirations to send to humanity via the winged messenger, Hermes.[3]

The seeking of special dreams to invoke the powers of the gods is called *dream incubation*. In ancient Greece, incubation occurred when a person slept in a sacred place after going through a ritual of purification. This usually involved abstinence from alcohol, meat, and sexual relations, along with an offering made to a selected deity.[4]

Many of the sacred Greek shrines such as Delphi, Apollo, and the temple of Epidaurus were advantageous to dream oracles; they were places where the deities were thought to reveal the secrets of inner knowledge. It was to these shrines that the sick would journey, hoping that Asclepius, the god of medicine and healing, would appear to them in their sleep. It's recorded that Asclepius offered advice during dreams in the form of herbal remedies and, on occasion, awarded instantaneous cures. He was thought to appear to his patients in their dreams, mixing potions and applying bandages to the sufferers' bodies, and in some instances summoning sacred snakes to lick the ailing areas. Those desiring a cure would sleep among nonpoisonous snakes, as they were thought to be symbolic healers. The association has carried forward in the modern caduceus, the symbol of two intertwined snakes signifying healing.[5]

It's interesting to note that in the yoga tradition, a coiled snake represents the Kundalini life force embodied in the base of the spine. Kundalini energy is believed to be the potency of the universe manifest within the human being.

Hippocrates, the ancient Greek physician and father of modern medicine, once said, "Some dreams are divinely inspired but others are the direct result of the physical body." He believed that the appearance of the sun, moon, stars, and natural phenomena were significant to the understanding of a person's health and well-being. If the sky in a dream was very clear, then the person's body was thought to be functioning normally. If the stars, for example, weren't clear or were falling from the sky, this signified a disturbance in the person's health. Hippocrates stated in his treatise on dreams, "It is a sign of sickness if the dream star appears dim or moves either westward or down into the earth or sea, or upward. Upward movement indicates fluxes [unusual discharges] in the head. Movement into the sea, disease of the bowels. Eastward movement, growing of tumours in the flesh."[6]

These symbolic interpretations might not be appropriate today, but they show the respect given to dream symbols in ancient times. It was noted in those ancient days that prior to the onset of disease, a dream would occur with the symptoms of that illness. In fact, these dreams today are called *prodromic,* which is derived from the Greek word *prodromos,* meaning "running before."[7]

Galen, the 2nd-century Greek physician, and Aristotle, founder of the science of logic, believed that dreams reflected the bodily state and could therefore be used to diagnose and treat illness. Plato considered the liver the seat of dreams, and in his famous work *Timeaeus* he claimed that prophetic dreams were received through the liver. Pliny held that dreams were supernatural in origin. In ancient Greece, dream interpreters were in great demand, much the same as medical doctors are today. Among the items looked for by dream interpreters were dream gates. In ancient Grecian dreams, two dream gates would appear, one consisting of ivory and the other of horn. If the dreamer saw the ivory gate, it was interpreted as a warning. If he or she saw the horn gate, the meaning was deemed prophetic.[8]

Several ancient civilizations revered dreams. In fact, four of the oldest civilizations—China, India, the Middle East, and Egypt— have left records indicating their use of dreams.

Dream incubation was widely practiced in Egypt from 4000 B.C. to 2000 B.C. The Egyptian pharaohs held dreams in great esteem, believing they were vehicles of guidance from the gods. Between the paws of the Great Sphinx is a slab of pink granite inscribed with the dream of a man who became an Egyptian king. One day while he was sleeping in the shade of the Sphinx, Ra, the sun god, appeared to him and told him that he would one day become the ruler of all Egypt. When he woke, he noticed that the Sphinx was covered with sand and in need of repair. He made a commitment that if he ever became the ruler, the Sphinx would always be kept in perfect condition. A few years later, true to the dream, he became Thothmes IV. Loyal to his promise, the ruler restored the Sphinx, and it has been maintained ever since.[9]

In Egypt, Imhotep was the equivalent of the Greek god Asclepius. In the shrine of Asclepius-Imhotep in Egypt reside records of interpretations of various dreams. One is inscribed, "A bed on fire means your partner is unfaithful to you."[10]

In ancient Syria, this was a special prayer for dreams:

My gracious god, stand by my side . . .
My friendly god will listen to me:
God Mamu of my dreams,
My God, send me a favorable message.[11]

In the Middle East, the practice of *istigara* was used to receive a dream that would answer a question. The *istigara* was a special dream prayer said just before falling asleep.[12]

Even the Old and New Testaments mention that God's will would be made known through the dreams and visions of the prophets. In fact, there are some 20 well-documented accounts that refer to divine guidance being given through dreams. In some cases, these dreams changed the course of destiny. Moses was instructed by God to listen for Him in his dreams. "Hear now my words. If there be a prophet among you, I, the Lord, will make myself known to him in a vision and will speak to him in a dream."[13]

In another account, an angel appeared to Joseph in a dream and said, "Joseph, thou son of David, fear not to take unto thee Mary, thy wife, for that which is conceived in her is of the Holy Ghost."[14]

In ancient Japan, dream incubation was practiced in both Buddhist and Shinto temples. Several Buddhist temples were famous as dream oracles. The procedure for obtaining a visionary dream was as follows: First, there was a period of abstinence, and a journey was made to the holy site where an offering was given. The dreamer would remain for a specified time of either 7, 21, or 100 days. These numbers were considered significant. The dreamer would sleep adjacent to the inner sanctum awaiting a special dream. It was believed that divinity dwelled in the inner sanctum. Often a healing dream would be requested (much as it would be in ancient Greece), and the Bodhisattva Kannon would appear in the dreams, healing ailments.[15] Regardless of which culture practiced dream healing, it was always the reigning deity who would come forth to effect the cure.

$$\mathcal{D} \mathcal{D} \mathcal{D} \quad \mathcal{D} \mathcal{D} \mathcal{D}$$

Chapter 5

Native Dreamers

The evening embers are dying. The lone cry of a solitary owl pierces the cold stillness. In the shadows, tribal members silently return to their tepees. The time of the big hunt is approaching, and tonight is set aside for dreaming. Tribal members embrace the quiet comfort of awaiting dream guardians, who are called upon to lend assistance and guidance. Tonight, their advice is sought as to where and when to hunt. Starry diamonds sprinkle the black sky. A shooting star punctuates the silence.

In the morning there's a gathering, and each dream is shared—and with each dream, certainty of the location and strategy of the hunt becomes clearer. The tribe knows that their survival depends on these dreams.

Native Americans gave special meaning to dreams. "Respect your brother's dreams" is a Native American proverb, and dreams were used by almost every tribe to predict the future, manage psychological problems, heal sexual difficulties, and cure ailments. Each tribe had very specific techniques for obtaining and understanding dreams. The study of the use of dreams among Native American cultures is a very complex one.[1] This chapter touches only briefly on their use of dreams.

To the ancient Native Americans, there existed only a thin line between the dream and wakeful states. They believed Mother Earth was a real entity and a powerful source of strength, and that the Creator pervaded all things in nature. They believed it was during the night that one could access the Creator, ancestors, and inner guidance. As a result, Indians gave great power to dreams.

In Mohawk villages, it was common for dreamers to become so inspired by images in their dreams that they'd create poems or riddles and would give or receive gifts based on whether other members of the tribe could answer the riddle.[2]

The Seneca tribe worked very intimately with their dreams. They demanded that each dream be acted out either symbolically or literally. It was this aspect of their culture that made their conversion to Christianity by the early French Jesuit missionaries extremely difficult.[3]

Each of the tribes of the Iroquois nation—Mohawk, Oneida, Onondaga, Cayuga, Seneca, and Tuscarora—called the Six Nations, participated in this unique daily dream ritual. Additionally, they'd gather each year for a special joint ritual sometime after the first snowfall. These determined Indians traveled great distances to attend the gatherings. When they arrived, they would each act out their dreams while wearing masks. Occasionally, they'd wear costumes along with the masks, and at other times, they'd perform naked except for a mask. The yearly festival of this traveling dream theater was known as the *Onoharoia;* it allowed many *Ondinnonk* (special dreams) to be acted out very dramatically. Many of the ritual masks of the Iroquois tribes were used in these ceremonies. Young men would perform in these dream shows, traveling from native settlement to settlement to act out their dreams.[4]

The people of the Iroquois tribes believed so strongly in the importance of *Ondinnonk* that they felt a person would become sick and even die if his dreams weren't acted out.[5]

The ancient aborigines of Australia believed in the power of dreams. Their rich and profound dream world encompassed much more than the dreams at night and still remains a mystery to the Western world. However, nighttime dreams were considered very important, and daily activities were often regulated by the sharing of dreams and their interpretations. Some aboriginal tribes believed that everything was a dream before the coming of white men.

Dream Guides

Central to most native tribes is the concept of a guardian or guide one can access while awake as well as during a dream. A psychologist might rationalize this as a gestalt conversation with an imaginary being who, in truth, is really an unacknowledged aspect of oneself. However, to the native people, the guide is very real. Their dream friends are as real as the friends they can touch during waking hours. Frequently, they fast in order to gain a dream guide, a special dream, or a dream song (a song presenting itself during sleep). Although native dreamers sometimes compose dream songs without fasting, the lack of food may, in some unknown way, enhance this mysterious creative process. Perhaps the thin air that's unique to the high mountains and rocky areas preferred by some Native Americans as places to fast also influences the quality of their dreams.

Research indicates that when individuals are involved in extremely quiet pursuits, they're more apt to experience a greater number of dreams than when busy with social activities. They'll also have longer REM cycles each night—as much as 60 percent more REM sleep. Increased isolation seems to cause an increase in dreaming, and total isolation can produce hallucinations in some people. Physical inactivity is also a factor in causing increased dreaming.[6]

Native American Use of Dreams

Ancient Native Americans had a variety of practical uses for their dreams. In addition to discovering times and places for hunting and planting, they also used dreams to determine names. They would incubate or ask for the name of a new child, and the name would come in a dream. Frequently, creative dances and songs came during dreams, and numerous cultural artifacts are believed to have had their origins in dreams. Some of the decorative patterns on blankets, paintings, jewelry, and clothing are also thought to have been conceived during dreams.

Common Traits of Native Cultures

The following traits are evident in all native cultures that possess a high regard for dreams:

- Dreams are considered vital to success in life. This attitude made it easier to recall and interpret dreams for the ancient people and remains true today.

- Supernatural figures appear in dreams, granting special powers or giving important information.

- Shamans (medicine women and men) are expected to use their dreams to acquire knowledge.

- Dreams are induced by utilizing techniques such as sleeping alone in a power spot or a sacred place, or by fasting.[7]

Interestingly, research indicates that 80 percent of all hunting and fishing societies use dreams to seek and control supernatural powers, while only 20 percent of all agricultural and animal-raising societies use dreams for this purpose. Thus, it appears that the more dependent a tribe was on hunting and fishing, the more likely it would be to use dreams for guidance and insights.[8]

To some extent, dreams are now considered relics of the human mind. However, in the recent past, native people had a direct path to them. They knew that as they lived close to nature and moved in harmony with all of the earth's cycles, it was far easier to access the mystical world of dreams, and they were able to interpret the meanings and images of their dreams. Now, as our societies have moved further away from nature, we've forgotten our ability to access our dreams directly and easily.

We can glean wisdom from the ancient Native Americans. Take off a day or a week and spend time in nature, away from electricity and machines. Rely on your resources. Get back in touch with the cycles of nature. Spend time in the moonlight, allowing it to bathe you. As a result of this gentle respite, you'll find it much easier to access your dreams and gain powerful insights from them.

※ ※ ※   ※ ※ ※

PART III

Dream Makers

In the beginning, the attempt of our crossing
is clumsy, unsteady, the way is
mysterious and unclear, our dreams
are woven of thick coarse wool.

Along the way, we find the vestiges
of our ancestors, ancient dream weavers,
left as guideposts, illuminators, lighting
our way, refining the quality of our weave.

— M. Anne Sweet

Chapter 6

Dream Recall

Your dreams can provide you with fantasy, adventure, and romance. They can serve as a mystical key to foretell the future and unravel the past. Your dreams can rival Hollywood in providing you with entertainment, but with *you* as producer, director, and star—all worthy of Oscars. However, if you want to recall your dreams, you need to remain cognizant and alert at all times or you'll forget the roles you've played. You also won't remember the other actors and the significance of each one. You'll undoubtedly forget the lines you spoke even before awakening. Just as it requires skill for actors to memorize their lines, it requires skill for dreamers to recall their dreams.

The single most important element in remembering dreams is motivation. To acquire that motivation, you must first perceive your dreams as worthwhile; regard them as valuable messages received from your subconscious. It's imperative that you believe they deserve to be heard.

Contemplate each dream as if it were a brilliant gem with each lustrous facet reflecting a clear and remarkable new insight into your inner being. Each dream is a portal that allows you to gaze deeply into your depths. From these different perspectives, you'll gain great wisdom in understanding yourself. Therefore, if you regard your dreams as valuable and useful, you'll be motivated to recall them.

Dream-Recall Blockages

If you're presently unable to remember your dreams, perhaps some attitude is blocking your ability to do so. To see whether this is the case, participate in the simple process outlined in the following pages. This will help you become aware of and release limitations—even those hidden in your subconscious—that are blocking your dream recall.

During this process, you'll be given a list of some of the more common attitudes that make dream recall difficult. One or more of the beliefs might apply to you. Take time to read the list thoughtfully *out loud*. If any of the statements seems to fit or feel right, be ready to jot down your experience.

On a separate sheet of paper, note the following headings, leaving room for a sentence or two after each.

Attitude

Thought response:

Emotional response:

Body response:

Affirmation:

Your Thought Response

If you read a specific statement (attitude) that seems true for you, notice the thoughts you have in response to it. (See pages 44–45.) Observe what you're thinking in terms of any denial or affirmation. Note whatever thoughts occur to you as a result of hearing yourself say this attitude out loud. Above all, remain honest with yourself, and keep in mind that there's no right or wrong thought. This exercise is simply to assist you in recalling your dreams.

Your Emotional Response

Observe your emotional response to hearing or reading the statement. What specific emotions does the attitude in question generate in you? Remember, don't judge your response; simply notice it. *The very act of examining attitudes will allow you to release them.*

Your Body Response

Notice your body's response. Even when it seems difficult to be conscious of thought or emotional response, your body will often send its own clear messages. It's responding, although subtly at times, to the attitudes spoken, and it's possible for you to become aware of these responses. As you state the attitude, practice learning to recognize even those slight changes within your body. It might only be a small tightening in the center of your chest or a twitch in your left eye. Your body is always giving you clues. Listen to it, for these signs can be used as a valuable indicator of concerns that are still blocking your dream recall.

Your Affirmation

The last section on your list, *Affirmation,* is something you create for yourself. An affirmation is a positive thought that reaffirms the direction in which you want your thoughts to go. Find or create an uplifting statement that will release the attitude that's blocking your ability to recall your dreams. Attitudes form pathways on which your thoughts journey. They're well-worn pathways you consistently choose, without thinking, just like you'd automatically take a well-traveled trail to cross a field of tall grasses. If a person has the attitude that "dreams are of no consequence," every time the word *dream* comes to mind, it's as if the mind runs down the path labeled *Dreams are not important.* This path can become so worn that it requires conscious effort to create a new one.

Likewise, a positive thought or affirmation, such as *My dreams are valuable and important,* will begin to create a new pathway. Eventually, if affirmed often enough, the new pathway will replace the old one. When a thought regarding dreams occurs, the mind will begin to travel the new path and reinforce the thought that dreams *are* valuable. As a result, it becomes easier to recall dreams.

At the end of this section are some suggested affirmations to enhance dream recall.

Attitudes That Block Dream Recall

To begin the exercise, say these statements out loud and write down each one that applies to you and note your internal response.

- I don't feel that dreams are important.

- I'm not sure I really want to know what's in my subconscious.

- I need sleep. Dreams prevent me from getting a good night's sleep.

- I might learn things about the future that I don't want to know.

- Maybe we're not meant to remember.

- Sexuality in dreams is disturbing.

- I might have nightmares.

- I feel out of control in my dreams, and that's uncomfortable for me.

- I might open myself up to psychic forces.

- It's distressing to do things in my dreams that are inconsistent with my waking values.

- Something difficult happened in my past, and I don't want to think or dream about it.

- It takes too much time and effort to remember dreams.

These are only a few of the attitudes held by people who don't recall their dreams. As you check to see if any of these are appropriate for you, see if there are others that apply to you as well. Remember, just becoming aware of and exploring attitudes is often enough to cause them to dissipate so that dreams can be more easily recalled. Following is an example of how your experience might appear on your chart.

Attitude

I don't feel that dreams are important.

Thought response:
I feel that they're important to *other* people who are having problems.

Emotional response:
When I say this attitude, I feel some irritation and even anger.

Body response:
After saying this attitude, I notice that I'm not breathing very fully and my lower neck muscles feel tight.

Affirmation:
There is <u>great</u> importance in dreams. My dreams allow me to unlock unseen potential within myself. I enjoy dreaming, and I remember my dreams easily.

Affirmations That Promote Dream Recall

- *I enjoy dreaming, and I remember my dreams easily.*

- *My emotions are valuable, and I appreciate my emotional dream life.*

- *I have all the time I need to remember dreams and to assimilate them.*

- *I accept my past unconditionally and know that everything that has ever happened to me in my life (and in my dreams) has been necessary for me to get where I am now.*

- *My dreams give me valuable perceptions that allow for more balance and joy in my life.*

- *Dreaming allows me to be more creative, and I love recalling my dreams.*

- *I don't judge my dreams. I know that every message from my subconscious deserves to be heard.*

- *Dreaming gives me valuable information about the future.*

- *I deserve sexual pleasure, and it's enjoyable to experience dream sex.*

- *I give myself permission to recall and understand the deeper meaning of my dreams.*

- *There is <u>great</u> importance to dreams. My dreams allow me to unlock unseen potential within myself.*

- *I enjoy dreaming, and I remember my dreams easily. So be it!*

Diary of Dreams . . . Your Dream Journal

I never travel without my diary. One should always have something sensational to read in the train.
— Oscar Wilde

A dream journal is a record of your inner journeys and quest for self-understanding. Recording just one or two dreams, however, won't provide you with nearly enough information. Carl Jung felt that true self-knowing comes from observing and interpreting a series of dreams over a long period of time, perhaps even years. He felt that in this way, individuals could begin to weave a tapestry of the recurring themes pervading their lives. As you continue your daily dream journal, you'll gain an understanding of your purpose and destiny, and it can actually become your personal book of wisdom.

Dreams are forgotten very easily (usually within ten minutes of awakening), and it can take an enormous amount of willpower to pull them back into conscious thought. Research has revealed that dreaming is accompanied by rapid eye movement (REM). Sleepers awakened during REM sleep were in the middle of a dream;

sleepers awakened immediately following REM sleep recounted completed dreams; and five minutes after REM sleep, sleepers remembered only fragments of dreams. *Ten minutes after REM sleep, the sleepers had virtually no recall.* Thus, it's literally within the first few seconds of awakening that a dream is still vivid in its entirety. Consequently, it's imperative that you write down your dream as soon as you wake while it remains fresh in your memory. Jot down as many details as you can recall. Lucid dreams, however, because you're a conscious participant, will remain in the memory for a much longer time.

What You'll Need to Record Your Dreams

1. An easy-flowing pen
2. A notebook, journal, or recording device
3. Flashlight or night-light (if using a notebook)
4. Easily seen clock

Easy-Flowing Pen

Be sure you have a pen that writes easily without pressure, such as a felt-tip pen. Don't use a pencil, as it writes too lightly for notes taken when you're very sleepy. Place both pen and diary next to your bed.

If you prefer pens that have their own lights, these can be bought at medical-supply shops. A less costly way to accomplish this is to purchase a penlight and tape it to your pen.

Notebook or Journal

The best kind of dream journal is a spiral-bound notebook. A loose-leaf notebook isn't as useful, as the papers can slide and move while you write.

Divide your notebook into two sections. On the left side, write the date, hour, and all the details of your dream. On the right side, note your interpretation (see the example on the following pages).

It's important to write the date in your journal ahead of time, as this sets up a positive expectation that you *will* record your dream on that date. Recording the date can also make it easy for you to notice and record a realization later concerning a particular dream on a specific date. For example, you may have had a powerful dream on October 24, and then later realized that it was your mother's birthday. While not being consciously aware of it at the time, your mind was responding to your emotions and feelings toward her. Later, having this information may provide you with valuable insights regarding you and your relationship with your mother.

You might also want to jot down the heading **Dream 1** in your journal. This again sets up a positive expectancy that you'll have more than one dream during the night. As soon as you've recorded your first dream of the evening and before you go back to sleep, write **Dream 2** in your journal, setting up the expectancy of a second dream.

When recording your recollections, also note the feelings you experienced in the dream. Jot down predominant colors, symbols, key words, themes, and emotions. Try not to get stuck on one small detail so that you forget the rest of the dream. If you heard a poem or an interesting expression or phrase, record that information first. Then record the visual parts you remember, as they tend to be retained longer than anything heard in a dream.

For individuals who find it difficult to wake up enough to turn on a flashlight or a tape recorder, there's an eyes-closed technique. As you awaken, feel for the notebook next to your bed. Then with your eyes still closed so that you remain involved in your dream, begin to write. You'll have to experiment to find a way to avoid writing over what you've already written. One method is to extend the little finger of your writing hand as a guide in finding the top or side edge of the paper; this gives you some indication of where you are. Some people who have difficulty reading their nighttime writing prefer to scribble their dreams on scrap paper and later transfer it into their two-sided notebook.

How to Set Up Your Dream Journal

Dream 1

Date:
Time:
Location:

[Here's where you write your interpretation of the dream.]

[Note everything that you can remember, every word or image. Write the first thing that comes into your head even if it doesn't seem like a dream.

Note your feelings while involved in the dream. Record anything you heard.

Note colors, symbols, key words, themes, and emotions.]

Example of a Dream Journal Entry

Dream 1

Date: *December 7*
Time: *4:20 A.M.*
Location: *Home*

My car isn't working properly. I look under the hood and notice that the radiator is empty. I keep adding water, but it keeps coming out of a hole in the bottom.

The feeling is one of frustration.

Interpretation

The radiator is the cooling device of the car. If it's empty, the car overheats. My car seems to symbolize my body or me. Also, to me, water represents spirituality. I keep emptying my spirituality out of myself. If I keep doing this, I'll overheat and I won't be able to run or function. I feel that this dream is telling me to spend some time being still and attuning to my spiritual side. I think it also means to drink more water. (I later found out that my steering fluid had leaked out during the night, giving the dream a somewhat prophetic aspect as well.)

Recording Device

The advantage of using a recording device is that you can usually stay more in touch with your vivid dream images than when you write them down. For those who have a hard time falling back to sleep after writing, a tape recorder or a recoding device is an excellent tool, enabling you to record more detail in less time. One disadvantage to using a tape recorder is that you will later need to transcribe the dream into your journal. Another disadvantage is that while it may seem that you're communicating clearly, in the morning you may not be able to understand your midnight ramblings. Very often your voice will sound as if you've come from another dimension, and, in fact, you have. If you use a recording device, you might consider getting the small handheld type that's used for dictation. In the dark, these are easier to use than the larger models.

Flashlight or Night-Light

A battery-operated light is valuable if you're writing in your journal at night. Although small flashlights work well, the small battery-operated lanterns sold in camping-supply shops seem to work best. Using one of these will keep you from having to juggle the flashlight as you write.

Easily Seen Clock

It is valuable to note the time of your dreams so that you can begin to see patterns in your dreaming, especially if you're working with the ancient Chinese meridians. (See Chapter 23.)

Begin to Record Your Dreams

- Put your tape recorder or journal next to your bed with your flashlight, pen, and clock.

- Lie in a position that allows your spine to be straight while you program yourself for dream recall.

- Choose one of the Before-Sleep Dream-Recall Techniques. (See below.)

- Sweet dreams!

Before-Sleep Dream-Recall Techniques

Tibetan Dream Meditation

As you lie down to go to sleep, *concentrate on your desire for dream recall.* Now focus your attention on the back of your throat. Imagine a glowing blue sphere in the throat area, and imagine putting your desire for dream recall within that blue orb. Hold that visualization until you fall asleep. Using this technique, you may find that your dream recall is greatly increased. It's interesting to note that this ancient Tibetan technique has an interesting physiological parallel. Research has shown that it's this area at the back of the throat (which is near the stem of the brain) that controls the activation of dream states. Thus, it may be by connecting with this potent area before sleep, you begin the simulation of dream activity and recall.

Water Technique

Fill up a glass of water and drink half of it before retiring. As you drink, affirm to yourself, *Tonight I remember my dreams.* When you wake in the morning, if no dream recall is evident, drink the rest of the water, saying to yourself, *My dreams are recalled, now and throughout the day.* Often drinking the second half of the glass of water stimulates dream recall. Sometimes that recall will occur spontaneously during the day.

Third-Eye Technique

This technique also uses water for dream recall. Put a bowl of water next to your bed. Right before sleep, dip two fingers into the water and lightly touch your throat. Then rub these two fingers on your forehead in the area of your third eye (the area between and slightly above your eyes). As you rub this area, affirm that you'll remember your dreams. The next morning, again touch these areas with water. Very often this will stimulate recall.

Spiritual Assistance

Relax your body, keeping your spine straight. Let your mind become still and receptive. Pray or ask your dream guide for assistance in remembering your dreams. (See Chapter 5.) Strongly affirm that you'll remember your dreams, and repeat this to yourself several times as you fall asleep.

Creative Visualization

As you begin to fall asleep, visualize yourself waking up, looking at the clock, noting the time, and writing down a dream. Continue this visualization forward in time until you see yourself waking in the morning and writing down another dream. Visualize yourself looking and feeling very satisfied because you've recorded your dreams.

Four Directions Technique

This technique has several parts and is an excellent method not only to remember, but to obtain a vision in your dream.

1. *When you enter the area where you'll sleep, smudge the area with sage, cedar, juniper, or sweet grasses.* Smudging means to offer or hold the smoldering herbs so that the smoke goes to each of the sacred directions—north, east, south, and west, and to Mother Earth and Father Sky (below and above). You can use a feather or a fan to direct the smoke. Smudge the area around your body for purification. This ancient ritual is for dedication and purification. It was felt that there could be direct communion with the Creator through smoke. One's prayers rise through the smoke, and the Creator sends messages or blessings down to the person through the smoke.

2. *When you get into bed, replay each action of the day, moving backward to the time when you woke in the morning.* Then begin the day anew in your mind, replaying each event from morning onward, changing your response to any situation in which you wish you'd behaved differently. For instance, if you judged someone wrongly, review the situation—but this time, with understanding and kindness.

3. *Say a prayer of thanks for the goodness in each day,* and affirm your intention to live a balanced and compassionate life.

4. *Imagine an upward-spiraling double helix of energy spinning through you* as you count backward from ten to one, affirming that you'll remember your dreams. Your very last thoughts before sleep are often the ones that affect your dreams.

5. *Ask for the guidance of the Creator in your dreams.* Ask for a revelation of the path you are to follow.

6. *In the morning, give thanks for all that you've received.*

After-Sleep Dream-Recall Techniques

Rolling Technique

Research has shown that dreamers usually roll over or change positions immediately after a dream. It's thought that this helps you move into a different brain-wave pattern (and also discharges the dream). If you can't recall your dreams, try changing your position, as sometimes this will spontaneously generate dream images if you happen to move back into the position that you were in when you had the dream. It seems that dreams are coded into the position that you were in while you had them, and gently rolling over can initiate recall.

Conversation

Immediately after waking up, share with someone what you remember. Just beginning to talk about your dream will allow more of it to rise to your consciousness.

Writing

When you write in your dream journal, just note whatever you remember, even if it's only a word or a feeling. If you don't remember anything, write: "I don't remember my dream." Very often this will stimulate dream recall. Or write down how you feel about not remembering, as this frequently gives a clue to the dream.

Imagination

When you wake in the morning (and don't remember your dreams), imagine that it's the night before and you're getting ready for bed—brushing your teeth, lying down, and going to sleep. Then just watch the images and feelings that occur, and imagine what kind of dreams that you might have had. Even though it might sound strange to *imagine* your dream, this exercise often spurs dream recall.

Doodle Technique

If you didn't remember your dream, begin to doodle in your dream journal. Often this right-brain activity triggers associations and sparks your memory.

Color Technique

In this process, get a sense of what color your dream *felt* like, and begin coloring or imagining that color to incite recall.

Gestalt

Place two pillows on the floor. Sit on one and say to the other, "Okay, dreams, why aren't you coming into my memory?" Then move to the other pillow and answer; for example, "You're always in such a rush in the morning, I never feel that I have time to come forward." Move back and forth between the pillows as the dialogue continues. Then ask, "How can I remember my dreams?" Notice the different voices and body positions you use for each one. The conversation can be written as well as verbalized.

Mood Savoring

With your eyes still closed, just before you get out of bed, notice your mood and indulge it. The mood you're in when you awaken often reflects the activity in your dreams. Exaggerating your mood often stimulates dream memory.

Dream-Recall Hints

Write it down. No matter how sure you are that you'll remember the dream, you most probably will not. Write it down.

Don't move. When you write in your journal immediately after a dream, try to move as little as possible. Research in dream laboratories has shown that movement often impairs recall. When people roll over as they're awakened from a dream, they have a more difficult time remembering the dream. (Use the rolling technique only if there isn't *any* dream memory.)

Watch those flashes. Often a dream doesn't appear, but you have a vague feeling that one is just around the corner of your mind. It's as if it's delicately perched on the edge of your consciousness, waiting for some familiar element in your waking life to stimulate recall. These images can be so fleeting that you must remain conscious of the images that suddenly pop into your mind. Watch those images that flash into your mind during the day.

Record the fragments. Even if it's only a dream fragment, don't dismiss it, record it. It can be important for self-understanding.

Record each dream as it occurs. It's difficult to record all your dreams every morning. Laboratory tests have shown that even if someone does remember all their dreams in the morning, they're less vivid and detailed than if they were recorded as they occurred. Just imagine watching four or five movies over an eight-hour period and then trying to remember them all at one time. Your memory is more exact if you record your dreams as they occur.

Sleep for shorter periods. Try to sleep two or three times a day. If you can change your sleeping patterns so that you have five hours of sleep at night and then one or two naps, you'll feel more energized because you're constantly refreshing yourself, and you'll recall your dreams much more easily.

Read and study. Learn as much as you can about dreams. Where intention goes, energy flows. As you increase your awareness in the area of dreams, you'll increase your ability to recall your dreams.

Name that dream! When writing in your journal, give each of your dreams a descriptive title. These are good reference guides for later.

Wake up naturally. Train yourself to wake up before your alarm. Waking up to a jarring noise often alters the quality of your dream.

Have a hard case? If you still don't remember your dreams, you'll have to find a way to sleep more lightly. Drink a lot of water before bed so you'll have to get up during the night to go to the bathroom. Sleep in a chair. Any way that you can think of to sleep lightly contributes to your dream recall.

Embrace your nightmares! Write down all your dreams, even nightmares and other dreams that you *don't* feel good about. Humans are not just "good." We are whole—a balance of light and dark, yin and yang, good and bad. We are total, infinite beings, and because of this it's important to honor and accept all aspects of ourselves. Every dream is important. As you write it down, affirm that this dream is indeed significant.

Resist the urge! Resist trying to explain away the dream by relating it to a late-night snack, a television show you saw right before bed, or a book you were reading. These activities are just triggers for you to reach into a deeper part of your psyche. Fifty other people seeing that same TV show would have 50 different dreams. Similarly, if you're awakened by a dog barking and you dream that you're surrounded by raging wild dogs, someone else, under the same circumstances, might dream about his favorite childhood dog bounding toward him. Each dream can be explained by the barking, but each dream has important symbols that are unique to the dreamer.

Don't feel guilty if you forget to remember a dream. Guilt will only hinder your progress. And if you do feel guilty, don't feel guilty about feeling guilty.

Interpret the meaning? You don't need to figure out the meaning of every dream. Often, just reviewing a dream several times will greatly contribute to your inner balance. Love and enjoy your dreams, interpreted or not!

Have fun! It's not necessary to record all your dreams. If you don't feel like doing it, don't force yourself. Dream recall and recording should be fun!

ᗡᗡᗡ ᗡᗡᗡ

Chapter 7

Dream Aids

Potions, totems, and nature's rhythms and cycles have been an integral part of the healing and visionary arts of shamans, kahunas, seers, magi, druids, and medicine men and women. Throughout ancient lore and recorded history, there have always been references to power objects used to facilitate divination and inner knowing.

Today, you can use these tools for deeper exploration of your dream realm.

Stones

Ever since man first appeared on this planet, stones have been held in great esteem for their perceived mystical qualities. The aboriginal peoples of the world, as well as mystical secret societies, have passed on their unique uses of stones to assist in understanding the unseen realms.

The stones discussed here are but a few that can be used to assist dreaming. It's important to remember that, of themselves, these stones can do nothing. It's your *intention* that activates them for dream use.

Moonstone

The moonstone, with its silver white light undulating on its surface, is sacred in India. It's thought to bring good fortune. Used as a gift for lovers, it's believed to arouse tender passion and give lovers the ability to see into the future.

In many cultures, it's felt that this stone changes with the phases of the moon. As the cycles of the moon are connected to dream cycles, the moonstone connects us more deeply with our inner dream states.

The moonstone is also soothing to the emotions. It's believed to enhance physical and emotional balance for women during their menses. As the cycles of the moon are very connected to dream cycles, the moonstone connects us more deeply with our inner dream states. Sleep with a moonstone near you or tape a small one on your third-eye area. As you fall asleep, dedicate your moonstone to your dream life by holding the intention that it will stimulate your dreams.

Selenite

This translucent crystal is ruled by the moon. It's named after Selene, the Greek goddess of the moon. This stone is used to gain understanding of one's personal truth. It can allow for a deep calming and the attainment of profound inner states. It symbolizes pure Spirit and can be used for spiritual advancement. Selenite is also an alchemic key to the past and the future.

Selenite is associated with your crown chakra and is a powerful tool for developing intuition and telepathic powers through your dreams. Use it for stimulating dreams of mental and spiritual clarity. It can also be an excellent stone for telepathic communication during the night. It, too, should be dedicated before sleep, to assist dream recall as well as to gain spiritual understanding through dreams.

Pearls

Not technically stones, pearls are ruled by the moon and are conducive to dreams. They're formed inside oysters, which come from the sea. The moon not only affects the tides and creatures of the sea, but it influences our dreams as well. The layers of the pearl are deposited in a concentric manner. Their spherical shape, soft luminescent color, and multiple layers are symbolic of the nonlinear nature of dreams. Pearls come from water, but even on land they maintain their connection to the ebbing and flowing and intuitive nature of the sea. Pearls from the ocean are more potent as dream enhancers than are freshwater pearls. However, having any pearls in your dream space will assist you in experiencing intuitive dreams.

Crystals

Crystals have been used since the beginning of mankind as objects of wonder and as a means of understanding and viewing unseen worlds. Their mystique spans time and culture alike.

The scepter of the Scottish regalia is topped by a crystal globe. Sir Walter Scott said that among the Scottish Highlanders, crystals were called Stones of Power. There are references to the power of crystals in ancient Greek and Roman writings. Egyptians in the 11th dynasty used crystals for viewing inner dimensions. In addition, shamans in Australia, New Guinea, Africa, and the Mayan area used these amazing stones. In ancient Japan and China, rock crystals were thought to be the congealed breath of dragons. To Asians, the dragon was emblematic of the highest powers of creation. Almost every major culture with an esoteric understanding has used quartz crystals for "seeing."[1]

Native Americans were especially adept in the use of crystals for power dreams. Apache medicine men and medicine women used crystals for inducing visions and finding lost property. Cherokee shamans used crystals for healing and inner "seeing." Sitting with their crystals, which they regarded as friends, they'd burn cedar and offer prayers asking for a dream or vision to guide them.

Many metaphysicians believe that crystals were used for dream work in the lost continent of Atlantis, and through the use of crystals, people could travel through time and space during their dreams.

Crystals are basically magnifiers and transmitters. They were used in the original radios. In fact, silicon, which is in the crystal family, is the basis of computer technology. It allows for the processing of enormous amounts of information by transmitting electrical currents over its crystalline structure. As there's a bioelectrical current within human beings, we can literally avail ourselves of the power of crystals to "transmit" or enhance dream states by transmitting our intention through its crystalline structure.

Using Crystals to Expand Your Dream States

The right crystal. It's preferable to have a crystal that's used just for dreaming and nothing else. A clear quartz crystal that is terminated (comes to a point) on one end is best.

Cleansing. The best way to cleanse a crystal dedicated to dreams is to leave the crystal outdoors on a clear night when there's a full moon. Place the stone so that the moonlight shines directly on it all night. If this isn't possible, try one of the following:

1. Rub your crystal with eucalyptus oil.

2. Let your crystal soak in water and sea salt.

3. Place your crystal outdoors in the sunlight for at least five hours.

4. Place your crystal in the ocean or a running clear stream for an hour.

Dedicating the crystal. To dedicate your crystal, hold it up to your third eye and say a dedication, either quietly or aloud.

Program your crystal for only one thing at a time. Here are some sample dedications:

- *I dedicate you, Dream Crystal, to dreams that will contribute to more joy in my life.*

- *I dedicate you, Dream Crystal, to dreams that will empower me with a strong belief in my own worth.*

- *I dedicate you, Dream Crystal, to dreams that will enable me to develop my unique creative skills.*

- *I dedicate you, Dream Crystal, to dreams that will allow my relationships to heal.*

- *I dedicate you, Dream Crystal, to dreams that will give me powerful insights into my future.*

- *I dedicate you, Dream Crystal, to dreams that will assist me in healing myself and others.*

- *I dedicate you, Dream Crystal, to dreams that will deepen my connection with Spirit.*

It isn't necessary to dedicate it again. However, if you're going to change its programming, cleanse and rededicate it.

Dream door. Put your dream crystal in a special place when you aren't using it. You can wrap it in black silk to hold the energy, or you can put it in a special spot where you can admire it during the day. At night, place it near your bed. Just before sleep, hold the crystal to your third eye and imagine that your consciousness is melting into it. Imagine that within it is a mystical door to your dreams. See that door opening. Know that you've opened the mysterious door to your inner realms. Then keep your crystal near you throughout the night.

Amethyst

The amethyst is in the crystal family. Its rich purple reflects the ability to move easily from one reality to another. The color associated with the third eye is purple, and this magical stone can be used to open the third-eye area for spiritual dreams. It is a calming, emotionally balancing stone. As it soothes the mind and emotions, our innermost nature can come forth in our dreams.

It's also excellent for people who have recurring nightmares. To use it for this purpose, place your amethyst on your forehead (on the area of your third eye) and program it for deep, calm sleep. It is also an excellent stone to place under your pillow for "sweet" dreams.

Dream Pillows

Whether there's some special ingredient in herbs that facilitates dreams or whether it's a behavioral response connecting your dream desire with the aroma remains unknown. The unique scent of the mugwort is thought to open the third eye (the door to dreams). Smelling it while you sleep isn't only believed to assist you in remembering your dreams, but also to revealing dreams of the future. When you sleep with a pillow filled with mugwort, a connection is established between the fragrance of the herbs and your desire for a special dream. What's important is that using a dream pillow really works. Other herbs that can be used in dream pillows are borage, lavender, and yarrow.

The best way to prepare and use a dream pillow is as follows:

- Make sure that the herbs are of the highest quality and, if possible, free of pesticides.

- Use a natural fiber when making the pillowcase. The best fabric is silk, as it's an excellent conductor of bioelectrical energy. Wool is also excellent. Many

meditators and yogis sit on wool or sheepskin because
this helps them align them with the bioelectrical
energy flows of the planet. Using wool or silk for your
dream pillow will help you experience dreams that are
more potent because your bioelectrical energy will be
more balanced.

- I suggest using lavender or purple material because
these are the colors of the portal to dreams and will
contribute to the power of your dream pillow.

- Use your pillow only for dreams so that it's the only
thing you associate with dreaming. You might keep
it in a special box or covering and take it out only at
night, just before bed. The fragrance will then be an
intimate reminder of the alignment between you and
your dreams.

- Hold the pillow close to your nose as you drift off to
sleep. Keep uppermost in your thoughts the desire for
a dream. In the morning, deeply inhale the fragrance
of your dream pillow. This will usually revive the
memory of a dream.

The Chinese Clock

Chinese, Japanese, and Indian cultures have all traditionally
thought of time as a nonlinear, circular process (as opposed to the
Western concept of linear time). In Chinese medicine, the day
is divided into hours assigned to different organs and different
aspects of the body.

For example, gallbladder time is between 11:00 P.M. and 1:00
A.M. It's interesting to note that two of the most potent dream herbs,
mugwort and yarrow, are also used to stimulate bile production
in this organ. It isn't a coincidence that the same herbs used to

induce dreams are also gallbladder herbs. Most individuals have their first dream of the night during gallbladder time. In addition to the innate dream-inducing qualities of these herbs, inhaling their aromas or drinking these herbs in a tea stimulates the governing organ (gallbladder) that allows your body to move into alignment with the natural rhythms of the universe. When your body is in alignment with the natural cadence of the universe, you'll have more powerful dreams.

If you go to sleep during, or just before, the gallbladder time, before going to bed, rub your fingers on the temple area above your ears to further stimulate your gallbladder meridian.

Notice what hour you go to sleep, then enhance your dream states by stimulating the corresponding meridian points before sleep.

Fall Asleep	Stimulate
9 P.M.–11 P.M. Triple-Warmer Time (Regulates some of the body's fluids, and is one of the meridians that distributes energy [chi])	Rub behind your ears
11 P.M.–1 A.M. Gallbladder Time	Rub above your ears
1 A.M.–3 A.M. Liver Time	Rub the area over the liver
3 A.M.–5 A.M. Lung Time	Rub indentions between upper ribs and shoulder
5 A.M.–7 A.M. Large Intestine Time	Rub the muscle between forefinger and thumb

Fall Asleep (cont'd.)	Stimulate (cont'd.)
7 A.M.–9 A.M. Stomach Time	Tap lightly under the eyes
9 A.M.–11 A.M. Spleen Time	Apply circular pressure over spleen, on the right side of the body just below the ribs
11 A.M.–1 P.M. Heart Time	Rub the armpit area of the left arm
1 P.M.–3 P.M. Small Intestine Time	Apply deep pressure around the outside base of little fingers
3 P.M.–5 P.M. Bladder Time	Rub the area where eyeglasses rest on the nose
5 P.M.–7P.M. Kidney Time	Rub the center of the sole behind the ball of the big toe
7 P.M.–9 P.M. Circulation/Sex Time	Massage middle fingers

(For more information about how to understand dreams using the Chinese clock method, see Chapter 23.)

ANCIENT CHINESE CLOCK

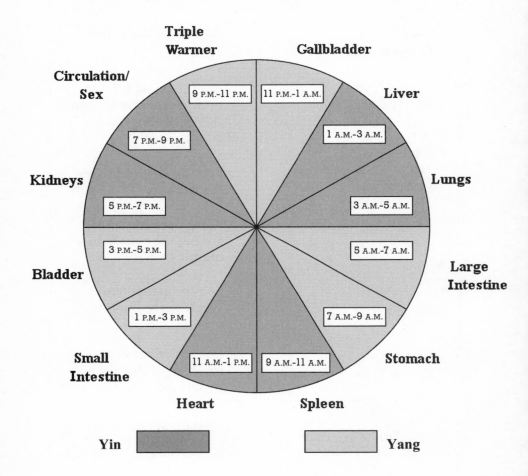

Bodily Alignment

When possible, sleep with your head toward magnetic north. This will better align your bioelectrical energy lines and thus contribute to better dream states.

Food and Drink

Your diet can greatly affect your dream states. If you eat foods that you have trouble digesting, this may contribute to dreams that are "hard to digest." Research has shown that pressure in the digestive system creates restlessness and causes us to wake up with only rambling dream fragments.

If you're properly digesting and assimilating your food, then you'll have dreams that you can "assimilate." It's best not to eat immediately before bed.

Melons. These are thought to contribute to vivid dream states. The high water content and round shape of melons suggest an alignment with the moon and the dream realms. Perhaps melons contribute to dreams because they act as diuretics, causing you to sleep lightly and thus allowing you to remember your dreams more easily. Perhaps there's some inherent quality to melons that contributes to dream recall. For whatever reason, they seem to assist some people in recalling dreams. For digestive purposes, eat melons separately from other foods. "Eat them alone or leave them alone" is the current maxim.

Vitamin B_6. For some people, taking 50 mg of this vitamin shortly before bed can contribute to dream recall, perhaps because of the diuretic effect of B_6.

Alcohol and other drugs. Alcohol and many drugs repress dreams. The person who regularly goes to bed intoxicated robs him- or herself of restful sleep and dreams. The ancient Greeks, masters of the art of dream interpretation, declared that anyone wanting to enter a dream temple had to abstain from alcohol for three days prior to entering. They felt that clear dreams were difficult to obtain for people who were under the influence of alcohol.

Moon water. Drink water that you've left outside in the moonlight for an hour. Be sure that the moonlight shines directly onto the water, not through the glass. Drink this moon water just before going to bed to enhance dreaming.

☞☞☞　☞☞☞

Chapter 8

Dream Incubation

The mother crane cautiously peers out through the rushes as the cold Canadian winds whip at the lake. Beneath her lie three perfectly formed eggs, warm and snug as their mother protects them from the elements. Sunbeams slant through a dark cloud, a chilling rain falls . . . and the eggs are safe. The evening darkens. The moon's reflection on the water is broken again and again by ripples created by the wind. Still the eggs are safe. Through the long, dark night the eggs incubate. The faint light of dawn accents the sounds of water dripping down the marshy reeds. Beneath the mother crane . . . three feeble, yet jubilant, baby birds.

Just as the crane incubates her eggs to allow them to come to birth, you can incubate your dreams. You can direct your dreams by consciously intending to do so. This idea isn't uncommon. We tell someone who is stuck in a problem, "Sleep on it." Then in the morning, as if by miracle, there's the answer that was needed.

Dream incubation is the concept that you can consciously guide the course of your dreams from the wakeful state. For example, a problem presented during waking hours can be resolved during sleep simply by making a conscious choice to do so. It can be done simply by giving a persona to your dream states.

Perhaps you're in a dilemma with one of your children. You might suggest, "Dreams, give me information that will help me resolve the difficulty I'm having with my son." You may also ask: "Dreams, what would be a valuable career move for me?" or "Dreams, why am I having a hard time losing weight, and what can I do to assist myself in this situation?" or "Dreams, I haven't been feeling well lately. Is there any specific nutritional guidance that will help me feel better?" Each of these is an example of dream incubation. You can even ask your dream persona about previous dreams with regard to specific understanding: "Dreams, why were there kangaroos in my dream last night? What was the meaning of that dream?"

As I mentioned, you've probably heard the expression "Sleep on it" in connection with problem solving. Sometimes, putting the problem in the background and getting a good night's sleep will lead to a solution or resolution through a dream. This communication with your dreams can give you answers to many questions in your life.

Almost everyone who studies dreams concurs that they allow us to get in touch with hidden parts of ourselves, tapping wisdom far greater than anything we're consciously aware of. Dream experts differ, however, about the source of the information that comes forth. Some believe it's from a force external to ourselves, such as our guides and/or God. Some are convinced it is our higher self. Other dream experts feel it's simply a segment of our psychological makeup that we aren't in touch with during normal consciousness. Nevertheless, through incubating dreams, it's been proven repeatedly that you can receive information that will assist you when awake.

It's up to us—the dream makers—to translate these nonphysical, nonmaterial expressions into images that make sense in our three-dimensional, linear consciousness. The goal of dream incubation is to create a dream that makes as much sense as possible—that's very clear and understandable.

You can also incubate dreams to test future probabilities. By imagining possible conclusions, you can examine future actions as well as compute the outcomes. This enables you to experience an outcome without actually taking an idea to its completion in your daily life.

When you incubate your dreams, it's likely that you may experience profound emotions in the dream state. Enjoy your emotions as you would a symphony. Be willing to experience the gamut of your emotions. Allow your feelings to ride the waves of the high and low periods that present themselves to you. Breathe in the excitement when listening to the crescendo and decrescendo of your symphony. Enjoy the anger, caress the sadness, experience the boredom—celebrate each nuance and variation as it occurs. Enjoy all aspects of your dreams; each is an integral thread in the weaving of life.

You can even incubate dreams simply for the enjoyment of it, just as you would enjoy a movie or favorite television show. They need not always be scrutinized for their significant meaning in your life.

If there's an area of your life that you'd like to explore, or if you desire a psychic perception about yourself, dream incubation can be valuable. Here are some simple guidelines.

— Choose a time when you aren't too tired and have had no drugs or alcohol. Make certain that you'll have plenty of time in the morning to process the information given during the night.

— If there's an issue that you want to incubate, first begin to contemplate the specific issue. Consider the solutions already presented, and get in touch with your feelings and emotions concerning this issue. Think about what you might need to release if that issue was resolved. Ask yourself, *Am I willing to have this resolved? Am I willing to let go of this difficulty?* Consider how different life would be if that problem was solved. Evaluate the issue from all perspectives.

— Place your dream journal or recording device beside your bed. Make sure your spine is straight. As you fall asleep, repeat your request several times, for example: "Help me understand my fear of the dark" (and repeat). Next, imagine that you're releasing all thoughts, attitudes, and feelings regarding that issue. Simply concentrate on your question, repeating it over and over to yourself. If you notice any distracting thoughts, allow them to filter through your awareness, then return to your proposed question. "Dreams, help me understand my fear of flying. Tonight, I release my fear of flying." Hold these thoughts in your mind as you drift off to sleep.

— Incubated dreams usually occur the same night as you request them. Occasionally, however, they will occur the following night. Trust any information that's revealed, even if it appears not to make sense at the time. Write down everything you received immediately upon waking. Be patient in waiting for the understanding. Frequently it isn't until the next day or even the next week that you're able to make any association between the dream and the issue from which it was incubated. Nevertheless, within that dream is the answer to your problem or dilemma. Any incubation efforts that you perceive as failures often prove to be quite valuable. Trust that a higher part of yourself has already solved the problem.

Dream incubation is often a valuable tool in releasing relationship difficulties. For example, Alice's father gave her a horse, and this seemed symbolic to her. Consequently, she incubated a dream that would help her understand what the horse represented. The dream revealed a past lifetime that Alice shared with her present-day father. (See Chapter 12.) In the dream he'd left her, riding away on a horse. Alice realized that for her, the horse symbolized painful abandonment. As a result of this one dream, she was able to release a great deal of anger she had felt toward her father. This opened the door for her to create what is now a deep and more loving relationship with him.

Incubation can be used to receive many types of information. An example of this occurred when I was preparing a new course on manifestation for my seminar curriculum. I'd been incredibly busy the week before and had been unable to spend much time on preparation for teaching the workshop. Early one morning the entire seminar appeared before me in a dream, so I leaped out of bed and wrote down all the details. The information I received was so extensive that I was unable to cover all of it during the daylong seminar.

The idea of dream incubation originated in ancient Greece. As mentioned earlier, research indicates that there were 300 to 400 temples built in honor of the god Asclepius. These temples were in active use for nearly a thousand years, beginning at the end of the 6th century B.C. and culminating at the end of the 5th century A.D.[1] Dreamers would go to a sacred dream temple for the purpose of receiving a useful dream from a god. They believed that by sleeping in holy places and appealing to a deity, they could obtain profound answers to their inner questions.

To participate in dream incubation now, it isn't necessary to sleep in a sacred place or to appeal to a specific god. However, I find that if I honor my place of sleep as an inner temple and appeal to Spirit, both the vivid clarity and the contents of my incubated dreams are enhanced. If possible, locate a beautiful place in nature, as was done in ancient times, and create a sacred sleep chamber. You might also consider creating a moon ritual. (See Chapter 24.) After selecting your form of ritual and purification, call on the Creator or your dream guide to lead you through the night hours, asking for the dream you desire. Ancient Indians, Chinese, Japanese, Egyptians, Hebrews, and Muslims practiced dream incubation in places of rare beauty found in nature.[2]

When you use dream incubation, anticipate that all your dream expectations will be met. In ancient times the dreamer would participate in purification rites, sacrifices, and other rituals and ceremonies. However, the same effect can be produced if you have a clear intention when you incubate your dream. The manner in which you phrase your dream incubation statement is very important. Instead of "I hope tonight I understand why my relationship with my aunt is difficult," say, "Tonight, I understand my relationship with my aunt." Your dreams will respond with clarity proportionate to your intention.

𝕯𝕯𝕯 𝕯𝕯𝕯

Chapter 9

Lucid Dreaming

Have you ever been dreaming and then suddenly become conscious that you were dreaming? In lucid dreaming, you're aware that you're dreaming during the actual dream.

You've probably experienced some degree of lucidity. Perhaps you had a frightening dream, only to find yourself thinking, *Hey, I'm okay, this is only a dream!* When you realize that some segment of your experience is a dream, it's called *prelucid dreaming*. A fully lucid dream is one in which you definitely recognize that you're dreaming. These dreams tend to seem as real and vivid as normal, conscious reality. Also, the senses of sound, sight, taste, and smell seem intensified.

Although lucid dreaming has received much attention from the metaphysical community in recent years, it isn't a new idea by any means. Lucid dreaming has always been an element of the spiritual practices of Taoism, Buddhism, and Hinduism.

The Tibetan Buddhists have expanded the practice of lucid dreaming into an art form. They believe that dreaming is a way to connect more deeply with your soul. They feel that each time you dream, you're experiencing the condition of your soul essence, and that if you die while dreaming, the dream will continue. The ancient text *The Tibetan Book of the Dead* gives instructions on how to pass through the different dream dimensions that occur after death. These dimensions are called *bardo states*. If you're unable to maneuver your way through the bardo states, you're forced to reincarnate into another life. However, if you successfully weave through these dream states, you return to God and total oneness. Obviously, then, lucid dreaming is of the utmost importance to Tibetan Buddhists. They consider it a means to release themselves from what they consider a world of suffering.[1]

The value of lucid dreaming is enormous. When people begin to experience lucid dreaming, the truth of who they really are and their personal reality expands. They begin to feel more expansive—as you do when taking in a deep breath of fresh air—and this feeling begins to affect other aspects of their lives. Personal limitations begin to dissolve, and there's a sense of being more in control of personal destiny. Intuition and imagination during waking hours are noticeably increased.

One of the goals of lucid dreaming is to transport your wakeful consciousness into your dreams and your dream consciousness back into your wakeful life without feeling a break. The purpose for this continuity in consciousness is that it allows the dreamer to recognize that the world of the wakeful self is a self-created dream as well. If you're working with lucid dreaming, an excellent affirmation to keep in mind is: *All that I see I can dream. All that I dream I can see, and I am aware of all of my dreams.*

Lucid dreaming can be regarded as a spiritual evolutionary process, a step toward remembering who you are and what your true destiny is. An Arabic mystic said, "A person must control his thoughts in a dream. The training of this alertness . . . will produce great benefits for the individual. Everyone should apply himself to the attainment of this ability."

Cultivate the skill of lucid dreaming as you would any other skill. Just as the ability to drive, swim, or paint can be developed and fine-tuned with practice, so can the ability to experience lucid dreams. It takes some discipline at first, but it becomes easier and, in time, effortless.

1. *Lucid dreaming techniques.* As you're going to sleep, say, "Tonight I'm aware and conscious that I am dreaming." Use the techniques in Chapter 6 to recall your dreams, and as you remember a dream during the night, while you're drifting back to sleep, say, "During my next dream, I remember that I am dreaming." Sometimes repeating the phrase *I am dreaming* several times as you fall asleep will be of help. Having made a conscious choice to experience lucid dreams, be vigilant and consistent. Over a period of weeks, it will begin to happen for you.

2. *Applications.* Once you're adept in this skill, you begin to alter the circumstances of your dreams. Choose some action you can take. Start with something simple. The Mexican mystic Don Juan told Carlos Castaneda to try to look at his hands while he was dreaming. Other simple dream actions could be picking a flower, opening your arms to the heavens in delight, or even hugging a tree. Give yourself a task to perform in your dreams.

Stanford University psychophysiologist Stephen LaBerge, a proponent of lucid dreaming, has developed sensors that detect the eye movements that accompany vivid dreams. A pulsing red light is then used as a signal to remind the dreamer that he or she is dreaming and thus help the individual have a lucid dream. Although mainstream sleep and dream researchers may be skeptical of this controversial technique, it demonstrates once again the interest being generated for a deeper understanding of our dreaming selves.[2]

ᛏ ᛏ ᛏ ᛏ ᛏ ᛏ

Chapter 10

Dream Gazing

Dream gazing is similar to daydreaming with an added dimension—it's daydreaming with discipline. It's one way to access the mystical world of dreams through your wakeful consciousness. As you glide deeper into the inner realm, the world of dreams begins to blend subtly with the world of your daily life. Just as it is possible to alter your life through your dreams during the night hours, you can also use daytime dream-gazing techniques to alter your life.

In an interview, author Richard Bach revealed the process he used in writing the magical book *Jonathan Livingston Seagull.* Bach described being in a kind of dream state while still awake, wherein he saw a vivid image of a little seagull flying in sunlight. The flash of inspiration gained from this vision grew into the beautiful photos and text of his book. Bach said that he transcribed the images revealed to him while still in the waking dream state.[1]

Bach was referring to the ability to dream while awake, which I call *awake dreaming* or *dream gazing.* To dream gaze, first allow yourself to become very relaxed. Suspend your normal thoughts.

Letting them go frees your mind and body to release all tension. Then simply imagine a dream. Create any dream you like, allowing it to be as unpredictable as one that would occur during sleep.

Start with a very simple, one-minute dream. Then write down exactly what the dream contained. This is especially valuable if you haven't been recalling your nightly dreams. You can become familiar with the world of dreams through daytime dreaming.

Another advantage of dream gazing is that it can help you deal with a difficult scenario in your daily life. You can create or imagine a dream simply by suggesting, "In regard to the situation or difficulty, I am now going to create a dream." Allow your mind to wander freely while you create this dream. Carefully notice the symbols and feelings that begin to well up. This will begin to assist you in resolving your difficult issues.

For example, if your elbow is giving you a great deal of pain because of an injury or illness, you might imagine a dream where you're scrambling through a jungle. Suddenly a huge black panther is right behind you in swift pursuit. You leap toward the safety of the dense underbrush, and when you look up, you're looking into the golden eyes of the panther! Without a second's warning, the panther jumps, gripping your elbow in its jagged teeth. You hear the fragile bone snap in two. The pain is excruciating. You're aware of an overwhelming sense of dread and abandonment. You realize you're totally alone. There's no one to help you, no one you can call for help. No one.

To look at this awake dream, write down the details and examine the different aspects of it. First, you're in the jungle, which may represent your primitive nature, your primordial self. The panther is chasing you. Perhaps the panther symbolizes your unconscious, the dark side of yourself, your shadow. You fear encountering your shadow, the primordial reflection of yourself. As the panther rips into your elbow, your elbow seems immobilized. You also sense being unable to move. Perhaps your awake dream represents fear of the primordial part of yourself, which is preventing you from moving forward in life. You may feel restricted in life because of that fear. As you're nursing your elbow, you're filled with an acute sense of aloneness because no one is coming to your rescue. By beginning to understand the underlying causes of your awake dream, you'll probably begin to feel relieved of the problem.

In exploring your awake dream more closely and in understanding its symbolism, perhaps you discover that the fear in the dream represents your fear of moving out into areas that are unknown to you. Then as you begin to affirm and strengthen your belief in yourself—for example, repeating to yourself something like, *I am able to move into the unknown easily and effortlessly*—you may find that your elbow has greater movement and is no longer in such pain.

For me, dream gazing is a powerful and useful technique. It enables me to move to the very heart of any difficulty and usually facilitates an expedient resolution.

🕉 🕉 🕉　🕉 🕉 🕉

PART IV

Dream Workers

Apprentices of subtle craft,
we have gathered much in the following
of this age-worn path:
journeymen to the Loom Masters,
we spin the tapestry,
pictorial odyssey,
crystallized visions,
loving designs of the heart.

— **M. Anne Sweet**

Chapter 11

Dreams for "Seeing"

As I raced down the beach, sharp stones cut my feet and tears stung my face as the wind whipped at my clothes. A thunderstorm marked the sky with jagged scars across dark clouds. Finally, I fell to the ground. Sobs ripped through me as I clutched at a rock and squeezed it until its edges cut into my hands. I wanted to die. I'd been betrayed. Empty and vacant, I got up and walked home. As I lay in bed, a fog of loneliness suffocated me. I'd never felt so alone. Gradually, the gripping tension lessened, and I drifted off into a restless sleep.

Hazy, dark shadows slip in and out of my dreams . . . misty specters aimlessly wandering in a chasm of darkness. In the distance, I can see a brilliant light. I'm drawn to its soothing glow, but shrouded beings tug at my arms. Wrenching away from their bony grasp, I glide to the light; its beacon is a relief to my hollow heart. I hear a voice say, "You've passed the second barrier, and you will never need to return this way again. I am with you . . . I am with you . . . I am with you." The sound of the voice seems to echo inside me, resounding with strength and power as it gathers energy, much like that of an approaching storm.

Slowly the image faded; and I fell into a deep, sweet sleep. I woke up feeling so refreshed. The night's storm had cleared the sky, and sunlight filtered softly through my bedroom window. I stretched and reached to touch the sunlight, caressing its warmth with my fingers. I felt so new. Something had lifted during the night. My grief had melted and there was an awareness of the beginning of a new day. Something mystical had occurred during the night hours. Someone had entered my dreams and soothed me. At that crossroads in my life, many years ago, a spirit visitor, vaguely familiar to me, pointed the way . . . and made all the difference.

Prophetic Dreams

Most people can recount at least one dream that provided them with a new understanding of life or that helped them during a crucial period. These dreams appear to reach beyond the ordinary boundaries set by most dream analysts. They are monoliths speaking of an ancient wisdom and a deeper magic. These are the prophetic or visionary dreams of old; and they originate from the wellspring deep within us, where the Creator resides. These dreams aren't necessarily ordered or commanded, but reach out to us in times of need. They lend assurance and guidance through the "dark night of the soul." The prerequisites to tracing the thread that leads to vision and prophecy in your dreams are an open heart and the willingness to ask . . . and listen.

Visionary dreams are different in character from precognitive dreams, which allow you to glimpse the future. Dream researchers state that these dreams are fairly common. Even Freud reported cases of precognitive dreams. One thoroughly documented case is the story of Clinton H. Elliott.

Back in the mid-1950s, Elliott dreamed that his sister would die in a matter of six weeks, which, in fact, she did. What was most amazing about this was that it added credence to his claim that he'd dreamed that he, too, would die soon. When he received this message, he informed his family and friends and began to put his affairs in order. He calmly made plans for his family's future and even told his wife the kind of funeral he desired. At age 66, death was easily a possibility, except for the fact that he was remarkably healthy.

Elliott was employed in the construction of a tunnel being built under Boston Harbor. Although his belief in his impending demise might have contributed to a slow, dwindling death, this wasn't the case. Elliott died by accident—a very strange accident. He was at his work site, discussing his prediction with the other construction workers, who, needless to say, were a bit skeptical. As Elliott finished his shift, an enormous crane, which had been checked thoroughly by the safety inspectors less than an hour before, suddenly collapsed, killing Elliott immediately. It was a totally unforseen accident to everyone . . . except Elliott. He had dream-predicted his own death.[1]

Almost all death dreams indicate psychological release or the death of old beliefs rather than actual physical death, but in this case, Elliott *was* able to see the future through his dreams. Dreams with prophetic import have often led to historical consequences. The Duke of Wellington was inspired to restore the Alhambra in Spain as a result of a dream in which he saw this beautiful Moorish palace disintegrating. President Roosevelt declared that Washington, D.C., needed a new airport because he'd had a disturbing dream that foretold of an accident due to the disrepair of the existing one. Cornelia, the wife of Caesar, had a prophetic dream of her husband's death and tried to forestall his attending the fatal meeting of the Roman Senate.

Often, our personal spirit guides give us information in our dreams. However, there are also disseminating guides, who, rather than work with only one individual, serve a purpose similar to broadcasting. When an idea whose time has come emerges, these spiritual beings begin broadcasting that information. People who have their psychic antennae tuned to that "station" will receive the information. This is exactly why inventions or discoveries occur at the same time in several parts of the world, often within days of one another. When people are sleeping, they are less mentally defensive, so they're more receptive to information being broadcast from the psychic realms. Hence, many discoveries have their origins in dreams.

Dreams of Those Who've Passed On

Often, dreams are a means for those who have died to communicate with us. It seems easier for us to hear them through our dreams. It's more for our sake than for theirs. Sometimes they come just to let us know that they're all right so we don't worry about them. However, at other times there's something we haven't completed in regard to this individual—perhaps something we didn't communicate—that has become a stumbling block for us. The visitation will often clear up those blockages.

There are occasions, however, when there's a message or warning that these departed ones feel we need to hear. Keep in mind, though, that just because someone has died, it doesn't necessarily mean that he or she has grown in wisdom. If individuals are lacking in wisdom when they're alive, they possibly will continue this way when dead.

So remember to weigh the advice that's given against your own good judgment.

If you need to resolve an issue with those who've died or feel a need for their comfort or solace, "call" upon them just before drifting off to sleep. The way to do this is to feel that you're touching their essence. Allow yourself to experience the connection you had with these individuals when they were still living. As you're going to bed, hold their essence close and ask them to come to you during the night; doing so can help ease your loneliness when those who were close to you have died.

Alien Encounters in Dreams

Some individuals have remarkable alien encounters during their sleep, and these types of dreams have been increasing. Over the past years, many best-selling books and top-grossing movies have concerned aliens. Either we've become more receptive to their tentative venturing, or *they* are becoming far more persistent. For whichever reason, the UFO phenomenon is here to stay and will become increasingly prevalent in our lives and play a more significant role in our dreams. For the most part, the alien beings that appear in dreams offer valuable advice and guidance. However, remember that even though they might come with lovely, lofty messages, first and foremost, you should follow your own inner guidance.

Deepen Your Ability to Have Visionary Dreams

There are very specific methods for increasing your ability to have psychic or "seeing" dreams. The first step is to incubate for your dreams. (See Chapter 8.) You can incubate for visionary dreams, precognitive dreams, past-life exploration, astral travel, or even to enter the realm of fairies and angels.

Whether these seeing dreams are "real" or the figments of a collective consciousness is irrelevant. The value comes from the experiences you have during the night. Ask yourself:

- *Are the messages gained from these dreams valuable?*
- *Do they contribute to my life?*
- *Do they expand my inner horizons?*

Any dream that allows you to look into the future, view the past, communicate with loved ones who've passed on, gain a vision, or even enter into other dimensions is a *seeing* dream. These special kinds of dreams expand your horizons into the realms beyond ordinary perception of reality. They allow you to reach below the surface of the human mind, to the place where the world isn't made of separate parts but is seamlessly joined in a rich tapestry of interrelatedness. In the deepest sense, your seeing dreams allow you to step beyond the confines of your life experiences into a much more profound arena.

These kinds of dreams are like holograms where an entire object can be reproduced from a small part of the hologram. A visionary dream may contain the innate structure for a larger segment of life. They are special dreams that allow us to expand our sense of self from the restriction of a limited point in time and space into a much more vast universe of awareness.

I'm often asked how you can tell if a dream is a precognitive one or just a psychological balancing of inner concerns. The following criteria have assisted me greatly in making this distinction.

How to tell if a dream is precognitive:

1. The dream is in color or the colors are unusually vivid. A precognitive dream isn't always in color, but this can be one of several determining factors.

2. You'll get the message in three different ways during the dream. The message may appear in three separate but distinct forms within one dream.

3. There will usually be a round or circular object within the dream. This can be a ball, a round plate, a circular mirror, or something similar.

If a dream that seems precognitive fits all three criteria, there's a very good chance that it's a foretelling dream. Sometimes you'll get a precognitive dream with all the criteria yet interpret it incorrectly. The following letter is an example of this process.

Dear Denise,

The following is what I believe was a prophetic dream. I used your method of dream interpretation to decipher this dream, and it met all three requirements of a prophetic dream: 1) There were three parts; 2) it was in extremely vivid color; 3) it contained a significant object that was round.

I'd been interviewed for a different job within my company a few weeks before this dream, and I was awaiting further developments. This is the dream; it was in three parts:

First, I dreamed that I received some news about a job. I was quite excited about it. Then there was a sudden change. In the second part of the dream, I was in an office. A couple of men, who were my new bosses, were talking. I looked down and noticed I was wearing a hideous pair of trousers. They were bell-bottoms with green, black, and white-striped designs. I was extremely embarrassed and tried to make myself inconspicuous. I wanted to change into another pair of trousers without the men seeing me. In the third part of the dream, I was in a big gymnasium. There was a huge piece of paper covering the entire floor. My new job was to fold and unfold the paper into different configurations, like origami, the art of Japanese paper folding. My co-workers and I created various shapes by folding them. One was a huge round hoop or a ring shape.

I was awakened by the telephone ringing. It was my mother informing me that the office wanted me to come in for a second interview. She'd been calling repeatedly, but I hadn't heard the phone.

As I drove to the interview, I was thinking this was going to be a piece of cake. I was sure I had the job because I'd so clearly had a prophetic dream in which I got a new job. The interview was difficult. The guy asked technical questions that I was unable to answer, and he cut me off every time I tried to tell him about myself. I remembered feeling embarrassed by the entire situation.

A week later, I found out that I hadn't gotten the job. When I heard the news, I thought maybe it wasn't a real prophetic dream after all, but later I realized that I just hadn't interpreted it correctly. In the first part of the dream, I received news about a job. That happened.

I was called in for the second interview. In the second part of the dream, I was feeling inadequate and self-conscious, which is exactly the way I felt in the interview because I couldn't answer the technical questions the interviewer asked me.

The paper-folding part was a little more obscure, but that was also prophetic. My search for another job is a large, convoluted task. I keep turning opportunities over in my mind, pulling them apart and putting them together in various ways, symbolized by my folding and unfolding the paper.

I learned from this dream that the obvious interpretation might not always be correct, especially when I'm too attached to the interpretation. I was so excited about the interview that I jumped to conclusions and didn't take time to listen to my feelings or really study the dream. I thought you'd be interested in hearing about this.

Shine on brightly,
Karl

The way that Karl learned from his dream, including the realization that he was trying to fit his dream to his expectations, was a valuable lesson. Dreams for "seeing" will allow you to expand your inner horizons, and as you do so, your outer boundaries will also expand.

ॐ ॐ ॐ ॐ ॐ ॐ

Chapter 12

Dreams for Past-Life Recall

The gondola gracefully swayed through the calm sea just off the coast of Venice. The oarsman bellowed off-key arias as we gently glided past one island after another. One particular island seemed to glisten more brightly than the others in the distant haze. As I pointed it out to my singing host, he gently headed the gondola toward it. It seemed to beckon mysteriously to me.

As I stepped onto the dock of the island, a slightly balding, round Franciscan monk rushed to greet us. He spoke some English and offered to give me a tour of the entire isle, which consisted of the Franciscan monastery and its grounds. (It's named St. Francis Island.) As I followed his rotund form, I had an overwhelming feeling of déjà vu. I was so comfortable there; I felt as if I knew exactly what was around each corner, even before we reached it. Images and forgotten memories flooded my consciousness. How could I know my way so clearly? I'd never even heard of this island. Suddenly, as we rounded another corner, I viewed a scene far different from the one I was "remembering." Unable to help myself, I blurted, "Oh, this is new!" With an astonished look, the monk replied, "It is new to the original structure . . . but it is more than 600 years old." To my amazement, I'd unearthed memories of being a monk on this lovely island hundreds of years ago. Thus, my journey into past-life exploration began.

Have you ever had the experience of being in a foreign place and sensing a familiarity too uncanny to describe? Have you ever listened to a particular piece of music and instantly found yourself transported to another time and place? Perhaps you met a stranger and experienced an instant rapport that you didn't understand, or you met someone new and took an immediate dislike to him or her. Have you ever had a dream in which you found yourself in a foreign place, or in foreign clothes, yet experienced a tremendous sense of familiarity? It could be that you were being reminded of someone or someplace from your childhood long forgotten, or it could be that you'd lived there before. Perhaps you were in that foreign town in a different body, in a different time. Could it be that you knew that stranger in another existence—in another incarnation? Could dreams be a key to past lives?

The concept of reincarnation was known long before recorded history. In fact, more than half of the people in today's world believe in reincarnation—the idea that the soul is eternal and, as such, returns to the Earth plane again and again, through rebirth in various bodies, in order to grow and learn. Each lifetime provides experiences that allow one, as Spirit, to become stronger, more balanced, more loving, and, eventually, to unite with God.

In one life, you may live in poverty to learn humility and resourcefulness. In another lifetime, you may be extremely wealthy to learn to deal with money fairly and in a positive manner. In one life, you may be blind in order to learn inner sight, and in another one be athletic, enabling you to experience and fully understand physical strength. You may be a woman in one life and a man in another, or be Caucasian in one and Asian in another. Past lives aren't so much building blocks as they are a jigsaw puzzle, with each life contributing to our evolution in becoming whole, complete, and balanced.

"As ye sow, so shall ye reap." This is the law of karma. Karma is the fate we create for ourselves as a result of our actions in this lifetime as well as in previous ones. The idea of karma gives us a clearer understanding of why one individual may experience adversity throughout his or her entire life while another has a seemingly easy path.

Reincarnation and karma provide us with a clearer picture of our purpose and mission in the present through our understanding of previous lifetimes. They also give us a better understanding of our destiny in the universe. Life isn't a onetime affair, nor is it a series of meaningless experiences strung together haphazardly. Rather, it's a mystical, ongoing journey that allows each of us to emerge as conscious, loving beings. *The search for the soul may be the most important work we ever undertake,* and discovering who we were in our far past can facilitate that journey.

Throughout history, celebrated philosophers have pondered the vast mysteries of life, death, and rebirth. The first record concerning reincarnation was discovered in Egypt. Those early philosophers believed the soul was immortal, and when the body perished, the soul entered another human body.

The ancient—as well as the present-day—Hindus believe that the soul is immortal and inhabits one body after another, in search of its true divine nature. In the centuries preceding Christ, Buddha shared wisdom regarding the cycle of reincarnation, the great wheel of life and death. Buddhists, similar to the Hindus, strive to be released from the death/rebirth cycle by attaining nirvana, or oneness with God. The Essenes, an early Jewish sect, are also said to have believed in reincarnation.

In 500 B.C., the Greek philosopher Pythagoras wrote of reincarnation and gave descriptions of his personal recollections of his various incarnations. Plato also believed in reincarnation and the continued evolution of the soul. Napoléon Bonaparte once admitted to having been Charlemagne in a past life. Voltaire, the French philosopher, observed that "it's not more surprising to be born twice than once." And the Spanish painter Salvador Dalí confessed that he was the great Spanish mystic St. John of the Cross. Even such diverse New World personalities as Benjamin Franklin, Ralph Waldo Emerson, Henry Ford, Walt Whitman, Henry Longfellow, Henry David Thoreau, Thomas Edison, and General George Patton ascribed to the teachings of reincarnation.[1]

Benjamin Franklin, in one reference to past lives, wrote his own epitaph, which has since been titled "the most famous of American epitaphs." It reads as follows:

The body of B. Franklin, Printer;
like the Cover of an old Book,
Its Contents torn out,
And stript of its Lettering and Gilding,
Lies here, Food for Worms.
But the Work shall not be wholly lost;
For it will, as he believ'd, appear once more,
In a new & more perfect Edition,
Corrected and amended By the Author.

There are many excellent books on the subject for those who are interested in seeking proof of reincarnation. My purpose here, however, isn't to refute any doubts regarding past lives, although I firmly believe in them. Rather, I intend to illustrate that your dreams can serve as a doorway to your past. By stepping through that door, you may expand the quality of your life beyond your expectations.

The value of discovering your past lives is immeasurable. Spiritually exploring past lives and other dimensions is a way to tune in to inner guidance and leads to personal integration. It will help you find yourself more often in the right place at the right time. It can also help you develop a strong relationship with your spirit guardians, as well as help you experience spontaneous spiritual awakenings.

To release problems without exploring the source beneath the symptoms is like attempting to kill weeds with a lawn mower. The problems will come up again and again until one removes the roots that created the difficulty. Someone who eats compulsively may discover that the roots of this problem lie in another life in which he or she starved to death and that fear has now resurfaced as an insatiable desire for food. By experiencing a past life either in your wakeful or dream state, you can begin to release the decisions made in past lives that are affecting you today.

Children are especially adept at recalling their past lives in the dream state. When my daughter was eight years old, she shared with me a remarkable dream in which she was a black man during the time of slavery. She described in detail how her trousers were ragged at the edges and how she tilled the soil with a dilapidated hoe. She confided that some of her present-day friends were also black slaves in that dream. Perhaps one of the most curious factors regarding this experience was that one of her friends, whom she'd seen in this dream, had had a similar dream in which she was also a black slave in the South.

In order to connect with your past lives during sleep, it's important to utilize the variety of techniques described in Part III. Each evening before retiring, repeat to yourself, "Tonight, I dream of a past life." Continue to recite this phrase as you drift off to sleep. When you first begin, you may find that you receive only a wisp of a memory that could be from the past. To receive more clarity, during your waking hours use your imagination to expand what you've received, regardless of how insignificant it may seem. For example, let's say you saw an ornate helmet in one of your dreams. When you wake up, imagine the kind of person who might have used that helmet. Imagine where he might have worn it as well as the circumstances of his life. Imagination is an invaluable resource in discovering your past.

Imagine a past life associated with your dream images, and more often than not you'll begin to see who you once were. Often, individuals who've obtained vivid past-life dreams have actually traveled to one or more of the places they experienced in their dreams and have discovered that their dream perceptions were accurate. Past-life recall can be fun in the dream state and enormously rewarding in your daily life.

❦ ❦ ❦   ❦ ❦ ❦

Chapter 13

Dreams for Astral Travel

I soar, frolic, and gallop with ecstasy to the lofty ceiling of my bedroom, and then dive for the comfort of my soft teddy bear. With a burst of glee, tumbling and twirling, I fly to the ceiling once again with reckless abandon, taking a moment to hover over my rag doll's cradle. My mother opens the bedroom door. "What are you doing, Denise?"

Innocently, I respond, "Oh nothing, Mommy."

"That's nice," she murmurs and closes the door. Only momentarily disturbed, once again, I'm jumping off the bed, arms outstretched, my body careening wildly through the air.

When I was a young child, I was always leaping off the end of my bed, flying through the air. I really believed I could fly. I didn't know that I was experiencing astral travel. As I got older, I forgot the ability to fly consciously. In my dreams, however, there were relics of this memory. Occasionally, I'd discover myself in a dream soaring over the rooftops and racing to the stars. In my 20s, I enrolled in a weeklong course on astral travel. There, I reclaimed a degree of the skill that had given me such joy as a child.

Astral travel is one category of dream experience not included in the definitions of dreaming or lucid dreaming. It's commonly referred to as an out-of-body experience. This is when your spirit is literally separated from your physical body, and it usually occurs during sleep. Numerous esoteric religions and philosophies are based on this experience. In addition to a sense of separation from the physical body, there's a self-awareness that's extremely vivid that accompanies astral travel. This is quite different from most dreams; however, astral travel isn't uncommon. In fact, during sleep, the sensation of a quick jerk may be indicative of a difficult astral reentry into your body. We often have out-of-body experiences yet fail to recall them.

Dreams of flying or of being in an airplane frequently accompany out-of-body experiences. Also, people who actually fly, such as pilots, in their waking life are often inclined to have out-of-body experiences. Research indicates that people who as children believed they could fly, or liked to jump off trees or roofs, also have this tendency.

There are records of such accounts occurring throughout history; and descriptions of these are similar whether they took place in India, Egypt, South America, or even in the Midwestern United States. Vivid out-of-body experiences are frequently triggered by an accident or a near-death experience.

In rare instances, they're generated by a deliberate, conscious attempt to leave the body. Most people find that these experiences tend to be extremely joyous and dramatically alter their beliefs concerning the nature of personal reality. Specific studies reflect that at least 25 percent of adults recall having had at least one out-of-body experience in their lifetime. Many didn't realize that they were having out-of-body experiences until the phenomenon was defined for them.

There appears to be no research indicating that damage results from consciously leaving your body. In truth, it's a very natural occurrence. It's interesting to note that when you're having an out-of-body experience, you don't experience time or space as you generally do. Another unique phenomenon is that you may notice—when you first leave your body—that you seem to remain very much in your present physical form. However, the longer you're separated from your physical body, the weaker that sensation becomes, and your "being" appears to transcend into a cloudlike vapor or some other amorphous substance.

There are certain variables that seem to influence the out-of-body experience. Alcohol appears to be a definite deterrent to this phenomenon. One thing that seems to slightly increase your ability to leave your body is the way you position it, particularly if you lie in the north-south direction with your head to the north. This alignment is also valuable in regard to deep sleep. If you desire a very restful night's sleep, placing your head toward the magnetic north is ideal; however, if you want to feel energized, placing your head toward the south works best. For astral travel, your head should be toward the north.

In a book by Carlos Castaneda, Don Juan, Castaneda's mystical teacher, instructed him in the arts of lucid dreaming and astral travel. Don Juan maintained that when one had mastered the techniques of dreaming, there was no longer any difference between the things one did while asleep and while awake.[1]

Author Oliver Fox astral traveled extensively and wrote about these experiences. He said that the scenes he encountered were more beautiful, glamorous, and mystical than anything he'd ever seen while awake. He described his sensations as exquisitely enjoyable and said that his mental state was one of extraordinary clarity, power, and freedom.[2]

When I began to astral travel as an adult, I remained close to my home. I observed myself wandering through the rooms in our house. Curiously, my traveling would often be in a different time frame—it would be daytime instead of night. The astral dimension is an arena that's outside the space-time continuum. As I gained more confidence in this area, I began to experience floating, and eventually, flying. At the start, I'd venture only a few feet above the ground because I was afraid that I would fall. As I grew in confidence, I felt the ecstasy of flight.

My first adult recollection of astral travel was a frightening one. It was a very humid night in Hawaii. Early that evening, I'd spent time with a good friend, casually discussing the art of astral travel. Neither of us had experienced it. We jokingly agreed to meet each other at 3:00 A.M. and selected a location. Before I retired, I said to myself, "Tonight I will meet Jennifer at 3:00 A.M. by the waterfall in the upper Manoa Valley."

At about 3:00 A.M., I awoke, aware of a very strange sensation. Although the room was dark, I felt a kind of rocking, floating sensation, as if I were drifting on a rubber raft in a swimming pool. I was startled. The ceiling, which was normally six to seven feet above my bed, was now only inches from my body. I was weightless . . . without substance. What was this? What was happening? I couldn't understand why I was hovering so near the ceiling. Was it a dream? I was fully conscious, and it seemed so very real. I was so light, so free. Then, almost as an afterthought, I rolled over gently and noticed that my bed was below—with me in it! The terror of seeing my body was so great that I immediately zoomed back into it with a harsh jolt. The shock was so profound that it was a long time before I ventured out again.

It was as if I had split into two different people. The part of me that I identify as "who I am" was free, light, and floating. The other part, which I associate with my physical body, was somehow me but not me, lying on the bed, a mere physical shell. This was the first of my many explorations into the nature of astral travel and out-of-body adventures.

History has given us many examples of astral travel. In the first century A.D., the writer Plutarch told of a soldier in Asia who, while unconscious, roamed for three days in another dimension. Native tribes have always taken out-of-body experiences for granted. American Indian shamans and African witch doctors have practiced rituals enabling them to escape their physical bodies. The Australian aborigines would go into a trance and venture out on an astral journey whenever their tribes needed guidance. This was shown in the movie *The Right Stuff,* when the aborigines were assisting the astronaut as he was maneuvering his space capsule. Legends from prehistoric days share the secrets of those who left their bodies and communicated with the gods.[3]

Even churches, throughout time, have recorded out-of-body experiences. Saints such as Anthony of Padua and Alphonsus Liguori were seen elsewhere while their physical bodies remained in a church or monastery. The scientific mystic Emanuel Swedenborg visited many dimensions, scripting detailed accounts of what he'd seen. English author Thomas De Quincey reportedly left his body while smoking opium.[4] And it is said that Napoléon, shortly before his death, traveled astrally from St. Helena to Rome to inform his mother that he was dying.[5]

The British Society for Psychical Research, formed in 1882, studied astral travel and other psychic phenomena. Richard Hodgson, William James, Sir Oliver Lodge, and others from the society investigated many of these cases. A number of universities throughout the world are now involved in research in this field. Out-of-body experiments have been designed in which the sleeper astrally projects to another building and then describes what he or she sees during the visit.[6]

Many out-of-body experiences are described by soldiers during war when they've literally leaped out of their bodies to escape the horrors of gunfire or other explosives. Occasionally, people leave their bodies simply to visit a friend or a family member. A mother will travel to see her daughter; a father, his son. St. Augustine related the story of a man lying in bed who suddenly looked up to see a philosopher friend standing in his room. They began to discuss Plato. When the two men met the following day, the man inquired about the experience. The philosopher responded simply, "I did not do it, but I dreamed that I did."[7]

In *On the Delay of the Divine Justice*, Plutarch tells about Aridaeus of Asia being knocked unconscious and immediately taken from his body. While out of his body, he saw his uncle who had died years earlier. His uncle greeted him, assuring Aridaeus that he wasn't dead and that his soul was in fact firmly attached to his body. "The rest of his soul," explained the dead uncle, "was a cord connecting it to the body. So long as the cord still remained attached to his physical body, Aridaeus would still be alive." Aridaeus also saw a marked difference between his double, or his astral body, and the astral body of his dead uncle. His body had a faint shadowy outline, while his uncle's was transparent. While observing this phenomenon, Aridaeus suddenly became aware of being "sucked through a tube by a violent inbreath," and he awoke once again to find himself back in his physical body.[8]

This tube is similar to the tunnel that many astral travelers experience when they're leaving and returning to their physical bodies. The astral body has different names in different cultures: The Hebrews call it *ruach*. In Egypt, it's known as *ka*. The Greeks knew it as *eidolon,* and the Romans called it *larva.* In Tibet, it's referred to as the *bardo body*. In Germany, it is *Jüdel* or *Doppelgänger* or *fylgja*. Ancient Britons gave it various terms: *fetch, waft, tisk,* or *fye*. In China, it was *thankhi*. The *thankhi* left the body during sleep, and records indicate that the astral body could be seen by others. Ancient Chinese people meditated to achieve astral travel and believed the second body was formed in the area of the solar plexus by the action of Spirit, and that it then left through the head. Many of these ancient Chinese teachings were discovered on 17th-century wooden tablets describing the phenomenon of out-of-body experiences. The ancient Hindus called this second body: the astral body, *pranamayakosha*. Buddhists referred to it as the *rupa*.[9]

Anthropologists studying various native tribes have found that astral travel is a very common event. The cultural beliefs of the astral traveler determine the pattern of his or her experience. In eastern Peru, the shaman imagines he is leaving his body in the form of a bird. Asian tribesmen view the silver cord—spoken of by modern metaphysicians—as a ribbon, thread, or rainbow. Africans perceive it as a rope; the natives of Borneo, as a ladder. Regardless of how the phenomenon is defined, it appears common among astral travelers that a type of silver cord remains as a connection between the astral and physical bodies.

The scientific view of these dreams is that they're ancestral memories from the days when, according to Darwin's theory, our predecessors were either aquatic or airborne creatures. Psychologists refer to astral dreams as a type of depersonalization, or a means of avoiding being grounded in normal reality.

Conditions of Travel

In order to fully experience astral travel, there are two very important prerequisites. The first is that you believe and appreciate the reality of an astral body. The second is that you believe you can do it and specifically focus your desire on leaving your physical body. If it were an easy thing to accomplish consciously, astral travel would be an everyday occurrence. However, I believe that anyone can experience the existence of an astral body if his or her intent is great enough. In any case, most of us do experience this phenomenon but simply don't remember it. If we strongly identify with our physical rather than our astral bodies, it can be a frightening experience. Fear is the greatest barrier we encounter to astral travel.

Fear

Even the most intrepid of us will discover, upon deeper examination, that at some time we've come face-to-face with the wall of fear regarding leaving the body. First and foremost is the fear of death—the frightening notion that if we're separated from our physical body, perhaps we'll die. Our automatic reaction may be to get back within the physical body quickly because this is where our life is, in the physical. We tend to have this reaction in spite of our emotional attitudes and intellectual thought processes. Only after repeating the experience many times can we hope to release the fear of death. It's much like beginning to swim and eventually realizing that your body will float—that you won't drown.

Another common fear is "Will I be able to get back into my body?" I can say with absolute certainty that you will do so. There's abundant evidence that those who experience astral travel are always able to return safely. Fear of the unknown is also faced by many astral travelers. There's no guidebook. The healthiest way I know is to work through your fear simply by allowing it to exist while still being willing to explore the unknown.

Astral Aids

Following are some guidelines to assist you in your astral journeys. The first thing to do is relax. You might take some stress-reduction courses or read about creative visualizations to help you to relax completely. You might also try self-hypnosis or post-hypnotic suggestions. A visit to a hypnotherapist may assist you in this. Meditation may also help you move into a deep state of relaxation. Placing your head toward the north and straightening your spine will also make a difference.

The next step is to move into the space between wakeful and sleep consciousness. This is a very delicate balance. It's where you're not yet asleep but are no longer awake. You might focus on an image or symbol that's special to you. As you move more and more into a deep state of relaxation, begin to observe the mind pictures or any light patterns that appear randomly. Frequently these are referred to as neural discharges. Don't encourage or deny them; simply allow them to move through, acknowledging an even deeper state of relaxation while maintaining conscious awareness. Perhaps you'll recognize that you're deepening your consciousness because your body will begin to feel either extremely heavy or light. Your senses of touch, smell, and taste will begin to fade. Occasionally, your hearing will also begin to fade.

As you are in this very calm, relaxed place with your eyes closed, focus your awareness outside your body. Begin to imagine that you're now at some point outside your body. If it's in another corner of the room, imagine that you're touching the wall. Be aware of the floor and all objects near you. Imagine that you're in this place. Often, as you begin to leave your body, you'll experience a tingling sensation or hear a vibration. At this point, it's crucial to simply allow the vibrations to increase in frequency. This will occur until the frequency is so high that you'll be almost unable to perceive it. Your body may feel slightly warmer.

The last step is to imagine that you're moving your hand. Imagine yourself reaching out for and touching any object that's near, while remembering that this isn't your physical body but your astral body.

Another way to enhance what you're doing is to imagine gently pushing against the wall. Then begin to increase the pressure. At this point, it will appear as if your hand or arm is actually going through the wall. Then carefully withdraw your hand.

The ancient Etruscans took part in a rolling technique where they'd enter into a very deep state of relaxation and then imagine "rolling out" of their bodies as a means to leave them for astral travel. Some travelers prefer a lift-out method, where they imagine floating up out of the body.

The important thing is that you experiment, discovering which method works best for you. Be gentle with yourself. Sometimes after long periods of practice without attaining any results, in that moment when you least expect it, you'll experience your first conscious out-of-body journey.

Returning to Your Body

Once you've learned to leave your body, you're free to explore and examine any thing and any place you desire. When you wish to return to your body, simply imagine moving either your fingers or your toes in your physical body. This will immediately bring your spirit back into your body. You can also swallow or move your jaw to bring yourself back. A simple guideline is to activate any one of your five senses, and this will return you to your body.

🏵 🏵 🏵 🏵 🏵 🏵

Chapter 14

Dreams for Healing

My thin cotton summer dress rippled in the warm wind as I stood high above the vast blue sea. I felt exhilarated as I stretched my arms toward the sky. I turned from my vantage on the chalk-colored cliffs that overstretched the sea and walked barefooted through the golden grasses. A lone seagull circled overhead. His slow-cycling shadow whispered over the undulating grasses that moved in response to the ocean breeze. In the distance was a black cottage. There were no windows or doors. It was completely black. Like heat radiating off a hot road, its image seemed to waver like a mirage in the distance. As I approached the cottage, I was aware that there was someone inside. Sue. It was Sue inside! "Sue, come out! It's so beautiful out here!" Inside I heard the timid feeble response, "I can't come out."

"Please, Sue," I urged. "It's so dark in there. You must come out into the light." There was no response, only the distant sound of waves below the cliffs.

I awoke from my dream. It seemed so real. I felt exhausted. That was the tenth time I'd had that dream in as many days.

Sue, a vivacious woman in her 30s, was dying of cancer. Initially, when I was called in to contribute to Sue's healing, I was astonished to see this once hearty woman reduced to a mere 98 pounds. She was as frail as a skeleton, with stretched-taut skin over her bones and deeply sunken eyes and cheeks. Every day I went to Sue's bedside to assist in her healing process, and every night I met her in my dreams. I assumed that my purpose in these nightly healing sessions was to encourage her to step into her own healing. On the 11th night, I dreamed the following:

I'm standing outside the cottage. As usual, the radiant rays of the sun bathe the summer grasses with fluid, golden light. I place my hands on the peeling black paint of the cottage. "Sue. Please, Sue, come out." A solemn, hollow voice from within replies, "I can't come out. My husband is here."

I assumed that she was attempting to tell me, through this dream, that she had a suppressed emotion concerning her husband that was preventing her from healing. Thinking that I might have discovered the source of the cancer, I began to work with Sue on undelivered communications concerning her husband. I thought this must be the path to her healing. We worked in depth on all difficulties regarding her husband that she felt were unresolved.

Sue continued to get weaker. This was hard for me to accept because everyone I'd ever worked with had improved and regained their health. I often contributed to the healing of those whom the medical profession felt were incurable, frequently with miraculous results. What was I doing wrong?

I stood on the cliffs, inhaling the essence of the slumbering sea below. As I walked through tall grass, I could feel the warmth of the earth radiate up through the soles of my bare feet. The cottage seemed to shimmer in the sunlight like a mirage of a desert oasis. I once again urged Sue to venture out into the light. Sue responded, "I'm not quite ready. My husband is keeping me here."

This dream made me feel that Sue and her husband still had things to resolve so that her healing could begin.

Sue's husband was constantly at her side. It seemed that he never left her, not even for a moment. Sue began counting the days until Christmas. She had two beautiful children in their early teens, and she desperately wanted to celebrate the holiday with them. The day after Christmas, the nurse asked Sue's husband if he would leave the room so she could change the bedding. Normally he wouldn't leave his wife's side for any reason.

However, in that moment, when he left the room, Sue's spirit soared . . . and her body died. But because it was Christmas and I was with my own family, I didn't hear the news of her death, but that night I had a remarkable dream:

I stood barefoot on the towering, majestic cliffs. The ocean had never seemed more radiant . . . more magical. It seemed to hold the very essence of life, the womb of all beingness. Shimmering diamonds of light danced on the ocean's surface. The air was heady with the fragrance of sea and foam. I became aware of a serene presence standing beside me. Turning, I was greeted by a softly swirling light being. "Sue?" I looked in the direction of the black cottage, and it wasn't there anymore. There was only the vast horizon. I'd seen Sue only when she was ill and emaciated, but the woman beside me was completely whole and radiated an exquisite beauty. This lovely woman said, "They think I am dead. I am so alive. If only they knew. You see, Denise, death can be a healing as well. I am healed and I am well. Please let them know that I am alive."

When I woke up, I knew that she'd died. I called the family and they confirmed her death; then I passed on her message to them. As a result of this experience, I realized that it can be as healing to assist someone in dying as it is to assist someone in living. I'd thought that in my dreams I was urging Sue to heal, but in retrospect, I realized that I was letting her know that it was safe to surrender her body. I was making it easier for her to release her physical form. She'd completed her incarnation and was ready to move on. Her husband's attachment to her had been holding her back (hence her comments about her husband that I'd misinterpreted). In the moment that he left the room, she went for the light, leaving her body behind. Sue allowed me to see a deeper aspect of dream healing—an aspect that contributed to my daytime healing practice as well.

Dream Healers

Many people practice dream healing every night, yet most are unaware of doing so. Often those who've incarnated to participate in dream healing will reincarnate around battlefields or other areas where there's a great need for healing. These beings help the dying make the transition from living to spirit. In war-torn areas of Europe during World Wars I and II, there were a large number of dream workers who were assisting the wounded and the dying to step into the light. They helped make that transition easier.

Dream healers can contribute not only to the dying, but also to the living. Frequently, knowledge of our cure lies deep within our psyche, too deep to access during the daylight hours. A dream healer can contribute to another's healing simply by touching deep within the psyche in sleep. The rules for daylight healing apply to night healing as well. Gaining an understanding of these tenets of healing will contribute to your intention to join the ranks of the Healers of the Night.

Dream healing is a powerful way to heal yourself and those you love. However, before learning dream-healing techniques, remember the following tenets:

We Are All Healers

Within each of us resides the ability to heal. When we remove the considerations and the doubts, each of us can tap into that gift. A common concern among those who are first entering the field of healing and dream healing is whether they know enough or have enough experience to heal anyone. My old Chinese teacher used to say that a healer would draw to herself those who wanted what she had to offer. So, whatever your level of ability, whoever comes to you, from the perspective of his or her higher self, knows what you have to offer. And what you have to give is what that person needs at that time. Don't doubt this. You have within you right now all that you need to be a healer. You already know enough.

We Are Not Our Bodies

While this appears obvious to many, there are those who don't realize that it is on this premise that great healing occurs. The body is an illusion. Remember that you aren't just working on the physical body or the emotional body. Rather, become aware of the spiritual essence of another.

While it's possible to heal another person by deciding what is wrong with him or her and "fixing" it, a more powerful way is to realize that we are *not* bodies; we are infinite, immortal, eternal, universal beings. Find the place that's universal in the person you're working with. Know that every person has the innate ability for self-healing, provided they feel safe. *Be* safe space . . . for safe space is sacred space. Go beyond the idea of separation, find oneness, and connect to it. Remember who both of you truly are in that moment. When you enter into the space of "there's nothing wrong here," then there will be healing. The essence of genuine healing is oneness.

Belief Systems Affect Healing

It isn't necessarily the method or technique in itself that heals. Most techniques can work. Rather, it can be your belief or faith in the technique that will heal. For instance, it's common in Western cultures to believe in the practice of medicine by the medical profession. Many people put their faith in their doctors and in this way have found the place where they can best heal themselves. However, in cultures where native healers are prevalent, often a traditional healer can gain better results than a Western-style doctor because of the prevailing belief system.

Go to the Source of the Problem

In symptomatic healing, the healer focuses on the symptoms. However, unless the true cause is addressed, the healing is usually only temporary and the patient will find the problems recurring or may develop other difficulties.

For example, if a young man has arthritis in his right hand, perhaps the underlying cause can be traced to earlier experiences with his father. If, when he was a boy, his father smacked the backs of his hands when he was misbehaving, consider the range of emotions the child might have felt at the time. He might have felt afraid, hurt, and angry. Perhaps he began to deny those feelings and just felt overwhelmed and powerless. Now, as a grown man, when he finds himself in a situation where he feels helpless or weak, his hands are subconsciously affected.

A symptomatic healer, using the dream state and various dream techniques, can help the man gain freedom of movement and relief from the pain in his hand. However, unless the young man can release the underlying feelings of powerlessness that originated in his childhood, the arthritis may return, or some other difficulty will manifest itself in another area of the body. A better way to heal is to go to the source of the problem.

The Body Reflects Consciousness

All the emotions and thoughts that you have in your life can remain stored in your body, as well as all the emotions that you may have denied or suppressed in life, and this can influence your health and well-being.

Normally, as a person goes through life, situations arise that can cause him or her to feel angry, sad, joyous, and so on. However, when the individual decides that it's inappropriate to have a particular emotion, he can "go numb" or deny what's happening to his body. He can find some way *not to feel* whatever is going on with him. Each of these un-experienced or suppressed emotions can create physical difficulties.

When there's a health problem, the emotions and situations that caused the difficulty are usually not those that have been experienced or felt. Rather, the problem arises from situations that have *not* been experienced: those situations where a person went numb or didn't allow himself to feel the pain, grief, or anger. It's only when an individual allows himself to examine and even experience those suppressed emotions that true healing can occur.

All Healing Is Self-Healing

The body always wants to heal itself. No technique or method in and of itself has ever healed anyone. It's the body's *response* to that method that heals. Two people with the same difficulty can be given identical procedures, and one will be healed and the other will not. This happens because all healing is basically self-healing. The person you're working with heals him- or herself. You are the facilitator.

The Only Person You Ever Heal Is Yourself

The greatest healers know that when they're healing others, they're also healing themselves. Each person you work with, on a spiritual level, is a part of you. It is "you" in a different body. This is a universal law. Know that each person you've drawn to yourself for healing is a different aspect of your own being, for we're not separate from each other.

For example, if someone who comes to you for healing has cancer, one way to start the healing process is to look first *within yourself* and ask, *Is there anything "eating away" at me?* As you begin to heal the emotions that are eating away at you, the healing process may begin within the person you want to heal.

My kahuna teacher said that it was a sacred honor to be allowed to contribute to the healing of someone else. If you want to contribute to someone's healing and that person is having difficulty receiving, look within yourself. First, allow yourself to know that *you* deserve love. Open yourself up to the deepening of this awareness. As you create that context for another's healing, you heal yourself.

As a healer, and particularly as a dream healer, you must *not* feel that you're sacrificing yourself for your patient. You must know that you're not better than the people you're healing. You are healed through helping others heal.

In any kind of healing, it's important to go beyond the feeling of separation. Reach that exquisite level of oneness. Remove any walls that you sense between yourself and another so you feel the unity that exists between the two of you.

Disease or Physical Difficulties Can Be a Gift

Physical difficulties can be a way of learning. If healers prematurely remove blockages before the higher selves of the ailing individuals have fully comprehended whatever they needed to learn from the imbalance, it will be re-created. It's important to provide a safe space for people to choose their own path. It isn't for you, the healer, to arbitrarily make that decision. Ultimately, you don't know what's best for another person. It isn't appropriate to decide what's wrong with someone and then "fix it." This response is associated with belief in the illusion that a person is just his or her body. When you dream for the healing of another, it's important to remember that beneath the ailment or injury this person is whole and perfect. We are *not* our ailments.

Love Is the Ultimate Healer

One aspect of the definition of love is unconditional acceptance of another's reality. This acceptance is at a deeper level than personality or persona. When you move into absolute acceptance of and connection with another's true essence, then there's nothing more you need to do to bring about healing. Your presence is enough to activate that process . . . in accordance with their highest good.

Health Is a Function of Service

True service isn't seeing that someone else is in bad shape and deciding to help him. This idea of "fixing" him comes from forgetting that he is divine and in the process of choosing his reality. It also sets you up as seeing yourself as better than he is, implying that you'll help him up but not quite "up" as high as you are. Allow people to go beyond you, and *you* will grow. This is true spiritual service.

My Chinese teacher used to say, "It is a poor student who doesn't surpass his teacher." Hanuman, the monkey god of India, said, "When I don't know who I am, I serve you. When I know who I am, I am you."

Do what you can to contribute to the world so that it will be a better place—not for the world's sake, as the world may be perfect just the way it is, but for your own sake. In the same way, do what you can for others for your own sake, remembering that the essence of each person is perfect as he or she is. Don't sacrifice—ever. Genuine service isn't sacrifice. Dream the world into wholeness. Let your healing dreams be a gift to the planet.

A Healer Is Compassionate

As a healer, you must maintain balance between having one foot in the reality of the physical world and the other in the realm of Spirit. In the spirit realm, you know that the world is unfolding as it should. Here, you know that there are no accidents and that everyone has generated their own illnesses and is responsible for their own lives. However, by remaining in an intense spiritual focus, you may become cool and lack compassion for the suffering of others. In contrast, by focusing only on the physical world, you become a player in a larger drama. In this reality most people get caught up in the misery of the world and begin to feel sorry for others. We forget that they aren't their bodies or their problems. It's easy to get into this frame of mind and fail to see beyond the suffering. But if we do this, we've forgotten who we really are.

It's important to be compassionate and sympathize with another person's pain, yet also remember his or her true essence. The individual isn't ill; it's the body that is ill. Find this balance, and you'll be an excellent healer.

The Most Important Part of Dream Healing Is Intention

Once you understand these tenets of healing, you can begin to enter the realm of dream healers. However, the most important aspect of night healing is your intention. As you prepare for sleep, become relaxed and comfortable. Use the dream-guide or dream-shield techniques. (See Chapters 17 and 18.) Allow your full intention to contribute to the healing of the person you have in mind.

To do so, first imagine him (or her) very clearly. If you aren't visual, get a sense of the individual. (Each of us has a unique energy or aura.) Get in touch with his essence, and say his name to yourself. You might even visualize him as very happy—see him running, jumping, and feeling exhilarated. Then go to sleep. Where intention goes, energy flows. You may not remember what good you contributed during the night; nevertheless, you'll have begun to move into the realm of night healers.

Often my clients tell me that they've been aware of me working with them in their dreams, and upon waking, they've discovered that their symptoms are relieved. Usually, I'll have no recall of having visited them in the night, or I'll have only a faint glimmer of a memory. Sometimes I've told individuals that I'd work with them in the night and then have forgotten to program myself before bed, only to hear the next day how effective the night healing was. So don't be discouraged even if you don't remember what you're doing in your night hours; it might be that you're still functioning as a night healer.

If you want to contribute to your own healing, as you go to sleep say, "Tonight, I am healed. Tonight, I am healed." Your body can heal itself through your dreams. Keep in mind that your soul may be trying to communicate an important message through an illness or disease. Use your dream state as a workshop to receive these communications, and this can help you heal.

$$\mathcal{D}\,\mathcal{D}\,\mathcal{D} \quad \mathcal{D}\,\mathcal{D}\,\mathcal{D}$$

Chapter 15

Dreams for Love and Sex

He moves with confident grace as he saunters down the beach. His back muscles ripple with feline certainty as he takes long, fluid strides. He hesitates . . . and turns to face me. We're no longer two strangers who happen to be walking in the same direction on a lonely beach. We've entered into a conspiracy of attraction. The look is brief. It's only the suggestion of a glance. Still, in that silent moment, a tangible current fills me with his soul. I walk on . . . and smile.

I woke up from this dream feeling a mysterious inner glow. The encounter with this dream lover had been brief, yet so fulfilling. I sang through the entire day.

Dreams can be a pathway to ecstasy. They can be a way to expand love for others and of self and can be used to work out sexual difficulties within your daily life. Dreams can even be a wonderful form of evening entertainment.

Sexuality appears regularly in the dream state. Men have erections frequently during the REM states, and women's vaginas moisten during these times. These are normal, natural occurrences. In ancient cultures, there was an innate understanding of this; in fact, sexuality and sensuality occurring in the dream state was considered a basic expression of all life. In the East, it was a means of expressing unity with Spirit. Sexuality was viewed as a path to mystical experience. An ancient Indian text states that "sexual union is an auspicious Yoga which involves enjoyment of all the sensual pleasure and gives release. It is a Path to Liberation."

In the East, it was thought that the underlying reality to all of life consisted of two dynamic energies called *yin* and *yang*. Yin was the receptive, feminine principle; and yang was the masculine, outgoing energy. Each was considered necessary for the harmonization of life. Yin was embodied in the receptive energy of the moon; yang was embodied in the projecting energy of the sun. Everything was considered either yin or yang, and all of life was an interplay between the two forces.

Human beings were considered the highest expression of these two powerful dual energies. A healthy sexual union was considered a way to break through the illusion of duality—a way to attain liberation and enhance health and well-being. When this sexual union occurred in a dream, it was supposed to be especially potent. Sexual union was a way to become closer to God, and dreams were considered a powerful arena in which to experience and express one's sexuality. Dream sex can provide you with spiritual experiences, deep insights, and lighthearted fun, but first you may need to overcome guilt about your sexual dreams.

Guilt

When you have sex in a dream, it's not uncommon to feel guilty or ashamed about it. However, it's important to know that there's no cause for guilt in any dream relationship. In ancient cultures that had a metaphysical basis, sex wasn't considered to be in conflict with spirituality or religion. Sex was both an art form and a normal part of each person's education. Sexuality was not shrouded in guilt.

In dreams, there's no such thing as promiscuity. Your dream lovers may simply be different aspects of yourself appearing in erotic form. Dream sex can be a way of uniting with disassociated parts of yourself. In addition to letting go of guilt over dream sex, it's vital that you work on releasing any shame from past sexual activities. As uncomfortable as those memories are, it's important to observe and release them. Any guilt that you cling to can create barriers; however, it can be processed and released in your dreams.

Whenever you feel the pain of guilt, remember this: if you yield to it, you're deciding against inner peace. Therefore, before you go to sleep, say to yourself gently, but with conviction, *I accept who I am and what I've done as well as what others have done to me. I accept and forgive myself and others.* This may not be enough to resolve all guilt as some is deeply rooted, but it's a good beginning. Your dreams can help you release shame and guilt.

Opening the Dream-Sex Channel

Another significant aspect of sexuality is the understanding of how energy flows through the body. Within the body are energy centers called *chakras.* In order to maintain a healthy view of yourself, it's imperative to have a harmonious circulation of your life-force energies through the chakras. When these energies become blocked, self-esteem is lowered, disease occurs, and vitality diminishes. Basic to this energy flow is your sexual energy, which can be likened to your creative energy. Often people involved in a spiritual movement deny or block this vital energy, and they become so "heavenly" that they're ineffective in their earthly pursuits.

We need to maintain a balance within all our chakras to be empowered in day-to-day life. The first chakra, the sexual center, is important to the maintenance of all the others, as it's our connection to the earth. It's the home of the Kundalini, the mysterious force dwelling at the base of the spine, which yogis strive to awaken. It is what's referred to in Asia as the "fighting spirit." This doesn't imply that you should pick a fight; rather, it simply refers to a zest and vitality for life. As this area opens, women discover that their menstrual flow becomes easier, hormones are vitalized, skin becomes softer and clearer, and they're rejuvenated.

You've probably seen a woman who seems illuminated by her own glow. This is usually someone whose first chakra is open and clear. When a man's first chakra opens, he'll feel more empowered in his life and will operate from a perspective of greater clarity and certainty. (You don't need to have sex to have your sexual energy open.)

Each of your chakras represents a different facet of yourself, and each deserves to be developed and opened. However, the first chakra is one easily ignored by those on a spiritual path because of guilt or denial. Your sexual energy is part of your God-given heritage. Use it. Allow it to open, and your sensuality and zest for life will increase.

One method to prepare for dream sex is to channel the sexual energy upward through the chakras to the top of the head, which in India is known as the aperture of Brahma. This can be done with the use of breath just before sleep. Eastern mystical teachings stress the importance of breath as a way to align and channel creative sexual energy. Your breath should be slow and deep, extending your lower abdomen when you inhale and contracting it when you exhale. This is the most natural way to breathe, and it's the way you breathe when you're asleep. However, most people breathe the opposite way, with the chest expanding on the inhalation. Once you've mastered this type of deep breathing, imagine a brilliant surge of energy entering at your feet, moving up through your entire body, and exiting at the top of your head. This exercise will begin to open your chakras, which often leads to enlightening, transformational experiences during sleep. Sexual dreams sometimes indicate the rising of the Kundalini, and many major forms of enlightenment occur as a result.

Once you experience this energy moving through your entire being, you might want to do the dream-lover meditation in Chapter 19. You might also fall asleep repeating expressions such as "This night, show me the highest potential of sexuality. Tonight, let me dream of divine intimacy."

Dream Sex and Creativity

An active sex life in dreams not only contributes to a sensuous waking life, but indicates self-actualization and confidence. Abraham Maslow, the noted American humanistic psychologist who presented the idea of self-actualization, said that people with potent, sexual dream lives are usually self-assured, independent, composed, and competent. The dreams of a less self-assured person are more likely to be symbolic rather than the openly sexual dreams experienced by the person with high self-esteem.[1]

One researcher discovered a strong correlation between sexual dreams and creativity. In a creative-writing class, the instructor divided students into groups of the most creative and the least creative, based on writing assignments. Then data was collected from both study groups. The students who were less creative had sexually passive or nonsexual dreams, and the more creative students had a higher proportion of overtly sexual dreams. The researchers concluded that freedom of sexual activity in dreams is related to freedom of creative thinking in all areas.[2]

Interpretation of Dream Sex

Occasionally, women dream of having a penis. Freudian analysts refer to this as "penis envy" and believe that these dreams imply a secret desire on the part of the woman to have a penis. However, these dreams can represent the woman's desire for achievement of traditional male characteristics that they may see symbolized by the penis.

However, certain dreams of sex are based on wish fulfillment, especially those portraying extremely satisfying sexual encounters when the dreamer has gone a long time without sex. Occasionally, these dreams can actually revolutionize a person's sex life. In some dreams, one may experience making love with an individual of the same sex (or opposite sex in the case of a homosexual). This isn't necessarily latent homosexuality or heterosexuality. Rather, it's most likely a desire to attain those qualities represented by the lover. For example, if a woman dreams of making love with another woman who's very strong, it may reflect her desire to incorporate qualities of strength into her own character.

In analyzing your dream, notice where your sexual encounter takes place. For example, a sex dream that occurs in a Victorian house may symbolize Victorian attitudes. If you're having sex in the basement, perhaps you're experiencing submerged or subconscious feelings concerning sex, or maybe your dream is indicating some area of sexuality that you consider crude or base. If your dream encounter is in the middle of a raging hurricane, this generally indicates that you're experiencing powerful emotions with regard to your sexuality.

Communal Dreams

One special aspect of dream sex is dream sharing. You can literally enter into the dream of a loved one. The ability to do this is enhanced when you sleep together because your auras are intermingled, and it's then easier to step into each other's dreams. However, communal dreaming can also be done from a distance. If you're separated from your loved one, it can be a way to continue your intimacy. To experience the most effective communal dreaming, discuss it beforehand and mutually agree to enter each other's dreams. As you go to sleep, affirm—with intention—that you and your partner will be together in your dreams.

Often, dream sharing occurs without preprogramming. Perhaps you've shared a dream with your lover. The following morning, you discover that you both experienced the same or a similar dream. Communal dreaming can be an excellent way to increase intimacy and develop greater understanding in relationships. Before beginning your dream sharing, it's helpful to do a simple meditation. The following is based on a Tantric Buddhist technique.

First, sit in a comfortable position directly facing your partner. Make sure your spine is straight. This is extremely important for this meditation. Now begin the natural deep breathing described in the previous pages. Remember, as you inhale, your abdomen expands, and as you exhale, it contracts. If you sense your chest expanding and contracting instead of your abdomen, simply imagine the presence of a balloon in the center of your abdomen. The balloon expands and contracts with each breath. It may take a short time to become accustomed to this type of breathing; however, the results will be well worth it. It's a very natural way of breathing; this is the way you breathe when you're asleep.

Allow yourself to feel very relaxed. Then imagine a current of energy originating in the center of the earth, moving up through your spine, all the way up through your entire being. This is your grounding cord. Visualize this energy moving out of the top of your head like a geyser, then cascading around you like a fountain. Look into the left eye of your partner and imagine a beam of energy flowing from your heart chakra (the energy center in the middle of the chest) into the heart chakra of your partner. Then imagine this same energy moving down his (or her) spine and penetrating the sexual chakra. This extremely potent energy then travels from your partner's first chakra area into your own and moves back to your heart chakra once again. This is the *circle of gold technique*. You may also reverse the flow of energy.

As you're practicing, allow yourself to experience the very deep and profound connection with your partner. Once you've completed this exercise, maintain silence and go to sleep immediately, programming yourself for an even deeper connection during the night.

ᘐᘐᘐ ᘐᘐᘐ

Chapter 16

Dreams for Children

A golden pool of melted butter floats in my morning oatmeal. My finger, finding a chip in the earthen bowl, idly plays with its rough edges. My ten-year-old daughter is in the middle of an engaging conversation concerning her dream exploits of the night before. I'm enjoying our family's breakfast dream sharing. When Meadow shares her dreams, a hazy look crosses her face as she vividly remembers the intimate details. Her dreams are usually long-winded sagas full of intricate details. They sometimes appear to span generations. She also pays close attention to details in her daily life. David's dreams are usually succinct and to the point—much like his personality. My dreams are usually active and whimsical.

When we take time to share our dreams and assist one another in understanding their secret messages, the quality of the day is more balanced. For each of us, our dream sharing is extremely significant for the consolidation of our family energy. It provides Meadow with a sense of acceptance and a deeper understanding of herself. She claims that she's more apt to remember her dreams and use their messages when we take this time to share our dreams over breakfast.

It isn't uncommon that when children recount their dreams, adults will nonverbally communicate that they aren't to be taken seriously. And when our children have had a nightmare, we rush to reassure them, saying, "Oh, it's just a dream. It doesn't mean anything." However, listening to your little one's dreams—even in the middle of the night when you're longing to crawl back into bed— can have an inspiring and transforming effect on your child's life.

Dream Importance

It's important to communicate to your children the significance and value of their dreams. You want to encourage your child's interest in dreams. Never, ever correct or criticize the child's behavior in the dream or belittle any of his or her feelings about it. Let your children know that you enjoy hearing about their dreams exactly as they occurred. And at the same time, it's all right to encourage a child to confront the beasts or other scary things in their dreams. Teach your children that they can call on a dream guide or guardian angel to help them out of a threatening situation.

Savanna, one of my daughter's young friends, told me that she was afraid to go to sleep at night because she thought scary monsters would come in the dark. I gave her a pointed quartz crystal that I'd programmed for use as a dream crystal. I told her that as she went to bed, she should hold the crystal in her hand and say out loud, "I command that all dream monsters leave now!" Savanna later informed me that since using the dream crystal, she hadn't experienced any nightmares and sleeps peacefully through the night.

It's valuable for children to feel empowered through their dreams. Let your kids know that they can have control over their dreams. If they have difficulty with this and have already attempted to change the course of their dreams without success, it's important to continue providing encouragement. Your children may feel worse about themselves because they haven't been able to alter their dreams. If this occurs, have them either act out or draw a specific dream and then create a more powerful and positive ending. Your emphasis should be on the flexibility and changeability of dreams. Listen carefully, and tune in to what your child needs in the moment.

Also let your children know that they can use dreams to develop a talent or ability that can then be incorporated into their daily lives. For instance, they can say before going to sleep: "I'd like to become a better swimmer [or skater or artist and so on]. Give me the dream that will help me accomplish this goal."

Dream Books

To help your children with their dreams, obtain a "dream book" in which they can record dreams. It can be a notebook, scrapbook, diary, or even a few blank pages stapled together. Allow your children to select what appeals to them the most, and explain that this will be a special book to be used only for dreams. Children can write about their dreams themselves, or, if they're too young, you can jot down their dreams for them. Then have your kids create a drawing of their dream alongside the story. They may want to draw a picture of how they were feeling or how they wished the dream had ended.

The dream book can also be utilized when children think of additional stories regarding their dreams. For example, if your son had a disturbing dream, he can go back into the dream and rewrite it, making himself the hero. Help him understand that it's all right to revisit the dream and make it end exactly the way he wished it had. Let him know that even scary things in the dream can be changed.

Dream Interpretation

It's crucial for parents to give their children enough time and space to interpret their dreams. It may be difficult at first for kids to figure out what their dreams mean; however, by simply allowing them to share their dreams, you'll empower them in their daily lives.

As you talk about the interpretation of your dreams, your children will feel safer discussing what they believe are the meanings behind their dreams. Dream guidance should be very gentle, and children should never feel that they're being pushed.

Nightmares

If your daughter (or son) has recurring nightmares, you can help by giving her crayons and paper and encouraging her to draw the object that scares her. When she draws the monster or scary creature, she can put it in jail, make it look silly, or even add in a dream guide who's bigger and more powerful. By doing this simple exercise, the child feels empowered, rather than victimized, and the nightmares often cease.

Dream Champions

If your children have difficulty in either scaring off the monsters or believing that they can change any part of a dream, you may wish to become a "dream champion." By doing so, you actually begin to fight the battle for your child in an improvised drama until he or she feels safe or empowered enough to take over and "finish" it.

For example, after your child recounts their scary dream you can hold an imaginary sword in your hand and say out loud, "Now I have the sword in my hand; the hairy monster is backing up.

Look how afraid he is of this bright sword! I'm so powerful that the monster is starting to run away, but I won't let him just run because the magic silver in the sword is going to destroy him so that he never comes back to scare you again!" If at any point in the drama you can give the imaginary sword to your child, do so. I've found that once the child feels safe and has some *sense of control,* he or she will often want to finish the job!

Communal Dreaming

One delightful way to introduce children to learning about their dreams is for them to have a "dream visitation" night. One time, when my daughter was young, she invited her friends Savanna and Roslyn to spend the night. These eight-year-olds had never done any dream work previously. Just before they went to bed, I said, "Tonight, why don't you all share your dreams. Tonight, why don't you enter one another's dreams." Following is what occurred as told in their own words.

Roslyn's Dream

Savanna and Meadow and I were walking to a rock shop. Savanna had brought her best crystal, I'd brought an orange one I found on the way, and Meadow had brought a crystal she'd found near her home. When we got to the rock workshop, everyone was cutting crystals into quarters. We sat down and started to cut ours. Savanna was very mad because she'd brought her best crystal, but she did it anyway. We cut them and then we had to glue them back together. Little chips were falling out, and we glued those back in, too. When we were done, we took our crystals and wrapped them up in paper and took them home. Savanna still had her best crystal, but it wasn't like it used to be. It still had little chips out of it that she'd forgotten to glue back.

Savanna's Dream

Meadow and I were sisters. There was a man who'd kidnapped a girl. I told Meadow about it, and she got so mad she threw him in the swimming pool. Roslyn was watching. Meadow was mad because she liked this man and he'd been pretending to be nice to her.

Meadow's Dream

[This is a condensed version—Meadow's dreams are epic novels.]

A few days ago, two of my friends were spending the night and my mom said, "You girls can share a dream tonight, if you like." It didn't seem like we all shared the same dream, but we all dreamed about each other, and I'm going to tell you about one of the dreams I had that night:

I was with my friend, Savanna, eating at her school cafeteria, and she started punching stuff into the principal's computer. I found myself and her in the principal's office, punching all these things into his big computer. Savanna remembered that the principal had all these rules, such as: "You'll have to die if you mess with the principal's computer." Then she remembered that we had to stick our hands in a window thing. We stuck our hands in this window, but when Savanna tried to pull hers out, something grabbed her hand with all these bones on it and it pulled her in.

I grabbed her foot and yanked her out. The principal began chasing us. We ran through all these things through the whole school. We had to do all these things or die. We finally got out.

Roslyn was there and all three of us ran to the town square. I asked them, "Do either of you have a quarter?" They said no.

Savanna said, "A quarter is a lot of money!" I ran up the hill to town and called her mother, Sandra, to see if she could come and get us. And for some reason, I was becoming quarterless during all this. Finally, my mom came, and I told her the story about the principal, and that he was chasing us. She started videotaping him and becoming friends with him. She was kind of the hero of my dreams because she made the principal all happy and then he forgot about chasing us. And then my mom picked me up and asked me how my day was, and I said, "Oh, nothing exciting." And then Savanna and Roslyn were picked up by Sandra. Everyone was safe and happy at the end of my dream.

[Meadow's note: "I think the meaning of this dream is to go ahead and take chances, and it will have a good ending. Take chances in life."]

It was interesting to note that not only did they recall their dreams, but each dream had all three girls in it. Without going into any in-depth interpretation, it's fascinating that two of the dreams (Roslyn's and Meadow's) had the idea of quarters in them, and two of the dreams had a male antagonist who was eventually overcome.

$$\mathcal{D} \ \mathcal{D} \ \mathcal{D}$$

One morning, Meadow (when she was eight years old) asked if she could tell me about a dream she felt was very significant to her. I've included it here because it demonstrates a method of dealing positively with a child's nightmares.

Meadow Talking about her Nightmare

A month or two ago, I had a dream about robbers, and this man, who used to be my mom's friend, was one of the robbers. I was so horribly terrified. That's my biggest fear—robbers, coming in and taking things and being there. It was probably the scariest dream I ever had, and I was really frightened.

And then, after talking to my mom about that dream, I got really scared just talking about it. She put out a pillow and said to pretend that it was the robber, so I began chopping him and hitting him with my hands and beating him. Then, the next night, I had another dream about robbers in the house. But this time, I had a plan. If we heard the robbers knock on the door, at the count of three, we'd open both doors—the back and the front doors. We had it all figured out. I woke up and was a little scared, and then I thought about killing the robbers, so I wasn't scared. I think that was a really good improvement, don't you?

Then right after that, I had a dream that me and my mom were where this man lives, who had been the robber in my first dream, and we saw this beautiful house. And, that's where he lived. And my mom said, "Oh, it's so nice to be back again." And, I wasn't mad at this person anymore, and he wasn't a poo-poo head anymore. So I think I've really changed through my dreams.

By showing Meadow that she could be in control of her dream states (that is, by hitting the "robber" pillow), she was able to feel more powerful than her dream enemy, and this feeling carried over into her daily life. Meadow is no longer afraid of robbers.

The man in the moon looked out of the moon
Looked out of the moon and said,
'Tis time for all children on the earth,
To think about getting to bed.
— **Mother Goose**

PART V

Dream Meditations

To become Loom Master is to weave
with the threads of the universe,
the thread of a thought,
of a breath on the wind,
drawn from the earth
from the moon and the stars,
a textile so fine, it is the
gossamer clothing of our souls.

— M. Anne Sweet

Chapter 17

Dream Guide

The three meditations contained in this section are inward journeys that you can either read to a loved one or record and play back to yourself before sleep. (If you do this for yourself, replace the word *you* with *I*.) The first meditation will allow you access to the assistance of a dream guide. Dream guides are spiritual beings who usher people through their dreams, assisting them in transporting gifts of wisdom back from the "other side." A dream guide is an entity who can guide you safely through the night and help you glean greater understanding of yourself and of the inner dimensions. Your guide may be someone you knew in a past life or someone you knew in your present life who has passed on. This loving being might even be an angel or divine being providing guidance during the night.

Dream Guide Meditation

You are about to embark on an inner journey to a sacred place within yourself to discover your dream guide. Once you've reached this place, you'll have access to a profound source of strength, power, and peace.

To set out on this journey, lie or sit in a comfortable position. Uncross your arms and legs, and become as comfortable as possible. Do this now. Good.

Allow your eyes to close softly. Now inhale. Completely fill your lungs with air . . . hold for three seconds . . . and as you exhale, feel yourself letting go.

Take another breath . . . even deeper than before . . . hold . . . exhale completely . . . and allow your entire body to relax. Now, one final, deep breath. Hold it for three seconds and exhale.

Good. Now focus your attention on your left foot. Feel your left foot relaxing. It's now completely relaxed. Focus your attention on your right foot, and feel your right foot relaxing. Your right foot is now completely relaxed. With each breath you take, feel yourself deliciously, pleasantly comfortable.

Now put your awareness on your left leg and feel your left leg relaxing. Feel it completely relax. Allow yourself to be aware of your right leg and feel it letting go. Be aware as your right leg totally relaxes. Now imagine a warm wave of serenity rolling up from your feet, extending up through your legs, your abdomen, your chest, up to your shoulders, down your arms, and all the way out through the tips of your fingers. Imagine one warm wave after another. Good.

Imagine your abdomen is a balloon. As you inhale, the balloon inflates. As you exhale, visualize that you're letting the air out of the balloon. As the balloon slowly, slowly deflates, you become even more relaxed. You may do this now. Good. Your entire body from the neck down is now warm and comfortable. Focus your awareness on your neck muscles, allowing your neck to relax. Feel your jaw and face relax . . . completely relax.

Imagine yourself in a natural environment on a starry night. It may be by the ocean; among trees in a lush forest; at the peak of a mountain with the moon glistening off the snow; or an enchanted meadow filled with fauns, fairies, and unicorns. It may be a place you've been to before or a place that exists only in your imagination. It's whatever is beautiful to you . . . whatever makes you happy.

Spend some time seeing yourself in this environment, using all of your senses. Listen to the sounds of the night. Imagine yourself thoroughly exploring this special environment. Make it as real as possible by using all of your senses to visualize it. Touch things, smell the air deeply, and see what's around you. Good.

Now, somewhere in this natural environment imagine a still pool—still . . . deep . . . serene . . . clear. This pond has moonlight secrets hidden in its depths. Its surface is satin, glass-clear water. You can see your reflection, but it's altered as if in a dream.

Take just a short while to really visualize the water. Then as you observe this pool, a mist is forming over its surface. The mist grows, beginning to swirl as if it has a life of its own. Whirling and twirling, the mist reaches out until the entire environment is wrapped in this mystical fog. You are safe and serene.

As you stand bathed in the moonlit mist, your intuition gently informs you that someone is approaching from the distance. The presence is coming closer and closer; you are aware of great compassion and strength radiating from this being as he or she comes closer . . . and still closer. You await this arrival with anticipation. Through the mist, you can feel the pervading love and acceptance that's flowing to you from your dream guide.

Your guide is coming forth to provide you with insight and give you assistance through the night. Your guide is very close now. This being knows you intimately and has awaited your call.

Reach out now into the mist with your hands extended toward your dream guide. As you do, be aware of your guide's hand gently slipping into your own. In this moment a profound relaxation fills you.

When you go to bed each evening, imagine your guide's hand in yours. Know that this being is with you, now and forever, to guide and lead you through the mysteries of the night.

The mists begin to clear, enabling you to see clearly the form and features of your guide. If you aren't able to visualize your guide, get a sense or feeling of this being. For example, you might not be able to see a waterfall, but you can get a feeling of the freshness of it.

Take some time to be with your guide, wrapped in the gentle silence of the moonlit night. If you desire, your dream guide will come with you night after night during your sleep to assist you in dealing with difficulties presented during the day. Your guide can also help you gain great wisdom from the future or from the past, as well as assist you in exploring other dimensions.

Say goodbye to your guide.

At this time, you may wish to drift off to sleep. If you wish to return to wakeful consciousness, however, simply take a deep breath and, in your own time and when you're ready, allow your eyes to gently open. . . .

ぢ ぢ ぢ ぢ ぢ ぢ

Chapter 18

Dream Shield

A dream shield is a personal power object for the cultivation of inner protection and strength. It can be used to experience a deeper understanding of the ancient mysteries and can help keep you and your loved ones safe. The symbols that you place on your shield are rudiments of your individual mythology and will allow you to be more in alignment with your life's purpose. The following is a letter received from someone who accessed the power of a dream shield.

Dear Denise,

I wanted to let you know what happened after I took your past-life seminar where we did the "dream shield" technique. On Sunday night following the seminar, I received a phone call advising me that my brother had died that morning after having a heart attack Saturday evening. I didn't communicate with his widow directly because there has been lots of "stuff and junk" between us for more than 20 years.

After the phone call, I talked with my good friend Gina. I commented that I probably wouldn't attend the funeral, as I was fearful of having a family confrontation. I had a major quarrel some years ago at my father's funeral with my brother and his wife. Gina indicated that the funeral could possibly be a means of deep healing for myself and that I might not have such an opportunity for a long time. I told her that I'd ask for dream guidance and follow that advice. We continued to chat about other things, and then I went to bed.

I didn't consciously create my dream shield as I turned off the light. I recognize now that my subconscious had already been programmed by the dream-shield process we'd done earlier in the day at your seminar. I went to bed and slept soundly. I woke up at 4:30 A.M. very surprised. Dream recall is a new process for me, as is visualization. My pillow was sopping wet, for I'd apparently been weeping. I had a vivid dream where I was standing at the cemetery under a canopy and was reading a farewell letter. I felt extremely calm, healed, and peaceful. I knew that everything was okay. I didn't have any anxiety about recalling the letter, for I "knew" that I could recall it at the office when I went to work later. Everything felt perfect and serene.

That evening, I received the details of the service and asked Carol, my brother's widow, if I could have the time to read my letter. My request was granted without argument even though I could sense some attempt to manipulate me. It was as though I was "shielded."

On Thursday at the funeral, I read my letter and felt an immediate sense of deep, deep peace with my brothers—with Fred, who had just died, and also with my other brothers. At the end of the reading, I placed a bouquet of rainbow-colored carnations on the casket. After the service, as we comforted each other, there seemed to be a feeling of intense compassion and a sense of true togetherness. His widow thanked me for the reading and asked for a copy. The gathering afterward was a very warm and friendly time for our friends and family.

It was an extremely healing process, and I had a profound sense of completion. This was much more than I ever could have believed was possible.

Love,
Vi Randall

P.S. I've included the eulogy that I wrote for my brother, as it was dream inspired.

Eulogy for Frederic

On November 8, the spirit of Frederic returned home. This is the autumn or "earth" season, the time of dying, of gathering home all things that will nurture and sustain life through the dormant winter or "fire" season. This was Fred's season, and he lived the essence well. He nurtured his family, he worked with his hands, and he enjoyed life to the fullest when in the company of his loved ones.

Today, November 12, I honor the spirit of my brother, and I speak words of love and send him many rainbows to help him return to the Great Spirit from which all life comes. Father Sky and Mother Earth are in harmony on this day to grant him a safe journey. During the last year, his mother and older sister completed their journeys, and he now joins them. We'll miss him, as we've missed Elsia and Rondalyn, but to all things there's a season. A time to mourn. A time to cry. A time to be born. A time to die. This is our time to honor our brother, our friend, our soul mate, in our own way. This is the time for our own reflection, a time to release our fears, our jealousies, our anger, our hate, and our mistrust. A time to acknowledge that we are all one family on this planet Earth. A time to come together, in spirit and harmony, to wish and grant each other the same love and peace that we wish Frederic. To his widow, I send understanding and love to sustain her during this transition. To his children,

I send knowledge that their father taught wisdom and faith. To his brothers, strength and serenity; to all his friends and family, unconditional love.

Let each of us honor Frederic in our own way as he is laid to rest with his father. His physical journey has been completed, but his spiritual journey continues. From Father Sky, I call upon the Wind to blow his spirit gently home. From Mother Earth, I call upon her to receive him home. May the spirits of Fire purify all thoughts, and may the spirit of Water cleanse and wash away his hurts, anger, and disappointments.

In closing, grant me forgiveness for my trespasses. I love you, Frederic, older brother and mentor. Thank you for being my teacher. I'll miss you.

$$\text{⚘ ⚘ ⚘}$$

The Dream Shield Meditation is based on ancient dream techniques. This is safe and easy, and is best done just before sleep. You can record this meditation and play it back to yourself before bed. Speak with a very slow, relaxed voice. You might want to include a musical background. You can also read it to friends or use it with clients.

Dream Shield Meditation

To begin the process, allow your body to assume a restful position, making sure your spine is straight. You may do this now. Good.

Now begin to take very easy, deep breaths. Inhale and exhale. That's good. It's almost as if *you* are being breathed. It's as if nothing else exists except your breath. In and out. All your thoughts and cares are drifting away as you continue to breathe. With each breath, you find yourself relaxing more and more. You find yourself moving deeper and deeper within yourself. Imagine that you're flowing into your body with the oxygen as it enters your lungs; then you're flowing out of your body as you exhale that oxygen. In and out, each breath taking you deeper. It's as if you're drifting and flowing with the very gentle ebb and flow of the air that you're breathing. There's a rhythm, a balance to the universe, and your breath is connecting you to that harmony. Breathe gently and evenly as you continue your journey into a very relaxed, yet aware, state. Allow your awareness to drift gently into your body and allow yourself to be aware of any tightness. Just notice it. Good.

If there's any tightness in your body, feel it melting away like ice on a warm summer afternoon. That's good. Now allow your imagination to begin to drift and float, and imagine that you're walking along an ocean shore on a warm, moonlit evening. Your entire body feels relaxed, and you're moving with grace and ease. The soft sounds of the ocean are lulling you into a calm place within yourself. In the distance, you're aware of a great shimmering light on the ocean shore. As you approach it, you see thousands of crystals lying on the sand, their luminescent beauty reflected by the light of the moon. Each crystal seems to have its own inner glow that's so magical . . . so mysterious. In the distance, you see a particular crystal . . . a special one that seems to draw you to it. Reach out and pick it up. The instant it touches your hand, tranquil electrical currents flow through your body. Take a deep breath and feel the power that's enveloping you.

As you put this dream crystal into your pocket, you begin to hear a deep tone. Touching the crystal has activated a resonance within you. Appearing before you in the moonlight is a shield. It seems translucent at first. It's only a veil of light and sound, but as you stand and observe it, it becomes solid. You're aware that carved or engraved on its surface is a symbol—a symbol that only you can see. No one should ever know what this symbol is. It is for you alone.

Now reach forward and grasp the shield. There's security and safety afforded you just by holding this dream shield. And as you hold it, watch the environment begin to change.

The ground begins to shake beneath your feet, as you feel mighty movements of the earth. As you walk, holding the shield, you observe the splendid scenes of the world being formed. Hills are moving and valleys are forming. Mountains are pushed up into splendid jagged edges reaching for the sky. Observe as the substance of Earth is moving through its creation. Earth is physical strength; it is being a part of the physical dimension. Touch your shield to the ground. Your shield has now been activated with the power of the element of Earth.

As you continue walking, the winds begin to rise and whip around you. Hold your shield to the wind and let the element of Air empower and activate your shield, unlocking your high ideals. It is the divine process of thought.

And now the air becomes still . . . nothing is moving. Then you feel moisture—one drop, then another, and then another falls. It's the beginning of the time of the Great Rains. Hold your shield over your head as torrents of rain cascade around you and your shield.

The element of Water is activating your shield; feel its strength. Water represents intuition and is spiritual. The power of Water activates your shield.

As the rains are subsiding, great bolts of lightning punctuate the sky. Again and again, lightning streaks through the atmosphere above you, and thunder reverberates around you. Raise your shield high over your head, keeping both feet firmly planted on Mother Earth. A bolt of lightning strikes your dream shield. Energy courses through your shield, down your arms, and through your veins; and the lightning grounds through your feet as your shield is activated with the power of the element of Fire.

Your dream shield is complete. It has been activated by the elements of Earth, Air, Water, and Fire. You are now ready for dream exploration and adventures.

Now you notice that you're beside a door. Take a short time to be aware of this door. Is it big or small? Is it old or new, ornate or plain? This is the mystic door to your dreams. Take just a moment to examine it. Your dream crystal and dream shield are the keys to open this door. Decide which area you wish to explore in your dreams. Do you wish to do problem solving for a difficulty in your life? Do you want adventure and romance? Do you want to explore the psychic realm? Do you want healing for yourself and others? Decide what you want to explore in your dream realm. You may do this now. Good.

Imagine that you're holding your dream crystal to your third-eye area (slightly above and between your eyes). Dedicate your dream crystal to your dream quest. Hold your shield with one hand and your dream crystal in the other and lightly touch the door with your crystal. The door begins to open. As it does, your shield and crystal become invisible but are still a part of your energy field. You are now welcome to enter the world of dreams.

You remember to accept unconditionally whatever occurs during this dream state. If you notice your mind making judgments, just thank your mind for its concerns and keep going.

And now, step into the realm of dreams. Use your imagination to enhance your dreams. You may do this now.

Prepare to leave the realm of dreams. It is a realm to which you can return night after night. Begin your departure by taking a deep breath. I'm going to count from one to ten, and as I do so, allow yourself to begin to return to wakeful consciousness. Or if you desire, drift off into a deep, restful sleep.

One: Every number you hear deepens your ability to remember your dreams.

Two: Your dreams are valid, and you understand their meaning.

Three: Every dream you have, whether it's remembered or not, greatly enhances your waking hours.

Four: You're feeling rested and rejuvenated.

Five: You're very rested and refreshed, and your body vibrates with excellent health.

Six: Your ability to be in the right place at the right time is greatly enhanced by your dreams.

Seven: You are one of the light workers of the night, and you contribute to the well-being of others during your sleep, even if you aren't aware of it.

Eight: If you choose sleep, it comes soundly and easily.

Nine: You are more and more awake, more and more aware.

Ten: If you choose, you can now move to wakeful consciousness.

Sweet dreams!

Chapter 19

Dream Lover

The dream lover meditation is designed to increase your awareness of your sensuality and sexuality. When your sexual/sensual energy is open and clear, you'll naturally experience and enjoy life more fully. You can use this meditation during your waking hours or just before sleep as a means of programming your dreams for sensual encounters.

My initial attempts at creating a lover in my dreams were less than the sizzling trysts I'd anticipated. My first dream lover was a pale, withdrawn, and insipid lad who looked about 21 years old (although he whiningly sought to convince me he was much older). This was definitely not what I had in mind, and I terminated the dream. My endeavor the following night centered around a robust, burly man (not my type, but a definite improvement over the spindly teenager) with a noticeable bulge in his trousers. Fortunately, with my dream "x-ray eyes," I could see the oversized potato he'd stuck in his trousers in the hope of luring me to his bed. I again made a hasty retreat. My next attempt was a dark, foreboding shadow of a presence who tried to force his attentions on me. Foiled again!

My fourth dream lover, finally, was a success. The dream was set in 18th-century Italy. This lover was neither too young nor too old. He possessed all the correct physical equipment. He was strong, kind, and romantic. He was perfect! I even met his entire passionate Catholic family. He then informed me that we couldn't make love until we were married, and our wedding wouldn't occur until his older brother had gotten married.

At least this last dream gave me a clue as to why I was having so many difficulties obtaining a desirable dream lover. My upbringing was making it unacceptable on a subconscious level for me to take a lover (any lover, including a dream one) because I was already married. While discussing the situation with my husband, David, he told me that he'd always had dream lovers and felt that they were important for his own sense of well-being. In short, he encouraged me in my nightly endeavors. So I intensified my efforts! After a few more feeble encounters, it *definitely* became worth the effort, and I strongly recommend it. One immediate benefit was that my dream escapades greatly enhanced the sexual relations I had with my husband.

Often men and women secretly desire to have an affair, not necessarily because they're experiencing any lacking in their present relationship, but because of a desire for change or variety. Taking a dream lover (or lots of dream lovers) is one constructive way to fulfill that desire while keeping your present relationship intact. It's also excellent for the single person, since a dream lover can appease the compulsive *need* to be with a partner. Consequently, you can be more empowered in your selection of a companion.

Preparation for Meditation

If you're using this meditation to make a recording for yourself, or if you're reading it to another person, first create a restful setting—phone off the hook, lights low. Be in a setting where you'll have little or no distraction. Use a very slow, sultry voice when doing this meditation. If you're making a tape, you may wish to have some music in the background. Select music that you find very sensuous and arousing.

Dream Lover Meditation

To begin, make certain that your body is completely comfortable and in a relaxed position. Good. Now check to see that your spine is straight and your arms and legs are uncrossed . . . that's good. As your body begins to move into very deep relaxation, notice that each breath you take allows you to move deeper and deeper within yourself. Simply watch your breath for a moment. You aren't encouraging or denying your breath, you're just observing your breath. In and out . . . day and night . . . light and dark . . . black and white . . . male and female . . . yin and yang. There are two opposing, yet complementary, forces existing in the universe. In this moment, you're aligning and becoming one with those forces . . . in and out . . . keep watching your breath. Good. Now allow each breath to become deeper and fuller . . . deeper and fuller. Nice, deep, full breaths. That's good.

Allow your imagination to take wing and see yourself in an enchanted, moonlit meadow. The moon is spilling out of the heavens in cascading waterfalls of light. A mist of scented jasmine caresses the ferns curled up for the night. A dream owl hovers overhead, its silvery reflection in the stream below seen only by the stars. There's a quiet magic in the air.

Now spend some time imagining yourself in this secret garden of the night. Make it as real as you can. Imagine yourself using all of your senses to experience this place of quiet beauty, and see yourself walking through the meadow. If you can't visualize it, get a sense or a feeling of being there. Your body feels graceful, sensuous, very relaxed, and easy.

You notice that in the center of the meadow there's a bed. It's a sumptuous bed—so luxurious and voluptuous. The pillows are soft and round. Take some time to imagine this bed, making it as real as possible. Make it your perfect bed. It might be a big four-poster like your grandmother's feather bed, or perhaps it's a canopied bed draped with gossamer fabric that's lightly caressed by the warm breeze. Really picture this bed. Now slowly and ever so sensuously, climb into it. Be aware of the opulent plumpness of the pillows. Feel the silky smoothness of the sheets as you slide easily beneath the covers. It feels so good to be in this bed. Fanned by the gentle fragrance of the night, you find yourself drifting off into a deep, deep, deep sleep. Deep . . . deep . . . deep . . . sleep.

Somewhere in the magic of the night, you gently roll over and stretch, and as you do so, your hand brushes against a warm body. Your eyes are closed, yet you intuitively know that this is your dream lover. While you tentatively explore the subtle curves of your lover's body, you feel the faint, stirring breath of your dream lover softly in your hair. Take just a few moments to imagine the most exquisite . . . the most remarkable lovemaking. Feel your spirit, your entire being, soar.

Dawn is approaching. As you lie nestled in your lover's arms, you drift off into a contented sleep. When your eyes open, golden morning light streams through the forest trees. Your dream lover has vanished in the silent whispers of the night. A prefect rose graces your pillow.

At the end of this meditation, you can either move into sleep or return to wakeful consciousness. If you wish to return to consciousness, count from one to ten and suggest that with each number, you feel more and more awake.

✿ ✿ ✿   ✿ ✿ ✿

PART VI

Dream Meanings

At the outset of our night voyage,
I am hesitant, overwhelmed
by the immensity of the crossing;
innate wisdom of my inner sage
speaks reassurances to my childlike soul—
I breathe and step out, the journey
is given when the spirit is ready.

— M. Anne Sweet

Chapter 20

Dream Symbols for Life

Golden sunlight streamed in through my frosty morning window. I sat watching the steam rise from my cup of peppermint tea, loving the way it danced in misty swirls like ethereal sprites. Abby, my amber-colored cat, stretched lazily and curled up again, nuzzling her nose into velvet paws. Ruffling my fingers through her tawny, warm fur, I reached up and randomly flipped on the television. As I took my first sips of hot tea, I watched part of a show about a blind boy and the difficulties he encountered in life. That night, I decided to catch the late news and *coincidentally* saw the end of a show featuring a blind girl coping with her life.

The next day, as I drove home after taking my daughter to school, I passed by a bus stop. Curiously, there stood two blind men leaning nonchalantly on their white canes.

Later, driving to the grocery store, a blind man suddenly stepped out into the path of my car. I slammed on the brakes, spun the wheel, and stopped just short of hitting the frail gentleman. I pulled over to the curb to collect myself. All day I'd gotten messages, but I hadn't been listening.

Every day, in every way, the universe is trying to tell you something, just as your dreams are attempting to give you messages during the night. If you see a blind person in your dream, you might interpret that symbol as something you are refusing to "see" in your life. Your wakeful symbols are no less viable or significant. At the time in my life when I was being made aware of "blindness," there was something that I wasn't "seeing" regarding my life, and these wakeful symbols were my higher self's way of letting me know. Unfortunately, I sometimes have to be hit over the head before I'll slow down and focus on what's being communicated! When I paused and looked more closely at the symbolic experiences I was having, I confronted and released what I'd been unwilling to see, or what I was being "blind" to.

Daily life is no less an illusion than dream life. In my Zen training, both wakeful and sleep images were considered illusions. We were urged to touch a deeper reality. Use the symbols that you notice in your life in the same way as you use your dream symbols. For example, just as your car may be a symbol for you and your body in your dreams, experiences relating to cars can be symbolic during your daily experiences.

One brisk September morning, Meadow and I were driving home from our country cabin. David had gone on ahead in our other car. Stately pines caressed low-hanging clouds as we sailed over the high mountain pass and wound our way past vacant ski slopes. Suddenly, the engine in my car began to rev uncontrollably. I laid all my weight on the brake, but my car continued gaining momentum as it raced down the steep mountain road. I grabbed the emergency brake and yanked on it frantically as I turned off the engine. Finally, my car skidded to a stop.

When I was able to get roadside assistance, the mechanic jumped out, looked over my car, and easily started it up. "There doesn't seem to be any problem with this car, lady." However, when I started the car, the engine sounded like someone had floored it. We towed the car 75 miles to town.

The next mechanic gave his diagnosis: "There's nothing wrong with this car, lady." Yet when I turned on the ignition, it almost ran through the back wall of the garage. *(If you listen to the whispers, you don't have to hear the screams.)* I finally found a mechanic who determined that the cruise control was broken.

What did my runaway car represent or symbolize to me? What was I trying to tell myself? To me, a car is a symbol of my body or my physical being. (See "Car" in Chapter 28.) My car was racing out of control; it didn't have the ability to cruise. The only way it could operate was to get completely wound up, and at that time in my life, *I* was completely wound up. I had a very intense seminar schedule and was spending most of my time thinking (or worrying) about the future instead of being in the present. My car problem was telling me to slow down and set my life's course on "cruise control" and enjoy life.

As I said, *every day, in every way, the universe is trying to tell you something.* A further example of this concept is the plumbing in my house. To me, plumbing represents my emotions. If the plumbing clogs or the pipes freeze, it can be a reflection that my emotions are backing up or are frozen. If I take the time to discover what it is that I'm blocking emotionally, and if I then allow my emotions to run freely, often the pipes will unplug more easily. I know this doesn't make any logical sense; it's just something that I've observed.

It's also valuable to notice the little bits of conversations you hear randomly in passing. One day as I was being led to a table in a Chinese restaurant, I overheard this from a neighboring table: ". . . don't go ahead with the project." Upon leaving the restaurant, I turned on the radio and heard a song: "Don't go, baby, don't go." On the newscast that followed, I heard: ". . . the engineers have been advised not to go ahead with the project." Was the universe trying to warn me not to go ahead with something? I'd been scheduled to go to Washington, D.C., to work on a project, but after listening to the subtle voices of the universe, I decided not to go. It was a fortunate decision. The plane I'd been scheduled to take was forced to land in Chicago due to a blizzard, and no planes were able to get in or out of D.C. If I'd gone, I would have missed my meetings and incurred a great deal of unnecessary expenses.

The people in your life can also be symbols of your inner growth. I'd moved to a new city and begun my healing practice. My first client told me that she was agoraphobic. I'd never heard the term before and found that the word literally meant "fear of the marketplace," and was applied to someone who was afraid of going outside. Curiously, my next client was agoraphobic as well, and then to my amazement, my third client was also agoraphobic. Three in a row and they didn't know each other!

When a symbol appears three times in my life or in my dreams, I begin to listen very carefully. I knew that I didn't fit the classic definition of agoraphobia. I was comfortable in crowds and could easily leave my home without feeling anxious. However, as I began to delve more deeply into myself, I found some raw truths. In our move, I'd left behind many dear friends. My new environment seemed cold and hostile to me, and emotionally I had no desire to venture out. The agoraphobics were symbols of my not wanting to explore my new environment. Once I became aware of these thoughts and began to take some emotional risks, not only did I begin to enjoy my new city, but I began drawing clients who were more outgoing. *Coincidentally,* my agoraphobic clients also began to get better.

There also was a time when the majority of my clients were women who hadn't been able to get pregnant. Knowing that I didn't want to have any more children, I was puzzled by this symbol, but when I began to "give birth" to a new self-understanding, the women with whom I was working began to conceive, one by one.

Everything and everyone in your life, as well as in your dreams, is trying to tell you something—from the billboards you see to the formations you observe in the clouds, from simple things like losing your keys to the gifts you're given. You can use the symbols noted in this book for both dreams and daily life.

☼ ☼ ☼   ☼ ☼ ☼

Chapter 21

Dream Methods

Each morning, we usually wake with a light mist of memory from the night before. However, these elusive fragments of our dreams quickly disappear, and the hazy images clear, once we realize that we're here, now, awake. Occasionally, however, a dream is so vivid that we almost feel we could walk back into it. Sometimes these dreams continue to tug at our consciousness, and we wonder what they mean for life today, yesterday, or tomorrow.

There are many methods you can use to interpret your dreams, and each may take you on a unique pathway in understanding yourself. How you interpret the dream is less important than the meaning that you personally derive from it. You may look at each dream as a separate and new revelation or view your dreams over time as a collective whole.

Following are some traditionally used methods of dream interpretation. You might work with several of them or use one at a time—there's no right or wrong way. Remember, have fun as you find the one that works best for you.

Keep a Dream Journal

Record every dream that you remember for at least three months. Watch for recurring themes, people, places, feelings, or situations. Important messages from the unconscious can be uncovered through this method. After you record a dream, notice any hunches or intuitive feelings. Your gut reaction about a dream can be a clue to its meaning.

Create a Dream Dictionary

Create a dream dictionary containing the symbols that are unique to you. Whenever you have a dream, write down the symbols that appear, and then list the meanings that you personally assign to them. Assemble your collection of dream symbols in dictionary form, and refer to this list each time you dream. The more you use your dream dictionary, the more insights you'll gain. This is a powerful way to increase self-awareness.

Watch That Dream Feeling

Think about the feeling or emotion you experienced as a result of your dream. Now look back over your life and remember the last time you felt that way, recalling the particular situation that evoked this emotion. Most often, either that earlier event or the issues underlying it have triggered your dream. This can be a real clue to finding out the significance of your dream.

Talk with Your Dream Guide

Ask your dream guide for help in understanding and interpreting your dreams. This is the method that works best for me. (See Chapter 17.)

"Gestalt" the Dream

Go back into your dream, and examine the role of each item and character. For example, if you dreamed about a man, a child, and a woodstove, you'd say, "I am the woodstove, and I represent ____." (Here you'd say what woodstoves represent to you—perhaps they represent contained warmth or family and friends.) Next, you'd say, "I am the child, and I represent ____." Continue to do this for each aspect of your dream until it is clearly defined.

Now have the different parts "talk" to each another. For example, put out three chairs, one representing the woodstove, one representing the child, and the last representing the man. Sit in the woodstove chair and talk to the other two chairs, saying, perhaps, "I represent family, friends, and inner warmth; and I think families should always be together as they are when they sit around woodstoves." Then, sit in the child chair, and say something like this: "I'm the child and I don't want to be with the family sitting around the woodstove. I want to be outside so I can run and play. I don't want to be tied down. I feel confined and stifled when I sit around with the family." Continue with this process until you have a clearer sense of the meaning of your dream.

Draw Your Dream

Draw pictures that illustrate the feelings or images you experienced in your dream. Use colors that reflect the tone of the dream; it isn't necessary to draw exact images. For example, a black horse you saw in your dream doesn't have to look like an actual horse in your drawing. You can draw the feelings of "black," "movement," or "power." This exercise can begin to free you so that some of your unconscious feelings can rise to the surface.

Use Free Association

Based on Freud's most acclaimed theory, this method consists of writing associations, or the first idea that comes to mind, for each part of your dream. This may offer you clues to the major themes you're dealing with in the dream. For example, imagine that you dream about a rabbit. A free association might be: "Rabbit . . . Peter Rabbit . . . my brother Peter who used to beat me up—hey, I'm feeling really beaten up by life these days!"

Pretend You Meet a Martian

Pretend that you're telling your dream to someone from another planet. The alien doesn't know anything about Earth. For example, if there's a broom in your dream, how would you describe it to your friend from Mars? You might say, "A broom is a long object that you hold close to you and then push away from you. It helps you get rid of things that you don't want." After you've described the broom, examine your life to see if there's anything you want to rid yourself of. It might be something that you're pulling toward yourself and then pushing away. As you begin to describe the parts of your dream to the alien using the most basic language, often the meaning of your dream becomes clear.

Complete the Plot

Go back into your dream in your waking hours and rework it in such a way that *you* end up the victor. You can change any uncomfortable part of any dream—*you* can be the hero. Conquer your dream enemies, and make your dream have a happy ending! Visualizing an ending to your dream can help you understand its meaning.

Act Out Your Dream

The Iroquois Indians regularly acted out their dreams in a drama. You can also do this in a group or on your own. The idea is to physically reenact different aspects of the dream, which begins to integrate the meaning of it more deeply into your daily reality.

Explore a Dream Dictionary

See Chapter 28 to find the symbols that appear in your dreams, and notice which ones feel right for you. No dream dictionary will be 100 percent accurate because dream symbols are very personal, but using a dream dictionary will get you off to a good start.

Use the Ancient Chinese-Clock Method

See Chapter 23 for a detailed explanation of this type of dream interpretation.

Try the Replay Method

Place your awareness of the dream in the right side of your brain. Play through the dream, staying in this mind-set (the right side is the intuitive side of the brain). Then shift your awareness to the left side of your brain (the side of the brain that analyzes). Replay your dream. Notice the difference in how your body feels when you run the dream on one side of your brain and then on the other. Pay attention to how this elicits different emotions, depending on which side of the brain you use to replay it. You may also find that your interpretation of the dream will change according to which side you use.

꽈 꽈 꽈 꽈 꽈 꽈

Chapter 22

Seasons

Everything that dwells on this planet is affected by the seasons in one way or another. In ancient times, understanding the power of the seasons was considered necessary in order to understand the mysteries of life. In 250 B.C., a secret "mystery school" was founded in China that centered its teachings around the esoteric comprehension of the seasons. The teaching was preserved through secret societies of the Middle Ages and eventually blossomed into the study of astrology. Each of the seasons has a profound influence on our psyches, and each season represents an integral part of who we are. Just as we have our cycles of learning and of resting, we also have monthly and yearly cycles. Dreaming, too, follows the cycles of nature.

Winter

> Under the winter moon
> The river wind
> Sharpens the rocks
> — Chora

Dreams during the winter months are often the most powerful and the clearest. They directly concern your spiritual awareness. This is your time of inner growth, of looking within. These dreams plant seeds for the year to come. This is the time when visionary dreams concerning war, religion, and politics are most likely to occur. You're more apt to remember your dreams in winter, and you're getting ready to blossom into spring. A winter setting in a dream often indicates a drawing inward of your energies.

Spring

> Yes, spring has come,
> This morning a nameless hill
> Is shrouded in mist
> — Bashō

Dreams that occur in the spring often have to do with new directions. They deal with your emotional self, your feelings about yourself and others. This is when you'll most likely have visionary dreams concerning motherhood, teachings, and disease. A spring setting in a dream generally signifies new growth and fresh beginnings.

Summer

> *The summer moon*
> *Is touched by the line*
> *Of a fishing rod*
> — Chiyo-ni

Many times, dreams in the summer have to do with your outgoing self; your thought processes and social concerns. Visionary dreams concerning invention and science occur more during this season than any other. A summer setting in a dream can represent carefree joy, and/or a very expansive time in your life.

Autumn

> *The autumn mountains;*
> *Here and there*
> *Smoke rising*
> — Gyodai

Dreams during autumn often have to do with completion and can concern your physical body. They have to do with sexuality, completion, and creativity. This is the time when you're most likely to get creative inspiration through your dreams. Dreaming about autumn often relates to harvest and abundance of ideas, beliefs, and material goods.

🌿🌿🌿 🌿🌿🌿

Chapter 23

Ancient Chinese-Clock Dream Interpretation

The veil of fog and mystique that has surrounded Chinese medicine has begun to part in recent years, and Western doctors are beginning to give credence to this ancient art. The Chinese were stewards of a sophisticated and practical medical system thousands of years before Western doctors even began bloodletting with leeches. Magnificent finds, such as the circulation of the blood, are mentioned in *The Yellow Emperor's Classic of Internal Medicine,* written more than 4,000 years ago.

In Chinese cosmology, the source of all things is the Tao, which is considered the law of the universe. From the Tao flows the one energy. The two opposing yet complementary forces of the universe that blend to form the one are the yin and the yang. Yin represents the female energy—it corresponds to that which is dark, soft, receptive, moist, cool, and declining; yang represents the male energy, corresponding to that which is light, dry, hot, active, and rising. It is the dance, the dynamic interaction between theses two forces, that creates the life force of chi, which is the energy that exists in everything, from the most etheric matter (such as light) to the most dense (such as granite).

All matter is imbued with chi and is divided into different aspects as it's manifested in the universe. These different aspects or elements correspond to the different seasons, the different organs, and the different hours of the day. They all are manifest within humankind, linking us with the rest of our environment. Each hour of the day corresponds to a different organ and a corresponding emotion.

ANCIENT CHINESE CLOCK

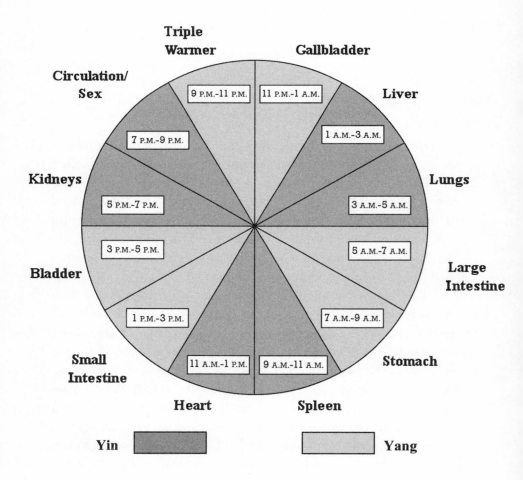

This system, based on Chinese philosophy, divides the day into different time periods. Each period relates to a specific organ or aspect of the body. Just as each organ is thought to have corresponding emotions and characteristics, the dreams that you have during each time period are considered unique to those characteristics. Thus, it's important to note the times of your dreams in order to derive the full benefit of this method.

On the following pages is an hourly guide that will help you interpret your dreams based on the times at which they occur.

11 P.M.–7 A.M.

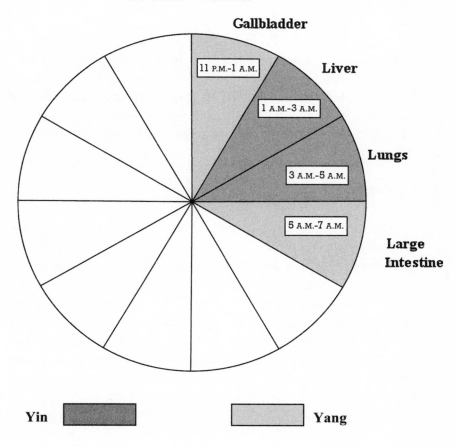

11 P.M.–1 A.M.

If you have a dream between 11 P.M. and 1 A.M., which is gallbladder time, your dream may likely focus around issues of unresolved anger, especially with regard to external circumstances. Any difficulty arising during this time period should be confronted within the dream state. This is also the time of courage. The courage you gain in your dreams will translate to courage in your daily life.

1 A.M.–3 A.M.

Dreams occurring between 1 A.M. and 3 A.M., liver time, might concern issues of self-anger, purification, and the will to live. Dreams within this time period can reveal areas that need to be cleansed or purified in your life. The liver is the one organ that can regenerate itself. During this period, your dreams may have to do with the future and with personal regeneration.

3 A.M.–5 A.M.

Dreams occurring between 3 A.M. and 5 A.M., lung time, generally concern issues of spiritual development, inner grief, receiving love, letting go, completion, freedom, and expression. It's during this time that you're most likely to experience psychic and transformational dreams. This is also the time when you're most likely to receive dreams that are other-dimensional, or dreams from a loved one who has passed on. This is an excellent time for astral travel. The ancient Chinese said that this was the beginning of the spiritual day. You'll have dreams during this time regarding new beginnings in your spiritual growth.

5 A.M.–7 A.M.

During the hours of 5 A.M. and 7 A.M., large intestine time, your dreams might concern things that are cluttering or clogging up your life. This is also a time of outer grief, discernment, caring for others, and self-empowerment. Often, it's a time to receive dreams concerning other people. In addition, dreams from the past and even past-life recall tend to occur within this period. It's a time for processing the information and experiences that you've gathered during the day.

7 A.M.–3 P.M.

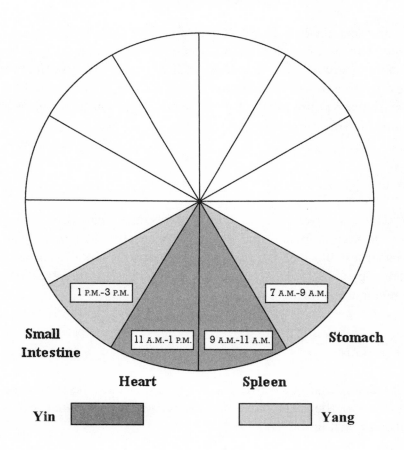

7 A.M.–9 A.M.

Dreams between 7 A.M. and 9 A.M., stomach time, tend to focus on the digestion of new ideas. They may also concern things that you can't "stomach" or assimilate in your daily life. These dreams can also deal with sympathy and empathy for others. It's a good time for the healing of others. This is also an excellent time for creative ideas to come through or to receive answers to problems that have been troubling you.

9 A.M.–11 A.M.

Dreams between 9 A.M. and 11 A.M. take place during spleen time. This is the period for self-acceptance, and dreams tend to focus on accepting the goodness of life. This is also the time of healing dreams—the time of the mystic warrior. It's the period for the humane killing of all that isn't working in your life. This is a powerful time for physical self-healing.

11 A.M.–1 P.M.

Dreams between 11 A.M. and 1 P.M. occur in heart time. These can be dreams of joy and celebration, or they can reveal the relationship blockages in your life. These dreams can also connect your spiritual self with your earthly self. This is another excellent time for astral travel.

1 P.M.–3 P.M.

Dreams that occur between 1 P.M. and 3 P.M., small intestine time, are for the purpose of absorbing and assimilating what you've taken in during the day.

3 P.M.–11 P.M.

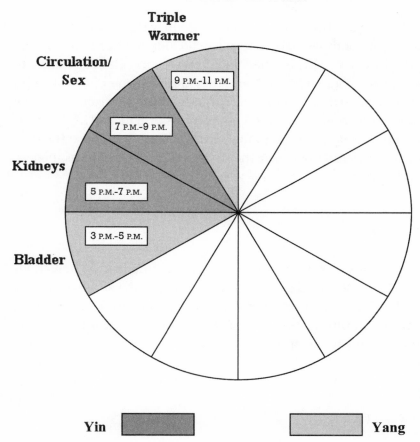

Triple Warmer

Circulation/ Sex

9 P.M.-11 P.M.

7 P.M.-9 P.M.

Kidneys

5 P.M.-7 P.M.

3 P.M.-5 P.M.

Bladder

Yin   Yang

3 P.M.–5 P.M.

Dreams during bladder time, from 3 P.M. to 5 P.M., reveal areas of fear, particularly outward fear. These dreams assist you in the release of old ideas and relationships that aren't working for you. They'll help you let go and allow the power of the Creator to flow through you.

5 P.M.–7 P.M.

Dreams between 5 P.M. and 7 P.M., kidney time, can assist you in letting go of inner fears. These may include the fear of being who you really are. This is when you'll experience dreams relating to fears from your childhood, and they can help you resolve areas of criticism and disappointment. The kidneys are connected with the element of Water, which represents transformation. This is a time of transformation through the release of fear. This is also the time of the transition between the death and rebirth of ideas, beliefs, and attitudes.

7 P.M.–9 P.M.

Dreams that occur from 7 P.M. to 9 P.M. are in the circulation/ sex time. These tend to be dreams regarding being at the right place at the right time. They often focus on inner-control issues. This is a powerful time for enlightenment dreams. It's interesting to note that within many spiritual communities, disciples sleep during these hours.

9 P.M.–11 P.M.

If you dream between 9 P.M. and 11 P.M., known as the triple-warmer time, you may have dreams concerning issues of control— not so much of yourself, but control of your environment. You may also receive dreams relating to the outer movement in your life, the breaking up of old patterns and the establishment of new ones. This is the time for establishing a balance between too little control and too much in your life.

🌀🌀🌀 🌀🌀🌀

Chapter 24

The Moon

She is the giver of visions—journeying silently into the night—an emissary from the land of dreams. She is the silvery white goddess, illuminator of the unconscious, and revealer of mysterious forces. All tides are hers: tides of the great seas, of the sky, of the inner realms of the night, of the secret tides of death and birth . . . and even the tides of the monthly cycles of women.

She is a celestial goddess of dreams. She carries the moon tides gently to the center of the soul . . . tides that ebb and flow. All these secrets belong to her, for she rules the great deep where all life began. She's the mistress of the inner tides that never cease, the ruler of fantasies and intuition. She is queen of the star-washed sky, bringing creativity and vision on the dream tides of the night.

Sleep and darkness are her gentle companions. She returns month after month with renewed strength, uniting opposing elements and transforming darkness into light. She's a source of physical and spiritual rebirth and illumination. She cascades from the doorways of heaven in waterfalls of light. She is the moon—a powerful spiritual force on our planet and ruler of the dream tides that ebb and flow in the night.

Moon consciousness, or moon awareness, arises from the deep core of our being; it's inherent to our internal instincts. To primitive people, the moon was a visible and revered symbol of our inner states of dreaming. Today, the moon touches a memory of the forgotten arts, one of which is the recall and understanding of our dreams. Ancient civilizations honored the moon because it played an important part in their everyday lives as well as in their dreams. They observed that crops grew seasonally and in tune with the cycles of the moon. Women's menstrual cycles synchronized with lunar rhythms. The moon was the ultimate symbol of fertility in the universe; her gentle light soothed dew-moistened plants after the heat of the day. The light of the moon invited life to come forth from the seeds during the night. With the same mystical force that drew plants from the earth, the monthly bleeding from women, and tides to and from the shore, the moon helped activate dreams. It was thought that the moon was the bearer of wisdom in the night.

In past times, an important relationship was acknowledged between one's dreams and one's daily life. Since nighttime, the special dominion of the moon, brought sleep and visions, dreams were revered as messages from the moon to be carefully followed the next day. The moon was also believed to be the originator of creativity.

Early civilizations observed that being in or out of sync with the rhythms of the moon influenced their health and balance. People measured all of life by the lunar cycles. Activities from planting crops to cutting hair to engaging in battle were acknowledged to be more successful when done in alignment with the moon cycles.

Our bodily cycles are one of the most basic aspects of our existence. These internal flows define the way we experience ourselves and the world around us. Just as the moon's magnetic pull affects the tides, and even slightly distorts the earth, its cyclical pull dramatically affects our body fluids, which in turn affects our dream states. Since the body is approximately 67 percent water, and in view of the fact that our blood has a chemistry very similar to that of sea water, it's easy to understand how our dream states and body changes synchronize with the ocean tides and the phases of the moon.

An intimate knowledge of and exposure to the moon can deepen your mastery of your dream states. Developing an awareness of moon cycles, as well as of your own life cycles, will provide you with greater insight into your dreams. To maximize your understanding and interpretation of your dreams, it's important to create an alignment with the moon and its cycles.

One of the universal principles that ancient peoples learned from lunar cycles was the basic pattern for renewal. Rest, meditation, and gestation were treated with the same reverence, as was productivity. The understanding of equal respect for all parts of the cycle has been most clearly retained in the Eastern concept of yin and yang and its adherence to the cosmic laws of balance.

Each cycle of the moon is divided into four smaller cycles: new moon, waxing moon, full moon, and waning moon. Each cycle lasts about seven days, and there's no set moment when one cycle ends and another begins. They simply follow a flow pattern, as does our physical energy.

The new moon (or dark of the moon) is the time of rebirth. During this time, rest, be still, and meditate. Dreams that occur during this period reflect the deepest and most internal movements of your inner self. This was a time when ancient Native American women sought retreat in nature in order to be still and commune with the Creator. Amid this stillness, your dreams are preparing the soil of your inner soul for the planting of seeds in the weeks to come.

As the crescent moon appears, be aware as your energy begins to expand. When the moon waxes, or as more of it becomes visible, begin to take action in alignment with the revelations you receive in your dreams during the new moon.

The full moon is the culmination of the seed planted in the new moon. During this cycle, release the fullness of your creative forces. Be alive and animated. Participate fully in life and enjoy the dance of celebration. Research indicates that this is the cycle when the most vivid dream activity occurs. In addition, the full moon is also the time when you're most likely to recall your dreams.

The waning moon is the time to assimilate and absorb all you've learned in the preceding weeks. Dreams during this phase will be ones of reflection and introspection. When you begin to integrate your life movements with the moon's cycles, you'll be flowing in harmony with the most primordial and powerful force in nature. Your dream life will become increasingly vivid and viable.

One way to integrate your life cycles with those of the moon is to create a moon ritual. In ancient moon rituals, visionary experiences occurred that were considered necessary to the balance of life, and without these states, one's understanding of the universe dwindled. It's essential to our individual and collective balance to regain an understanding of these states of being. This can be achieved by creating a moon ritual for yourself.

A moon ritual is the channeling of energies utilizing the moon as a focal point to usher yourself into more expanded levels of consciousness. A ceremony can be used to change your perceptions of reality and is a symbolic event; it can either be simple or complex in nature. Moon rituals symbolize all the mysteries and powers of the subconscious. It is those elusive energies with which the moon priestesses of old desired to merge. The ceremony attempts to make tangible an event that's occurring on an inner plane, and the transformation of personality is implied in every ritual. It's a way to experience connectedness with the entire universe.

Here are some simple moon rites that you can use to enhance your dreams.

- Stand at a window or outdoors when the moon is up during its different phases.

- Lift your arms to the moon as ancient people did. Feel its energy surge through you, filling your being.

- Take a moon bath, allowing rays of moonlight to bathe and cleanse you—washing over you like waves of the sea.

- Dance in the moonlight. Allow yourself to move with wild abandon.

- Leave water out in the light of the moon; then drink it just before you go to sleep.

A ritual is a stylized series of actions used to bring about change; its origin is deep within the psyche of each individual. You already possess the ingredients within you to trigger all the experiences you desire. So create a moon ritual that speaks to your life and your needs, using symbols and artifacts that for you are representations of the inner qualities of your dreams.

The dream moon ritual I created for myself is simple. I lay out a circle of sticks or special stones, which signifies wholeness and my dream world. Without beginning or end, the circle represents the source and eventual return to the source of life and unity. Within this circle, I place things that are special to me and that represent the mystical world of dreams. Among these is the stone selenite, a name originating from the moon goddess Selene. This stone is an excellent tool in assisting dream recall and understanding.

To enhance the ceremonial aspect of my moon circle, I begin by dedicating my energy to the living spirit in all things and to my dreams. I then compose a simple dream song and create a dream dance that will invoke the power of life and my own inner nature. Once I've completed my ritual, I carefully gather my treasured objects and store them in a special place until next time.

When you first create your moon ritual and begin to participate in it, you may feel foolish or awkward. However, as you go beyond that point, you'll soon experience the sacred center. At the beginning of the ritual, your true emotions are buried under layers of linear and rational thinking, but as you persist, the right side of your brain will take over and the inner reality of the acts performed will come through. As a result, you'll feel yourself in harmony with the inner cycles of nature, with your dreams, and with the inner wisdom of the night.

𝕯 𝕯 𝕯 𝕯 𝕯 𝕯

Chapter 25

Colors

There's no doubt that color plays an important role in almost all of our lives, and in our dreams, colors provide us with valuable insights into the hues and shades of our experiences.

There are several theories concerning whether or not we dream in color. Calvin Hall, a dream researcher who's collected records of thousands of dreams, states that two-thirds of all dreams are in black and white. He believes that only one dream in every three is colored or has some aspect of color in it. Hall relates that few people dream entirely in color, and some individuals never experience color in their dreams at all.[1]

This view, however, isn't shared by everyone. Gladys Mayer, another dream explorer, says that all dreams are in color. She maintains that just as we all dream, yet perhaps don't remember our dreams, we all dream in color but don't recall the colors.[2]

In his book *Heaven and Hell,* Aldous Huxley states that dream symbols don't need to be in color to be effective. "It is worth remarking that, in most people's experience, the most brightly colored dreams are those of landscapes, in which there is no drama, no symbolic reference to conflict, merely the presentation to consciousness of a given, non-human fact." He believes that when symbols express psychological conflicts, color isn't necessary. Therefore, the color occurs in those areas without conflict. Some dream researchers disagree with this theory, claiming that all dreams appear to embody some type of conflict. Another disagreement with this theory is that some people always dream in color regardless of conflict.[3]

One theory holds that the presence of a specific color in dreams can signify a diseased condition. For example, a hypothesis purports that dreams containing a great deal of green indicate disorders of the liver, and dreams in which red predominates warn us of the possibility of hemorrhage or of circulation and cardiac problems. I believe that while there may be some validity to this theory, the *shade* of green or red is also a factor. A forthcoming disease can be indicated by disturbing shades of colors in dreams, but a clean spring green in a dream can signify a major healing force, and a clear brilliant red can represent physical strength and sexual potency.[4]

Yet another theory contends that those who dream predominantly in color are far more color conscious than the average individual and are exceptionally talented artistically. The proponents of this theory suggest that painting lessons will trigger dreams in color.[5]

Knowledge of color significance in dreams is one of the simplest yet most effective tools for understanding our dreams. As we look around us, everything within our sight reflects color. Where the colors change, where the shadows meet—this defines the form and shape of everything we see. The use of color to understand dreams has been practiced successfully for thousands of years in most cultures that have esoteric traditions. To understand color is to understand the essence of energy.

We're living in an expansive ocean of energy consisting of vitally alive vibrations of different speeds and varying degrees of intensity. This ocean of energy is a swirling dance of ever-changing matter. It is energy in the various stages of solid, liquid, and gas, each finding its temporary niche in the universe. Light and color are vibrations in this eternal play of energy. The warm colors of red, orange, and yellow have a slow vibratory rate on the electromagnetic scale, while the cooler colors of green, blue, and purple have a very fast rate.

Sir Isaac Newton, in 1666, was the first man to break sunlight into its component colors. Using a prism, Newton produced a spectrum dividing natural sunlight, or white light, into seven bands of color: red, orange, yellow, green, blue, indigo, and violet. Light is actually a vibrating, radiant energy traveling at 186,000 miles per second in the form of rays or waves. These wavelengths are measured in terms of frequency; the shorter the wavelength, the higher the frequency.

You, too, are a series of energy fields. Your entire body is constantly vibrating in fields of energy, some subtle and some manifest. You are constantly involved in movement and motion. Your body's energy fields are affected by the constantly changing energies in your environment, such as sunlight and wind, the energy fields of other people, and the energies of the food you eat. Your body—indeed, your entire being—is continuously affected very deeply by the energies of colors.

Even though we might not be consciously aware of it, we acknowledge the power of color in our lives. Our language reflects this in our expressions: *I'm feeling blue today. It was a blue Monday. She's feeling in the pink. He looks at life through rose-colored glasses. He saw red. She was red with anger (or green with envy or purple with rage).* The list goes on. Color plays an important role in every area of our lives.

There was a time when color was perceived as far more significant to humanity than is currently acknowledged. In fact, it wasn't until recently that color began to be thought of as merely decorative or entertaining. In human history as a whole, color was considered one of the most vital symbols in the world, and the profound meaning of each color was an integral part of all ancient civilizations involved in dream exploration. Mesopotamia, Egypt,

Greece, China, and Tibet, as well as the traditional cultures of Native Americans and even medieval Europeans, harnessed the power of color. Today, however, psychologists and scientists are acknowledging the use of color for therapeutic and medicinal purposes.

Researchers have discovered that certain colors trigger similar responses in people regardless of their cultural background. Orange red is perceived as stimulating, whereas dark blue produces a relaxation response. It appears that color psychology cuts clear across divisions of nationality, race, and culture in a way similar to music.

Of course you'll have different shades and hues of the seven major colors in your dreams. Often, the clearer the color is, the more accurate the meaning of the symbol. The muddier the color, the more that area is blocked for you.

Red

The color red in a dream corresponds to the first chakra, the area at the base of the spine. Our drive for existence and survival is represented by red, which energizes the physical body to respond and act in an assertive manner. Red stimulates the heart and increases the vibratory rate. It's no accident that restaurants use red in their decor, for its stimulating effect increases the appetite. Red is also associated with sexual energy, relating to sensations of pleasure. Red brings on reactiveness and physical excitement.

Red can also be related to anger. Pronounced red in a dream can symbolize clear anger; and a muddy red represents suppressed anger, in the form of pugnacity, aggressiveness, sensation, tenseness, or physical strength. Our perception of time seems longer when we're exposed to red; therefore, it isn't an appropriate color for waiting rooms.

Red relates to direct action, active employment, will, and power. Strength, courage, steadfastness, health, vigor, sexuality, sexual love, and danger are other attributes closely associated with red. Having this color occur in a dream can be extremely vitalizing and stimulating; and it can assist in overcoming inertia, depression, fear, or melancholy. It's a great aid to those who are afraid of life and inclined to feel like escaping. The red ray helps us plant our feet firmly on the earth. If you don't feel grounded because you dwell on the future, having red within a dream will help root you in the present—in the "now." It supplies the energy and motivation necessary to reach and accomplish goals. Red is a "doing" color, a "get the job done" color.

Orange

Orange in a dream corresponds to the second chakra, located about three inches below the navel on most people. Orange represents our drive for social acceptance. It is a warm, energizing color, but it's both lighter and higher in vibration than red, so the energy translates to broader fields in the body. It stimulates involvement with assisting in group and social functions, rather than concern with self-survival. Orange is a happy color; it's used by clowns the world over. It boosts optimism, expansiveness, and emotional balance; and relates to the herding instinct, ambition, agitation, restlessness, exploration, and business. It can relate to pride as well as to the movement of sexual energies. It may drive thought processes that bring about the interest in politics.

People whose favorite color is orange are likely to be sensationally ambitious, competitive, expansive, optimistic, warm, or hospitable, with humanitarian instincts. They seek social contact and acceptance. They are ambitious with respect to their community, their nation, and their business; and they appreciate projects of worldwide scope—that is, they love to expand their viewpoint.

Orange in a dream symbolizes optimism, confidence, change, striving, self-motivation, enthusiasm, and courage. This color is a social ray. The tendency to believe too readily, without skepticism or discrimination, can be healed by this ray. Therefore, if you tend to be suspicious, mistrusting, have selfish pride, or are even seeking power, having orange in a dream can assist in creating balance and discrimination.

The healing energies of orange in a dream stimulate the inner knowing that we are all one. It pushes the consciousness to rise above the self. Essentially, orange in a dream is expansive, exploratory, and social.

Red is sensual, while orange is social. It's the drive to find reality through other people, the drive for fellowship. The red energy is a passion for self-preservation and self-gratification. With orange, the drive and concern is more for social preservation—the preservation of society, family, and social gatherings. Orange indicates being unafraid to dance and sing and proclaim yourself as a lover of people.

Yellow

Yellow is intellectual, corresponding to the third chakra, located at the solar plexus. It's the last of the warm, extroverted color rays. In a dream, it can signify your thinking processes. The energy of the yellow ray stimulates your logical, linear thinking and relates to left-brain activities. Yellow helps you respond with mental discrimination, organization, attention to detail, evaluation, active intelligence, discipline, administration, praise, sincerity, and harmony. Thus, yellow offers heightened expression and freedom, which translates into the joy within a dream.

Those whose favorite color is yellow often feel the need to analyze everything and know the "what" and "where." They require a logical framework before they can understand things. They desire originality and change and are highly creative, seeking expression in art; literature; music; and talk, talk, talk. They're flexible, expressive, eloquent, and intensely self-aware individuals who are efficient in planning and organization. The spontaneous reactions to stimuli or events unique to both red and orange energies are not experienced by stimulation by the yellow ray.

Instead, there exists a more detached understanding of how the events originated—that is, where they took place, when they'll be brought to focus, and so on. Yellow understands the larger scope of life. It stimulates the need to live in an orderly world and to express our individuality and our need to understand.

The healing power of the yellow ray in a dream works on fear. Often, when you're afraid, your stomach feels queasy. Through various incarnations, a tremendous amount of fear may have been locked away in your solar-plexus region, and you can't understand the cause of your anxiety. Yellow in your dreams will gradually release the tension centered in your solar plexus and can ignite courage.

Yellow is incredibly healing for judgmental, critical, and verbally aggressive individuals. It increases flexibility and adaptability to change. When we harmonize with the yellow ray, no problem will remain unsolved under the scrutiny of our intellect. We also learn that it's better to work to change ourselves rather than others. The need for balance between our heads and our hearts remains clear.

Green

Green in a dream can represent security and balance. It corresponds to the heart chakra, the fourth energy point of the body's energy field. Green is the balance between the warm, extroverted spectrum of red, orange, and yellow; and the cool, introverted colors of blue, indigo, and violet. Thus, green stimulates feelings of love, harmony, peace, brotherhood, hope, growth, and healing. I often find that my clients tend to notice a lot of green in their dreams during their healing periods. People whose favorite color is green are usually generous, vital, openhearted, and nurturing. Green establishes an inner stability, stimulating our need to feel secure, certain, assertive, powerful, and to love and be loved.

Green in a dream is very beneficial for any deep, brooding feelings of regret. It's also helpful in overcoming limiting attachments, as many anxieties are created in the heart through various attachments. While it's valuable to enjoy whatever you have in the moment, it's also important to your peace of mind to develop the art of being unattached to "having."

Green is found everywhere in nature, symbolizing the abundant, replenishing forces of the universe. There will always be enough. The U.S. dollar is green and has been strong for many years; however, when a pink tinge was added to the paper used for the bills, it corresponded with a decline of the dollar on the world markets. New Zealand's money used to be green, and when the color was changed, there was a decline in the worth of their dollar. These might be coincidences, but they're very interesting ones!

Green energy is also extremely healing for doubt and insecurity. Through meditation on the purity of green, we can call on our true, expansive, compassionate, and openhearted nature. When the heart is open and we feel the love of the universe streaming through our being, we experience the greatest security and self-confidence. We learn to live without attachments and with fewer possessions. Green is a very healing color in dreams.

Blue

Blue, the first of the cool-spectrum colors, is conceptual and associated with the throat chakra. Blue stimulates you to seek inner truth. Blue in a dream helps you attain inner peace and emotional security and also helps you live out your ideals. Blue boosts spiritual security and the desire for inner understanding.

People whose favorite color is blue are apt to be idealistic, patient, and enduring souls. They tend to be nostalgic, committed, devotional, peaceful, and loyal. These highly sensitive individuals have very strong commitments to their idealistic thoughts and feelings. They seek contentment and peace of mind, and they aren't prone to change.

Blue in a dream represents inspiration, creativity, spiritual understanding, faith, and devotion. The concept of time flows quickly, and memories of the past are stimulated. Blue is an ideal color for waiting rooms and places of study. If there's a lot of blue in your dreams, this usually reflects gentleness, contentment, patience, and composure. However, a murky blue can sometimes indicate depression.

The color blue is beneficial for people who act compulsively without stopping to think. It's also extremely liberating for those who've become rigid and resistant to change. The blue ray has the power of synthesizing and combines separate elements into a complex whole. "True blue" sincerity manifests in all relationships in life. When we're sincere with ourselves, we can be sincere with others.

Purple

Purple relates to the brow chakra—intuition—and is the color most closely associated with dreams. Listen carefully to dreams that contain purple, indigo, or violet, as these stimulate your need to feel at one with the universe, have conflict-free relationships, and be in the forefront of human development. Along with the color blue, the effects of these shades of purple are calming, soothing, and comforting. Very often when you experience purple in a dream, it's indicative of psychic awareness and intuition. Pay attention to these dreams.

When a predominance of purple is in a dream, we're often afforded a vision of the future, like an eagle looking down as it soars high above the plains. From that vantage point, we can see what is near but also what is beyond. Therefore, when we see purple in a dream, we're seeing beyond; these tend to be dreams of prophecy. A person whose favorite color is purple is usually abstract, inspired, trustful of the future, and able to tune in to the inner world of others. Purple stimulates our spiritual perspective and intuition.

White

White in a dream can relate to imagination and the crown, or top, chakra. Its vibrations are the fastest and have the highest frequency in the color spectrum. Its effects on us are divine realization, humility, and creative imagination. It can be purifying, like white snow in winter, and it can represent purity. White encompasses all colors, so dreams containing this color should be observed carefully.

White has the energy and power to transform the focus of the imagination. It's a useful color for those who tend to daydream or have trouble manifesting. The white and violet rays are the creative imagination leading us toward higher spiritual attunement and divine love through our dreams. People who are strongly attracted to this color have a deep sense of wonder, bliss, and self-surrender. White is also a great healing color for anyone who has a negative self-image, for its energy holds the power of transformation. (In cultures where death is represented by the color white, it can also represent the end of a relationship, project, or era.)

Red

Inspires: Freedom, determination, honor, willpower, strength, action, alertness, independence, motivation, initiative, leadership

Releases: Anger, frustration, confusion, violence, destruction, revenge, rebellion, impulsiveness, impatience

Orange

Inspires: Optimism, courage, victory, confidence, enthusiasm, encouragement, attraction, abundance, kindness, expansion

Releases: Superiority, mistrust, pride, superficiality

Yellow

Inspires: Joy, expression, clarity, mental discrimination, organization, attention to detail, evaluation, active intelligence, discipline, administration, courage

Releases: Restraint, lack of focus, confusion, frustration, fear

Green

Inspires: Encouragement, generosity, love, vitality, power, security, openheartedness, nurturance, self-assertion, compassion, expansion, sharing, harmony, balance

Releases: Self-doubt, possessiveness, jealousy, selfish attachment, envy, insecurity, mistrust

Blue

Inspires: Wisdom, gentleness, acceptance, trust, understanding, detachment, kindness, compassion, patience, forgiveness, sensitivity, contemplation

Releases: Self-pity, self-rejection, separateness, isolation, worry, depression, passivity, anxiety, coldness, detachment

Purple

Inspires: Inspiration, vision, farsightedness, trust in the future, intuition, extrasensory perception, supersensitivity

Releases: Inability to live in the now, spacing out, forgetfulness, lack of discipline, resentment, separateness, arrogance, pride, contempt

White

Inspires: Mystical instinct, creativity, spiritual inspiration, meditation, reflection, deep inner wisdom, grace, delight, spiritual unity

Releases: Obsessiveness, martyrdom, restriction, intolerance, "daydreaminess," criticism, negativity

Chapter 26

Numbers

Numbers play an important part in dreams, for each represents spiritual power and significance. Through increased understanding of numbers, you can gain new insights into yourself. Essentially, numbers are only symbols; alone, they don't elicit change, but they do offer keys into your inherent potential and the energy that surrounds you. A number or series of numbers is significant if it clearly appears in a dream—for example, a number on a house, such as 723. In addition, notice the numbers ascribed to similar objects as they appear in your dreams.

Pythagoras, the Greek philosopher, metaphysician, and mathematician, took the art of divination through numbers to new heights. It was Pythagoras who first experimented with the essence of numbers, creating a science of numbers in 540 B.C. Fortunately, his teachings weren't lost in the great fire that destroyed most of his library. Century after century, his secrets were passed from master to student. As the student became a master, he'd teach the mysteries to an initiate. This process has continued to the present day.

The following are some of the metaphysical perceptions regarding numbers and what they may mean in your dreams:

1: Independence, new beginnings, oneness with life, unity, self-development, individuality, progress, creativity

2: Being a couple, a balance of male/female energies, a balance of the yin and yang energies (the polarities) of the universe, needing people, self-surrender, putting others before yourself, dynamic attraction to one another, knowledge comes from the balance and marriage of the two opposites

3: The trinity: mind, body, and spirit; it's the threefold nature of Divinity; expansion, expression, communication, fun, and self-expression; also relates to giving outwardly, to openness, harmony, and optimism: "Third time's the charm"

4: Security and foundations; it's the four elements and the four sacred directions; self-discipline through work and service; represents productivity, organization, wholeness, unity

5: Feeling free; five is self-emancipating, active, physical, impulsive, energetic, adventuresome, and resourceful; associated with travel and curiosity; it's the number of the free soul, of excitement, and change

6: Self-harmony, particularly through service by meeting responsibilities; family harmony; compassion and love; social responsibility; beauty; the arts; generosity, concern, and caring; it relates to children, balance, and community service

7: The inner life; inner wisdom; seven chakras; birth and rebirth; religious strength; sacred vows; tendency toward ritual, particularly spiritual ritual; the path of solitude, analysis, and contemplation

8: Symbolizes infinity, material prosperity, self-power, abundance, cosmic consciousness, reward, authority, and leadership

9: Humanitarianism, selflessness, and dedicating your life to others; the number of completion and endings; symbolizing universal compassion, tolerance, and wisdom

10: Wholeness, perfection

11: Self-illumination, intuition, clairvoyance, spiritual healing, and other metaphysical faculties; a higher expression of the energy of the number two

12: Power within wholeness, 12 disciples, 12 planets, 12 months

22: Unlimited potential of mastery in any area—not only spiritual, but also physical, emotional, and mental

33: The inner sanctuary, the spiritual teacher, cosmic consciousness, all things are possible

If any numbers appear in your dream that aren't listed above, here are some guidelines to assist you. Pay attention to the individual numbers. For example, with the number 43, look at the meaning of 4 and then check the meaning of 3. Or in accordance with numerology, add the numbers together, creating the new number 7. Now look for the meaning of 7.

Another way to analyze numbers that appear in dreams is to explore the possibility that they refer to some significant age or date in your life. The dream number may also symbolize a specific item, such as the number of children you have or will have, the number of years it will take to reach a goal, or the number of an address you had as a child.

Chapter 27

Animals

Animals that appear in your dreams are always significant. Throughout history, different meanings have been associated with animals, and they've always had spiritual significance as well. To native people, the spirits of animals could act as guardians, and in most tribes, it was virtually impossible to be a medicine woman or medicine man without seeking help from the animal kingdom. Each animal spirit represented a particular human ability or strength, and having an animal appear in a dream meant that the qualities of that animal spirit were being bestowed upon the dreamer.

In Native American tradition, the coyote is traditionally the "wise prankster" and represents mischievousness. The owl can be a symbol for transformation and wisdom, and the bear can represent healing and strength. Thus, to dream of one of these animals can help you embrace its qualities in your life. Children, and individuals who are close to nature, tend to dream of animals considerably more than most adults. When people begin to align with the cycles of nature, animals will play a greater role in their dreams, and they'll begin to assimilate the associated qualities.

In some shamanistic practices, when individuals dream of the same animal three times, it signifies their power animal. Shamans can have many power animals, or totems, but more often than not they'll have one main totem.

An animal appearing in your dreams may be your totem; it may also represent the *qualities* associated with the animal. Animals appearing in dreams can symbolize that someone was "acting like an animal." In addition, they can represent the animals you've owned during your life and the love you've had for them, and they can even represent the qualities normally associated with that particular animal.

Calling Animals

As you begin to enter the animal kingdom through your dreams, you'll notice a deeper connection with the natural world in your waking life, perhaps in a similar way to native people. Native Americans were (and continue to be) closely interwoven with the animal kingdom. These First People developed the skill of "calling" animals as a necessity for survival. They learned to speak with the elk, deer, and buffalo spirits, asking for guidance in regard to the hunt. There was reverence involved in any taking of life, as it was believed that the spirit of the animal evolved through sacrificing itself to provide sustenance for the tribe.

The ability to call animals leads to a deepening of your connection with the earth's cycles. I've discovered that even those who are certain that they can't master the technique are able to do so once they connect with the animal kingdom in their dreams. This practice has definitely helped me in reaffirming my connection to Mother Earth.

🌊 🌊 🌊

I recall an incident in Mexico. It was 4 A.M., and I was resting quietly on a dark beach in a small fishing village far north of Puerto Vallarta. I hugged my knees close to my chest and felt the deep rhythm of the ocean. As I watched a lone seagull silhouetted against the predawn sky, I found myself wondering about my life's purpose. I generally don't think of such things—as I don't believe in a random universe—yet in that early morning solitude I was wrestling with questions about God and the meaning of life.

As night receded into the golden warmth of a new day, I walked slowly back to the bungalow I shared with my family. David greeted me on his way out to go fishing with a local man. I'd never fished in the ocean before, but I thought it might ease my questioning heart, so I decided to accompany them.

As we glided swiftly in our small boat, I focused my awareness into the calm water, hoping to connect with the Spirit of the sea. For many years, I've had the ability to call animals, perhaps due to my Native American heritage. I generally bond with the spirit of one particular species at any given time. However, that morning, I simply wanted to connect to the entire Spirit of the sea. Although my earlier mood had left me doubting my ability to connect with any spirit at all, I asked to experience some of the wonders of the sea. I didn't have anything specific in mind.

Suddenly, right next to our boat, a whale shot up from the depths of the sea like a giant missile—30 feet of raw energy that left a shimmering trail of ocean spray. Again and again, whales surged up out of the water with the power of charging locomotives, leaving spray and foam in their wake.

Then, just as sudden, there was only the sound of our 12-foot boat rocking gently on the sea. The majesty of those moments of power and grace held us stunned. Then, piercing the stillness, within feet of our small boat, a younger whale arced out of the depths and seemed to hang in the air. Rivulets of sparkling water streamed down its sides and back into the ocean foam. Just as serenely as it had appeared, it was gone.

The old Mexican fisherman, who owned the boat, was overwhelmed. Although he'd been out on the water nearly every day during the last six fishing seasons in that area, he'd never seen anything like that morning's display. We three sat quietly, pondering what we'd witnessed. Then David's eyes darted to the horizon.

"Sharks!" David said urgently, shattering the mood.

As our eyes followed his, we saw ominous black fins moving toward us. All the images from the movie *Jaws* flashed through my head. Then there was a burst of joy dancing skyward from the sea, and dolphins were playfully dipping in and out of the water near us. The fins belonged to dolphins, not sharks!

There were at least 50 dolphins near the boat, and they were so close that I could reach out to within inches of some of them. The fisherman, unnerved by so many of them near his boat, accelerated the engine and tried to speed away . . . but no matter how fast the little boat went, the dolphins kept up with us! Finally, the pod began to trail off, but two of them remained nearby. As we slowed our speed, the pod kept its distance. We watched the sun dance in reflections off their backs until they blended into the blue of the distance. The very confused fisherman could only mumble something about "mating season."

This unforgettable connection reaffirmed how much we are a part of all things and the power of calling upon the animal kingdom.

How to Call Animals

Learning to call animals helps you connect to the unseen realms and also assists you in entering the unseen realms of your dreams with comfort and courage.

First step: Embrace the reality that you can indeed connect deeply with plant and animal spirits.

Second step: Begin to program your dreams to connect with the animal kingdom.

Third step: Before bed, reach out in your imagination to the spirit of a particular animal or plant. You can also do this in the middle of the day when you're awake. For example, if you're trout fishing, you might imagine what the trout spirit would be like. (This is the method that Native Americans use.) Then converse with that spirit with humility and respect.

"Greetings, Trout Spirit! I come to you in gratitude and love of the trout kingdom. I ask that you send forth one of your members in dedication. We know there's no death . . . only transformation . . . and as one of your species comes forth, we accept this gift as a great service, and you will be honored."

At about that time, expect a tug on your line.

Fourth step: Each animal and plant has its own sound or vibration. Imagine what the sound is, and then attempt to duplicate it vocally. If you have difficulty with this, imagine that you hear the sound in your mind, or imagine that you're making the sound. This is the "call." Remember not to doubt yourself or your ability to do this. Doubt is the greatest barrier to success with this technique. You can also practice the call just before sleep. Call for a particular animal to come in your dreams, and then listen carefully to the message given in each dream.

My calling has sometimes backfired. Once, when I noticed a swarm of bees in the neighborhood, I impulsively decided it would be wonderful if the bees could hive in our backyard so that my daughter could watch them through the window. I'd never attempted to call anything in the insect world, but I imagined it wouldn't be that different from calling a plant or an animal.

First I tried to find the vibration, tone, or resonating quality of the bee kingdom. Once I had a sense of the tone, I repeated it mentally. I sent out the call and waited . . . nothing happened.

About an hour later, I heard my daughter screaming. I ran outside and was greeted by a huge swarm of *wasps!* They were settling in to make our backyard their new home.

The Meanings of Animals in Your Dreams

Here's a partial listing of animals and some of the traditional, cultural meanings commonly associated with them.

Land Animals

Antelope: Swiftness, speed, agility
Ape/Monkey: Protection, family, ingenuity
Badger: Ferociousness, courage, tenacity, boldness
Bear: Healer, strength, stamina, introspection
Beaver: Persistence, group harmony, productivity
Bison/Buffalo: Abundance, courage, determination
Bull: Strength, stubbornness, determination, power, fecundity
Cat: Independence, cleverness, mystery
Cougar/Mountain Lion: Silent power, self-confidence
Cow: Fertility, contentment
Coyote: Cleverness, playfulness, family orientation
Deer/Stag: Grace, fertility, regeneration, strength
Dog: Loyalty, protection, faithfulness
Donkey/Ass: Sure-footedness, determination
Elephant: Patience, royalty, power
Elk: Stamina, nobility, warrior spirit
Fox: Camouflage, cunning, quickness
Giraffe: Farsightedness, achieving goals
Goat: Sure-footedness, reaching new heights
Hippopotamus: Birth, the Great Mother
Horse: Power, freedom, grace
Leopard/Panther: Valor, elusiveness, hidden knowledge
Lion: Self-confidence, radiant power
Moose: Balance, gentleness yet strength, majestic yet awkward
Mouse: Discovery, attention to detail, invisibility, scrutiny
Opossum: Strategy, stillness
Panther/Leopard: Intuition, inner power

Pig/Boar/Sow: Courage, cunning
Rabbit/Hare: Fertility, intuition, quick thinking
Raccoon: Adaptation, creativity, dexterity
Ram/Sheep: Staying in balance in precarious situations
Rat: Cunning, assertiveness, intelligence
Rhinoceros: Ancient wisdom, great strength
Skunk: Self-respect, self-confidence, courage
Squirrel: Energy, intelligence, discovery
Weasel: Stealth, cunning
Wolf: Family, loyal, strength

Aquatic Animals

Dolphin: Joy, peace, sacred messenger, wisdom
Eel: Grace, power
Fish: Fertility, Christ light, abundance
Octopus: Ancient wisdom, tenacity
Otter: Joy, playfulness, receptivity
Salmon: Spiritual knowledge, determination
Seal: Grace, joy
Tuna: Ancient power, strength, mobility
Whale: Trust, faith, balance, harmony

Winged Creatures

Bat: Transformation, primordial darkness, rebirth, initiation, sacred mysteries, the Great Mother
Blackbird: Ancient wisdom, inner knowledge, mysticism, hidden insights
Bluebird: Joy, confidence, gentleness, modesty, contentedness
Blue jay: Courage, speaking one's truth, adaptability
Canary: Sacred sounds, sensitivity, opening of throat chakra
Cardinal: Confidence, vitality

Chickadee/Titmouse: Cheerfulness, joy, enduring, fearlessness

Chicken: Service, sacrifice, fertility

Cock/Rooster: Sexuality, alertness, fertility, enthusiasm

Crane: Longevity, focus, discipline, vigilance

Crow: Magic, mystery, great intelligence, messenger from realm of Spirit

Dove/Pigeon: Peace, feminine energies, maternal instincts, gentleness, love

Duck: Emotional balance, domestic harmony

Eagle: Illumination, spirit, power, creation

Falcon/Kestrel: Speed, grace, power, absolute determination to reach a goal

Goose: Sacred quests, transformation, mystical journeys, community

Hawk: Visionary, strength, messenger from Spirit, decisiveness

Heron: Dignity, self-reliance, individuality, patience

Hummingbird: Joy, tireless energy, delight, hope

Kingfisher: Peace, prosperity, love, luck

Ostrich: Grounded, balance between ancient wisdom and practicality

Owl: Wisdom, visionary, magic, feminine energies, ancient secrets

Parrot: Optimism, joy, confidence

Peacock: Magnificence, sacred protection, dignity, self-confidence

Pelican: Generosity, self-sacrifice, buoyancy, prosperity

Raven: Messenger from Spirit, ancient mysteries, shape-shifting

Robin: New beginnings, joy, activation of creative inner force, happiness

Seagull: Emotional balance, communication, spiritual messengers

Sparrow/Wren: Cheerfulness, love of home, fertility, boldness

Stork: Fertility, balanced home, new beginnings
Swallow: Daring, freedom, grace
Swan: Transformation, intuition, grace, higher wisdom, inner beauty
Turkey: Blessings, generosity, service
Vulture: Death and rebirth, prophecy, Great Mother
Woodpecker: Industrious, focus, sacred rhythms

Amphibians and Reptiles

Chameleon: Adaptation, willingness to change, art of invisibility, sensitivity
Cobra: Royalty, power, wisdom [See also **Snake**]
Crocodile/Alligator: Ancient power, initiation
Frog: Transformation, purification, new beginnings
Lizard: Guardian of the Dreamtime, divination
Snake: Wisdom, initiation, transformation, creativity, healing
Toad: Prosperity, abundance, Earth Spirit
Turtle/Tortoise: Longevity, stability, home, Mother Earth

Spiders and Insects

Ant: Industriousness, stamina, community
Bee: Fertility, abundance, concentration, love
Beetle/Scarab: Metamorphosis, creation, resurrection
Butterfly: Transformation, transmutation, joy, beauty
Dragonfly: Dream messenger, joy, light
Spider: Creativity, fate

Mythical Creatures

Centaur: Mystical masculine power
Dragon: Immense spiritual power, protection
Griffin (half lion/half eagle): Connection between heaven and
earth
Pegasus: Spiritual inspiration, grace, holiness
Phoenix: Transformation, rebirth, new beginnings
Satyr (half man/half goat): Nature Spirit, music, dancing, joy
Sphinx (half human/half lion): initiation, Dark Mother
Unicorn: Love, gentleness, strength, purity

Chapter 28

Dream-Symbols Dictionary

Any dream dictionary can instill a false sense of security in the interpreter and stop any further search for understanding. For example, Freud's view of cylindrical objects as phallic symbols may direct the dreamer into a particular frame of mind; and it's interesting to note that people who are seeing a Freudian therapist tend to have Freudian dreams, while those working with a Jungian therapist tend to have a predominance of humanistic-type dreams. Likewise, those involved with psychic phenomena tend to have psychic dreams. Our belief systems seem to program the content of our dreams.

Dream authorities don't often agree on what dream symbols mean. The use of a dream dictionary is, at best, a vehicle to help you find your *own* interpretations. Since authorities in the field can't agree on definitions, it's wise to remember that *only the dreamer can know the true meaning of a dream.*

For example, a dream that contains green apples could be explained many ways: One dream dictionary claims that green apples indicate a loss through one's own foolishness. Another suggests an upset stomach, and yet another associates the apple with the Garden of Eden and points out the aspect of temptation. However, for you, green apples may relate to your visits to your grandfather's orchards. Perhaps your grandfather took you along as he walked among the trees, and you were able to share his pride and pleasure as he saw the results of his hard work. Your memories may include a variety of feelings, from the love you felt for your grandfather to the anxiety associated with the hard work necessary to bring forth the harvest. Your dream may relate to any of these emotions.

Sometimes you'll find that the symbol is a metaphor. The pine tree in your dream that kept appearing in the strangest places may have to do with something you're longing or "pining" for. The panting dog that seems to be so "hot" may be a residual childhood memory of eating a ballpark "hot dog" with your dad.

Remember, only the dreamer—not the interpreter or a list of meanings—can know the true meaning of his or her dreams. So use the suggestions in this book as a place to start. Some of these dream meanings are literal, some are common symbolic interpretations, some are metaphors or puns, and some are just plain intuition. (For more in-depth symbol definitions, see my book *The Secret Language of Signs,* and for more animal listings, see Chapter 27 in this book.)

When you wish to examine a dream, use the following keywords to locate the specific topic (the list is in alphabetical order and includes objects, feelings and physical sensations, and so forth). Then read over the interpretations to see if any of them seem to fit. Find out what meanings you assign to that symbol. Rather than being a definitive guide, this list is meant to stimulate *your* inner knowingness.

𝔇 𝔇 𝔇

Abandoned
Feeling left out or not included; may be subconscious issues from childhood or a past life • Leaving behind people, circumstances, or

characteristics that aren't necessary anymore • Need for self-acceptance, or to find your own inner truth • Time to throw off inhibitions . . . enter into a state of abandonment; abandon the chains of convention that have shackled you • Portents of abandonment can occur just before you become more independent and "on your own."

Abbey (See also *Church, Home/House, Monastery, Temple*)
Usually an old and holy place that can be a powerful symbol of the ancient holy and divine place within yourself • Can represent your spiritual essence

Abdomen
Often represents the second chakra; this energy center, located in the area beneath the navel, is associated with emotions • Vulnerability • A health issue that needs addressing in the area of your abdomen • Digestion issues, digesting life's lessons, absorbing what you need and releasing the rest

Abduction
Feeling out of control or that you have no control in a situation

Aborigine
The primordial part of you; your instinctual self • Part of your basic nature that may still be foreign to you

Abortion/Abort
Fear of loss of new birth within yourself or loss of some new potential in your life • Miscarriage of justice • Sudden changes in your life

Above
Inspiration; the higher self • Things looming above you; fears that seem bigger than you are • View the situation from a higher perspective.

Abyss

Bringing to consciousness a fear that has long been buried • An impassable chasm in your life • Impending danger . . . either internal or external • An ego death

Accident

Going too fast in life; a need to slow down and integrate • Not paying attention • Feeling like the victim of sudden change • Premonition of an accident; take time to relax; be careful and conscientious

Ace

Hidden talents; an ace up your sleeve • Excelling at something

Achilles Tendon

A place of vulnerability

Acorn

Great self-potential

Actor/Actress

The roles you play in life are only illusions. • Deception; false appearances • Are you satisfied with the way you're acting in life? • Glamour, excitement, larger-than-life, center-stage attention while basking in the admiration of others • *Act now!* Do it!

Addict

Giving away power to someone or something

Adolescent

Great change; a time when one is seeking to define self and direction in life • Gathering power for new beginning • Turmoil

Adrenals

Anxiety; an adrenaline rush • The gathering of power for a new beginning

Adultery
Conflict between duties and desires • Being drawn to a quality in another that you feel you lack

Aggression
Hidden aggression within yourself that you're denying • Someone who's being aggressive toward you even if you aren't consciously aware of it

Airplane
High ideals • Striving toward higher consciousness or spiritual aspirations • Soaring to new heights • Liberation, release, freedom, and expansion • A consuming drive for success; a thrusting upward at the greatest possible speed • Plane crashes can symbolize falling from great heights or a sign to stay off of airplanes for a while. • Could represent astral travel.

Airport
Time to take a journey or risk a new venture • A desire for adventure

Aladdin
Life can be magical; you can have your wishes fulfilled.

Alarm
This can be a warning; be cautious, for danger may be afoot.

Alcohol
Dulling the senses; not feeling • Denial of self and escape from the reality of life • May symbolize camaraderie; wine, women, and song • May relate to transformation (Jesus said, "This is my blood," in reference to the Last Supper)

Alien
A part of yourself you aren't acknowledging • Unfamiliarity • The "enemy" • Going home • May represent higher wisdom • Fear, such as "alien abductions"

Allergy
Sensitivity to the external environment, not being able to resist or assimilate external stimuli

Alley
The back side behind the façade we show to the world

Alligator
Hidden, formidable strength and power • Trouble below the surface

Altar
A focus for worship and honoring the spiritual aspects of life • A place dedicated to remembering what's truly important • Sacrifice

Ammunition
Gathering ammunition for one's own causes

Amputation
Giving up that part of yourself associated with the limb in the dream (an amputated leg may mean you feel you don't have a leg to stand on; a hand may signify an inability to grasp a situation) • Releasing parts of yourself that you thought were integral to your identity but that aren't really a part of your true being • A lack of mobility in your life • Cutting off people, situations, or parts of yourself that should be integrated instead of released

Anchor
Strength; being grounded • Attachment to a person or place

Anesthesia
Being numb to your senses; an inability to perceive what's going on around you • An avoidance of life

Angel
A spiritual messenger; our most divine ideals (many prophets' visions are based on the appearance of an angel in a dream) • Listen carefully to what's being said. • To see an angel in your dream is to be blessed.

Anger
Subconsciously feeling angry about something

Animals *(Also see entries for individual animals in Chapter 27 and in this dictionary)*
A primal, instinctive part of your being: if the animals are wild and ferocious, they can represent the primitive, aggressive part of your nature; if the animals are tame, they can represent the controlled expression of your instinctual nature; and if they are wild and free, they can be connecting you to nature

Ankh
Ancient Egyptian symbol of spiritual wisdom; this perhaps can be a sign from a past life

Ankles
Mobility

Anorexia
Lack of self-acceptance • A desire for total control

Ant
Industrious, productive, and busy • Strong; they carry more than their own weight • Community or social cooperation, sometimes to the detriment of individuality

Antenna
Transmitting and receiving ideas and energy • Awareness of the world around you; tuning in

Antique
A connection with the past • An old pattern or belief system that's no longer useful

Antlers
Protection of the divine masculine part of yourself

Anxiety
Not trusting that everything will turn out according to a greater plan for your life; examine your life to discover where the source of this may be

Ape
Primitive power • Mischief maker • Copying, imitating, or mimicking others rather than finding your own truth

Applause
Self-acknowledgment; needing acknowledgment from others

Apple
Wisdom • Healing potential • Wholeness • Health and vitality; "An apple a day keeps the doctor away" • Temptation, such as Eve being tempted with an apple in the Garden of Eden

Archery/Archer
Specific direction; clarity; single-mindedness • Pointing to one specific thing

Architect
The need to make plans in your life or create a blueprint for the future

Arctic
Frozen feelings and emotions

Argument
Parts of yourself are in conflict. • Perhaps there's someone in your life whom you'd like to argue with but it doesn't feel safe.

Ark
Safety and protection amid the waters of emotion

Armor
Protection • Being sealed off

Arms
Reaching out • Open arms symbolize being open and reaching out to life; closed arms are closed to life. • Weapons • Being defensive

Army
Major obstacles to be overcome • Opposition

Arrow
Clear direction; a goal; a straight course

Artist
Creative expression in life • Potential artistic ability

Ascent (See also *Climbing, Ladder,* and *Mountain*)
Ascending in life; your energy level is rising and life is on the up-and-up • A need to come down to Earth; you are too lofty or idealistic • Life is an uphill struggle; know that life isn't meant to be a struggle and that you can relax and enjoy yourself.

Ashes
Spiritual purification • The transitory nature of life • Sorrow and humiliation • In some cultures, ashes have purifying power. • They can also be a sign of death or absence of life or vitality. • The very essence of something

Ass
Plodding, patience, or long-suffering • Being an "ass" in your life •
Someone being an "ass" to you

Asthma
Inability to get enough oxygen may indicate suppressed grief. • Going
too fast; not being able to catch your breath • Stress; not feeling
connected with life

Astronomer
Looking ahead • Highest ambition

Atomic Energy
Incredible energy potential; a need to harness that power • Tuning in to
the collective-conscious fear for global and personal safety • Kundalini
fire awakening within; great potential for spiritual expansion

Attic
High ideals (the top floor represents the upper chakras) • Old issues
from your personal or familial past that you've put away

Audience
Congratulations! • The audience responds positively: an
acknowledgment of self-acceptance. • The audience responds
negatively: you need to work on self-acceptance.

Aunt
The industrious part of yourself (ant) • May refer to your aunts; the
qualities you associate with a particular aunt may be projected aspects
of yourself • Feminine aspects of the self

Aura
The energy field surrounding a person or thing; it's invisible to most
people, yet very real • Bright and clear: clarity and good health • Dim
and close to the body: lack of clarity; health disturbances

Avalanche
A completely overwhelming experience of previously frozen emotions
(see also *Water*) • Too much to do

Awake
If you're awake and aware during a dream, this is probably a lucid
dream (see Chapter 9).

Ax
Fear of loss • Wielding power with certainty • Cutting away that which
isn't needed • The executioner's ax—a powerful symbol of judgment

Baboon
Community-minded; social • Live by instincts and stay close to nature.
• Oafishness

Baby
A new birth within yourself • A positive outcome for the future • Birth
of a new idea • Potential for growth • Desire to become pregnant •
Many women notice babies everywhere (both human and animal)
right before they get pregnant (this includes unplanned pregnancies).
• A yearning to be babied and pampered and the center of attention

Back
Support; strength • Retreat; back up • Pay attention to the health of
your physical back, which is the support of your body.

Badger
Baiting or teasing

Baggage
Unnecessary things or thoughts that you carry around • A desire to
"pack your bags" and get out of a present situation

Ball

Completion; wholeness; unity • A social occasion; suggests joy • Can have sexual connotations • "The ball's in your court" means that it's now your turn to take action.

Balloon

Unrestrained joy • Soaring to new personal heights • If the balloon breaks, an illusion is shattered. • A balloon that's afloat can mean you're at the mercy of the "winds of change."

Bank

A bank is a reservoir of financial resources. • Invest in yourself; draw upon your inner resources. • You need to reconsider your banking habits.

Basement

The base or root of a problem • Your physical energy (very often a house will represent your body, with the attic associated with upper chakras and the basement with the lower chakras) • May indicate the subconscious or what is hidden or buried from your normal awareness

Bat

Fear of the unknown • "Batting" around an idea • Navigating in the darkness • An old, scolding woman • To the Chinese, the bat is symbolic of long life and happiness. • To the tribal people of the Americas, the bat is emblematic of shamanistic initiation and rebirth; the bat goes into the womb-like darkness of the cave only to emerge again.

Bathing

Purification • Washing your hands of a situation • Baptism or rebirth

Battlefield

Deep inner conflict (the antagonists are either those you feel hostile toward in waking life or are symbolic of inner conflict; remember, every person in your dreams is most often an aspect of yourself)

Beach

The border between the subconscious, emotional part of you, represented by water, and the earthly, physical side of you • Balance • Purification; rejuvenation

Bear

Mother Earth • The protective, mothering, female aspect • Force and power • A time of introspection and subsequent renewal • Many Native American people consider the bear to be a totem (or sign) of the healer • Teddy bear: cuddly and lovable; take time to be soft and cuddly • Return to the simple joys of life

Beaver

Busy; industrious • Prosperity through your own efforts

Bed

Sexuality and intimacy • Comfort; security; eternal womb • Rejuvenation; nurturance • The connecting point between conscious and subconscious and your dreams • Impending illness and the need to rest more • Repressed memories about things that have happened in bed in your past

Bedbug

Something unpleasant that's covered up • Small nuisance

Bee

Busy; industrious • Social cooperation • The possibility of hidden sweetness • Feeling "stung" by some circumstance or remark • In ancient Egyptian hieroglyphics, the bee was associated with the royal social order. • In ancient Greece, bees symbolized work and productivity. • In the Romanesque period in Europe, bees were symbols of diligence. • Just *be!*

Beetle
Represented eternal life to the ancient Egyptians • May indicate good luck

Bell
If the sound is clear: a resonance within the wellspring of life • A warning • Joyous developments

Bill
Karmic payment • Someone named "Bill" • Overdue bills or something you owe to another • Duck's bill

Bird
Soaring to new heights; soaring above your problems • Omen of good fortune • If singing, may be the harbinger of good news • Freedom • Birds are messengers to and from Spirit. • A need to connect more with the divine source present in everything that surrounds you • The need to distance yourself from a situation to gain perspective • A "flight of fancy" or flight of the imagination; let your creative imagination take wing! • A longing to return to the sweet purity of nature • A bird in a cage may symbolize feeling a loss of freedom. (See bird listings in Chapter 27.)

Bird's Eggs
New beginnings • Eggs in a nest can signify money

Birth
A powerful sign of renewal, rebirth, or new beginnings • A new phase in your life, either inner or outer • The spiritual awakening or unleashing of powerful creative forces within you • The corresponding and necessary death or release of something old—perhaps an old, negative attitude or limiting pattern • Feelings of vulnerability or dependence

Birthday
New beginning • Celebration of life • An anniversary of accomplishments

Black
The unknown; fear; your shadow and your unconscious mind • Inner darkness • The expression "in the dark" means feeling confused • Depression and despair • Mourning • Strength and power • The need to retreat and withdraw within yourself; nuns, monks, and renunciants wear black

Bladder
Fear of letting go; holding on to old beliefs and attitudes • Being "pissed off" means being angry.

Blind
You are being "blind" to something or "turning a blind eye."

Blizzard
Emotional upheaval • A "snow job" on someone or on you

Blood
Life force; nourishment; power; energy • Psychic energy • If you were bleeding: an energy drain for you • A young girl's defoliation or a girl maturing into womanhood • Memories of an early childhood sexual experience that's buried in the subconscious mind • The renewal of life • In a woman's monthly cycles, her inner cycles are sometimes symbolized by her bleeding. • Pain, suffering, and injury • "Blood sucking" can mean that someone's taking advantage of you. • "Blood brothers" indicates unity and commune. • The blood of Christ is a holy sacrifice.

Blue
Blue as a color is soothing, emotionally healing, peaceful, and relaxing; it also can represent mystical perceptions in life. • Depression is often

called "the blues." • When someone is "turning blue," it means that they're growing cold. • A need to "cool it" or relax and slow down for a while • "Growing cold" toward somebody or a situation • Turning blue can also indicate a symbolic lack of oxygen; a need to breathe more freely in your life. • Feeling bruised from a recent situation; when someone becomes bruised, their body becomes black and blue • The blue sea can represent the subconscious, the feminine, the Great Mother, and your deep secrets. • The blue sky can represent the conscious mind, the masculine, the Great Father, and the open, expansive part of yourself.

Boar
Someone or something is boring • A swinish personality • Ferocious, primitive, aggressive power

Boat
Traveling through emotional times (the water symbolizes your emotions, and the boat represents you and how you're handling your emotions) • Leaving for distant shores—leaving the stability of the land and trying new waters in your life • Clear sailing

Body (*Also see definitions for specific body parts; all have particular symbolic associations*)
The right side of body can signify the projecting, masculine, moral (right) side of yourself and your outer strength (if you're left-handed, reverse meanings). • The left side of body can represent the receptive, feminine, inner part of you. • The lower part of the body can represent the primordial, instinctual part of yourself; can also represent your lower chakras, groundedness, and sexuality. • A naked body can represent vulnerability or openness, while an overly clothed body can represent hiding yourself.

Bog
Feeling "bogged down" by a project or situation • Being in an emotional bog

Boil

A situation about to erupt • Suppressed anger • An acute infection • Water boiling can indicate emotions purifying, moving, and changing.

Bomb

An explosive situation in your life • Emotional, potential power • An emotional failure, as in "the concert was a complete bomb"

Books

Wisdom and knowledge, as well as lessons in life • "Booking" an appointment or an event

Boss

Taking authority in your life or mastering a situation • Feeling "bossed around"; submitting to another's will

Bottle

Feeling "bottled up" • Notice the size and color of the actual bottle and whether the cap was on or off; a clean bottle signifies more clarity in your life than a cloudy one; a bottle with the cap off is more "open" than one with the top securely fastened. • A message in a bottle can be an answer from an unexpected source.

Box

Self-imposed limitations • Pandora's box can represent all that you fear (in mythology, this originally meant "all gifts" or "all giving"; eventually, when male deities rose and female deities were denigrated, Pandora and her box were symbols of ill will and fear. • Freudians would say that a box represents the vagina or the womb; this can be the inner feminine aspect of a man or woman.

Boy

The masculine child within us all; in a man, it can represent his own childhood

Bread
Communion with others • Abundance • Often a powerful symbol for life; hence, the "bread of life" • Money or abundance

Break
A sudden and unexpected change coming in your life; an old situation may be about to break up • If things are constantly breaking around you, slow down and be more careful than usual, especially if you're the person breaking them. • Time to break off a relationship or situation. • A breaking of illusions or broken faith

Breasts/Bosom
Unconditional love and nurturing • The Universal Mother • If not vibrant, then maybe it's time to get a checkup

Brick
Strength, endurance, and strong foundations

Bride/Bridegroom
The peak of the feminine force within you • New beginning • The communion of the masculine and feminine forces within you

Bridge
Connection between one realm and another • A powerful symbol for change and transition; change of your personal experience of reality • If the bridge is crossing over water, it may indicate an emotional transition in life.

Brother
The religious male aspect of the self • Common tie; brotherhood • Something about you and your actual brother(s) • Feelings associated with the word *brother* as a carryover from childhood

Brown

The earth and the ground; a need to be more grounded • The leaves turn brown in autumn; this indicates a need to pull your resources inward.

Brush

The word *brush* might be related to phrases such as "brush with fate," "brush with disaster," or "brush with death"—all signifying a close call. • Thick underbrush can mean you're feeling stymied or that you can't move ahead in life. • Brushes used for cleaning, from scrubbing brushes to tooth brushes, can mean that you need to pay more attention to cleaning the spaces around you—either the physical spaces surrounding you or your inner spaces. • Perhaps you're overly concerned with cleaning.

Bubble(s)

Childlike joy and exuberance • Isolating yourself, as if in a bubble • Bursting bubbles can signify a disappointment in your life.

Bud

A bud occurs on a plant in springtime; this sign can represent new life and a fresh beginning for you. • "Bud" can also be a homophone for a buddy or friend.

Buffalo

Abundance; harvest; plenty • Sacred to the Native American

Bug

Small annoyance • Inconvenience

Building/Build

Creating new foundations in life (see also *Home/House*) • Specific types of buildings will have individual meanings: for example, a church might suggest religion, spirituality, or rigid adherence to a belief system; a government building might symbolize authority and organization or politics; a fortress could suggest that you're fortifying yourself against outside influences.

Bulb

A flower bulb has untapped potential for beauty. • A light bulb brings light where there was darkness or may indicate the coming of a great idea.

Bull

Great strength; force; power • Optimistic sign • Sign of fertility, of the masculine principle penetrating the feminine principle • In astrology, the bull is equated with the sign Taurus, which is tenacious, sensuous, earthy, and practical

Bulldog

Tenacity; holding power • Defiance • Seize the opportunity and don't let go

Bulldozer

Clearing the way by pushing through obstacles; go for it! • Trying to "bulldoze" someone, or someone trying to "bulldoze" or force you into doing something that you don't want to do

Burglar

Someone robbing you of energy or of something that's rightfully yours • A sign to safeguard your valuables against being robbed in the future

Burial

Death of old patterns and thought forms • Denial of a situation

Butter

The richness in life • Can connote flattery, as when you "butter up" someone

Butterfly
New beginning on a higher plane • Rebirth; inner beauty; transformation • Romance and joy; social success • Gentle enjoyment

Buzzard
Feeling picked on or preyed upon; preying on others • Contemptible; rapacious

Cabin
A cabin in the woods may symbolize peace and contentment (if the cabin is on a boat, see *Boat.*)

Cactus
A prickly situation • Something or someone that can't be touched

Cage
Self-imprisonment through fear • Feeling trapped

Cake
Celebrate the sweetness of life! • When you've accomplished or completed something, it's important to celebrate.

Calf
Happy, carefree youth in healthy surroundings • May refer to the calf of the leg

Camel
The ship of the desert; a way to get through a difficulty • Endurance

Camera
Keeping a distance between yourself and life • Preserving the past; preserving fond memories

Camp
A kind of temporary home: it may be a retreat where you go to get away from it all and connect to nature; or out of necessity, as when you're between permanent living situations and feel like you're just "camping out" in the meantime • Making fun of something through exaggeration

Can (See also *Box*)
You "can" do it; you *can* achieve it—yes, you *can!*

Canal
Childbirth • A directed and narrow emotional path

Canary
Music; harmony • May indicate tattling or telling of secrets

Cancer
Something is eating away at you emotionally. • The horoscope sign "Cancer" • Perhaps it's time for a checkup.

Candle
Your spiritual life force; your true inner light

Candy
Treat yourself to the sweetness of life!

Cane
A need for some support in life • A cruel form of punishment • Sugar cane, a natural source of sweetness; extract the joy from your life

Cannibalism
Feeling like you're being "eaten up" by a situation • Taking the energy of another instead of using one's own energy • "He's so cute I could just eat him!" • Cannibalism could also symbolize extreme possessiveness: are you wanting to devour someone, or do you feel like someone wants to consume you?

Canyon

A vast opening of unconsciousness • A seemingly impassable chasm

Capsize

Falling off your course; being dumped into emotions (water)

Captain

A person in control • You're at the helm in the emotional waters of your life • Time to take control

Car

Your physical body or yourself • Notice where the car is going, the condition of the car, and who's in it. • A failed brake may mean that you need to put the brakes on in your life. • If your radiator keeps overheating, ask yourself if you need to stop, cool down, and relax. • Bald tires can mean that you aren't getting the traction you need in life. • Constant window fogging might be pointing to something you aren't willing to see.

Cards

The game of life; your destiny • If they're Tarot cards or any other cards being used for fortune telling, then this symbol relates to a sense of fate: the cards hold your future; whatever specific feelings you have about the cards can be indicative of future trends in your life.

Carpenter

Making repairs in your life • Rebuilding physically, emotionally, and spiritually (Jesus was a carpenter)

Castle (See also *Home/House*)

A castle can be a kind of fortress; it can also refer to a magical realm.

Cat

The intuitive self • The feminine essence or part of yourself; the goddess within

Caterpillar
Unharnessed potential of which you are unaware

Cave
A powerful symbol • Your great spiritual wealth; your unconscious self • Consolidating your energy • Feminine principle; womb of the Mother Earth • A refuge from life's difficulties • Repressed traumatic memories that are emerging

Cemetery
Rest; peace • Fear of death

Center
A place of community activity where people come together to achieve a common purpose • In almost every tradition throughout the world, the "center" is considered to be the residence of the Creator: Hindu tradition says that God resides in the center of the cosmos; some ancient Chinese portray God as being a point at the center of concentric circles spreading outward; and in Native American tradition, the center of the Medicine Wheel is always Great Spirit. • A need to get to the center of a situation or yourself; when you go to the center, you're integrating all the parts of yourself and bringing them together within the center of your being

Chain
Many together, building strength • Feeling "chained" to a situation

Chair
Your position or attitude; where you "sit" in regard to the matter • Rocking in a rocking chair may indicate an out-of-body experience or a building of psychic energy.

Chalice
A powerful sign that points toward that which is sacred and holy • The Holy Grail and Christ • The divine feminine spirit

Chameleon
Adaptability; flexibility • Whimsy • Capricious; changing • Not showing one's "true colors"

Chaos
If everything around you is in chaos, you may be in a process of renewing your life. • In some ancient traditions, it was said that the cosmos was created by chaos. • A stagnant pond can be made clear again by adding clean spring water, but there will be a period where the water seems more murky and in great chaos; eventually, however, the old putrid waters are flushed completely out, leaving a crystal clear spring.

Chase/Chasing/Being Chased
Running from something or someone • Being afraid to face something in your life • Pursuing something in life

Chest
Inner treasures; the potential that exists within you • Might relate to your heart chakra (the emotional center of love)

Chicken
Cowardice; timidity • Counting on something prematurely

Children
The child within you; those inner aspects of yourself, such as playfulness, joy, and openness • The child part of you isn't being acknowledged • The subconscious desire to have children; very often before a woman becomes pregnant, she'll begin to see children everywhere, even if she doesn't consciously desire children

Christ
The God force within you • Love • Sacrifice • Martyrdom

Christmas

If this sign appears out of season, it can mean a celebration of friends and family. • A spiritual birth • Old memories surfacing

Church

Faith; hope; love • The temple of the soul • Sanctuary; haven; safety

Cigar/Cigarette

Examine your emotional response to the cigar or cigarette: if your associated feeling is relaxation, then take more time in life to relax; if it's anxiety, ask yourself what you are substituting for gratifying the basic needs in life; and if it elicits guilty feelings, this may be a sign or an inner admonition to give up smoking.

Circle

A very powerful universal symbol • Harmony; beauty; balance • Completeness; totality; wholeness

Circus

A need to step into your own childlike joy; laugh and enjoy yourself in life • Life is a circus; there's too much going on

City

The perception that you have of the city is usually a reflection of what's occurring within you. What thoughts or feelings do you have of the city: excitement, entertainment, chaos, business, commerce, crime, or pollution?

Clam

Someone isn't talking; lack of communication • Concern over something that must be kept secret

Clay

A desire to mold your life as you want it • Someone trying to mold you in a way that you aren't happy about

Cliff

A big life change • Taking a risk and going where there aren't any guarantees or certainties • Get ready to take a leap of faith; trust that your life is guided. • A critical time in your life; a time for decision

Climbing

Going up; personal ascension toward a business or personal goal; reaching the top of the ladder in your profession • May have sexual connotations; sexual excitement • In Jacob's dream, he climbed to heaven. • Climbing down can mean the opposite of ascending; the exploration of your subconscious

Clocks

Being tied to time • A need to be on time more often • Running out of time • Time is passing you by.

Closet

"Closeting" yourself from self or others • Coming "out of the closet" • Skeletons in your closet

Clothes

Your outer persona • The roles that you play in life

Clouds

A positive, healthy sign • Clear clouds: spiritual uplifting; inner peace • Storm clouds: spiritual questioning; a personal storm is brewing

Clown

A need to laugh at yourself; be happy and don't worry; enjoy life. • "Clowning around" when you should get serious in life

Cobra

The power of Kundalini energy

Cobwebs
Memories that are hidden away or talents that are unused • Feeling that you're caught in someone's web, or caught in the "web of intrigue"

Cock
Strutting; proud; egotistical • Masculine energy • About to erupt or go off, as when a gun is cocked

Cockatoo
Showy • Talking without thinking

Cocoon
Incredible potential awaiting transformation • "Cocooning" or separating yourself from others and even from reality

Coffee
Stimulation or relaxation, depending on your personal associations

Coffin
Completion; the end of a situation • The death of a relationship

Coin (See *Money*)

Cold
Shutting down your feelings and withdrawing inwardly

Collision
Severe inner conflicts or deep unresolved issues in your life

Colon
Elimination of things from the past

Colors *(See also Chapter 25 or specific colors in this dictionary)*
Each color has a specific meaning: In general, red equates with dynamic energy and sexuality, orange is social and fun, yellow is uplifting and

communicative, green is healing and abundant, blue relates to peace and spirituality, purple is linked to spiritual wisdom and psychic perceptions, pink is love, black is the unknown and darkness, white is purity and light, gold is illumination and wealth, and silver is related to moonlight and the magical and mystical.

Comet
Heralds tremendous personal and spiritual expansion • A powerful symbol

Compass
Feeling lost or disoriented • The direction you want to go in life

Conflict
Unresolved or suppressed inner conflict, even if you feel calm and balanced on the surface

Confusion
Something in your life that you don't want to look at or confront

Constipation
Holding on to things, situations, or people in your life that you no longer need • Need for a change in diet

Convent (See also *Monastery*)
Going within to touch the divine feminine within yourself • A sanctuary from worldly life; a time to be still and simple • A symbol for hiding from yourself by withdrawing

Cook
Nourishment • Material comfort

Cooking (See also *Cook*)
Synthesizing the ingredients in your life

Corner
Feeling cornered in your life

Court
A part of yourself or a situation in which you're judging yourself or others • Your inner royalty

Cow
Feeling peaceful or needing to cultivate more peace in your life • Patience and passive endurance • In some cultures, the cow is identified with the earth, the moon, and mothering. Many lunar goddesses wear the horns of a cow on their head. In Hindu belief, the cow and the bull represent the regenerating forces of the universe.

Coward
The fear of confronting something • A need to face your fears

Crab
Scuttling around issues in your life instead of facing them straight on, or going sideways around a situation • Being "crabby" or in a bad mood • The crab is the sign of Cancer in the horoscope; as the crab is one of the symbols of the sea (which is the cradle of all life), this can be a life-giving, nurturing sign.

Crack
A situation that's about to break through • A situation that seems sturdy on the surface but actually has some cracks in it • "Cracking up" mentally • Something that causes great amusement

Cradle
Caring and nurturing • The need to be cradled and cared for

Crash
A powerful symbol that says "Slow down"

Cricket
Joy • Domestic happiness; peace at home • Long life

Crisis
A time to search for meaning in life and turn to spiritual connections • A crossroads in life or a turning point

Critic
Being overly critical of yourself or others • The need to be more discerning of situations that you're involved in • Others are critical of you

Crocodile
Trouble beneath the surface • Dishonesty; a show of false feeling as in "crocodile tears" • Hypocrisy; it's a "crock"

Cross
A universal symbol of infinite balance and wholeness from the most remote times • Jesus; Christianity

Crossroads
A time of decision is ahead

Crow
The crow and raven are of the same genus and in some respects have similar meanings (see also *Raven*). • A portent of change in your life • Fear of death and inner darkness • The idiom "as the crow flies" means traveling in a straight line, so walk your talk; travel straightforward with clarity and decisiveness in your life. • "To crow" means to exult loudly, as over another's defeat, to boast; also to articulate sound that's expressive of pleasure or delight • For Native Americans, the crow has mystic powers. There is a similar meaning for the ancient Celts, the Germanic tribes, and the Siberians: the eye of the crow is thought to be the entrance to the supernatural realms and the inner mysteries of life; the crow also carried messages from the spirit realm. • Native people

consider the crow to be a shape-shifter with the ability to expand into other realms of consciousness; the shape-shifter can be in two places at once and take on other physical forms.

Crowd
Anonymity; secrecy • Strangers or something strange • Your perception of the crowd's opinion of you is your subconscious opinion of yourself. • Feeling a part of something larger than yourself

Crown
A pinnacle of accomplishment • Inner royalty

Crucifixion
The ultimate sacrifice • Feeling that someone is trying to emotionally crucify you, or you're allowing yourself to be crucified

Crutch
Feeling unable to support yourself • The need of support at this time in your life

Crying
Emotional release of something still in the subconscious during daily reality • Joy from resolving a difficulty or releasing an attitude that isn't serving you

Crystal
Spiritual transmitter and magnifier • A powerful symbol of clarity and spiritual energy: the symbol of the mystic; listen carefully to this dream

Cutting
Depending on the context, this can refer to the cutting away of undesired opinions, habits, attitudes, and beliefs. • If you're cut and bleeding, you are losing your vital force.

Daffodil

The purveyor of spring, which is the time of beginnings • Fresh potential; renewal; new life

Dam

Pent-up emotions about to release

Dancing

Joy; the dance of life • Sexual enthusiasm; wholeheartedness

Danger

A very deep-seated, internal conflict that needs attention • There is a dangerous situation in your life.

Dark

The unknown; your subconscious • Your fears • The womb-like power of the deepest parts of your being • The Dark Goddess, your ancient inner wisdom • Death or the dark night of the soul • Depression or gloom

Daughter

The female-child part of you; may be your daughter • Eternal youth

Dawn

A new awakening • Can mean someone named "Dawn" or "Don"

Deaf

Something in life that you don't want to hear • You're closing your ears to something.

Death/Dying

Not a bad omen • Transformation; the death of old patterns and programs; making way for rebirth • Very rarely indicates the imminent death of one who had died in your dream; usually indicates the death of an old belief system of yours, represented by the dying person

Debt
Something you owe or is owed to you

Deep/Depths
Your unconscious mind • Something beneath the surface

Deer
The gentle aspects of yourself • A sign of feeling victimized and defenseless

Delay
Your timing is off • Wait, not now

Desert
Jesus went to the desert for spiritual rejuvenation. • Desolate; forsaken; barren

Devil
The internal struggle between the parts of you that you consider "good" and "bad" • Fear • Someone in your life isn't acting in ethical ways.

Diamond
The many facets of your pure being • When coal is under great pressure, it creates diamonds; those areas of your life that seem like pressure, in fact, may be helping you achieve the crystal clarity of a diamond.

Diarrhea
Unresolved areas of fear in your life; animals (and people) get diarrhea when frightened • Not assimilating what you need to assimilate in life

Dirt
Grounding; connection with Mother Earth • Something in your life needs to be cleaned up.

Disease
Disharmony; dis-ease

Diving
Delving into the subconscious, especially regarding emotional issues, as water usually represents emotions • Getting in touch with subconscious motivations or fears, or the deep wisdom that dwells within you • A sexual symbol, as water can represent the feminine principle, and diving is a penetration into this

Divorce
A split within your inner psyche, such as between head and heart, or your male and female parts of self • A situation or person you wish to divorce yourself from • A hidden desire to end a relationship • Fear that your relationship may end in divorce

Doctor
Your inner healer • Perhaps it's time to see a doctor for a checkup.

Dog
Faithfulness; loyalty • Protection; rescue • Friendship

Dolphin
Unharnessed joy; playfulness; spontaneity • Intelligence • Spiritual enlightenment • A significant dream symbol

Donkey
Patience • Stubbornness

Door
Great opportunity for new adventure and self-discovery • An open door: you are ready; closed door: it isn't quite time • Significant symbol

Dove
Peace; freedom • Someone or something you wish to make peace with

Dragon
A powerful symbol • Life force; great potency • Dragon fire is very purifying. • "Slaying the dragon" is confronting and overcoming fear.

Dream
If you dream that you're having a dream, you're most likely lucid dreaming (see Chapter 9).

Drowning
Feeling overwhelmed by emotions

Drum
A powerful sign of connecting to your inner rhythms • To the Native American, one could travel to the inner spiritual realms on the vibration of the beat, and thus enter into a state of ecstasy.

Duck
Get out of the way of something.

Dust
Represents something inside you that hasn't been touched or is a forgotten part of yourself

Duty
Forgetting your duties to yourself or others • Feeling guilty about not conforming to external conventional notions of right and wrong

Dwarf
Feeling dwarfed by a situation • Limiting your potential • The symbolism for dwarves might come from the classic fairy tale *Snow White*, where the dwarves were her guardians and true friends.

Dynamite
A sign of an explosive situation that's about to erupt

Eagle
Very significant to the Native American • Profound personal power • National power • Your spiritual, soaring self • The ability or need to be farseeing

Ears
Being willing to hear the truth

Earth
Mother Earth • The female, receptive, rejuvenating principle of the universe; womb; sensuality

Earthquake
Great change approaching • Fear of the change you're undergoing

East
The place of the rising sun and new beginnings • A spiritual reawakening

Echo
What you put out will come back to you.

Egg
Wholeness • New life; new potential • A powerful symbol

Eight (See also *Numbers*)
By virtue of its shape, this number has been associated with the caduceus, the two intertwined serpents that are the sign of the healer. Also because of its shape, it symbolizes the DNA helix and the spiraling nature of the heavens. In Pythagorean numerology, the number eight is of the material realm and can signify infinity, self-power, abundance, cosmic consciousness, reward, authority, and leadership. In China,

the number eight is associated with wealth because it rhymes with the Chinese word for money. This number can signify that through organization, discipline, and work, you can achieve success in the material world.

Elastic
A sign to be flexible; stretch yourself into new areas of life

Electricity
The bioelectrical systems that surge through you; the life force

Elephant
Something that needs to be remembered • Thick-skinned • Ponderous, powerful, and wise

Elevator (See *Climbing*)

Elf (See also *Fairy*)
A sign to be more mischievous in life; take time to be madcap, impish, and childlike • Have fun; enjoy yourself and your own inner magic.

Elk
A reassuring sign • Power; beauty; dignity • The ability to overcome obstacles

Emerald
A sign of the magnificent healing power within you • Emerald was used for its healing properties in many cultures; it was used by the ancient Egyptians and has also been called the jewel of Venus and of love. • The magic within you; just as Dorothy sought the Emerald City looking for the Wizard of Oz, it can be a sign for you to seek your own inner magic

Emotions

Whatever emotions you perceive in the people around you are usually a reflection of your own inner emotional state. If you're aware of an array of sad people in your dreams (even if you aren't consciously feeling sad), this is a good indication that you're repressing inner sadness. If everyone around you seems angry, even if you think you feel calm, look within to see if perhaps you have some unresolved anger. Conversely, if everyone around you seems happy and balanced, even if your surface emotions are a bit wobbly, most likely your inner emotional state is healthy and happy.

Empty

A sign to simplify your life • Empty yourself of your concepts, patterns, and ideals. • Being empty is potential waiting to be filled. • Feeling empty and alone

Enemy

A sign that there's a war going on inside of you; reconcile with the parts of yourself that you've denied or disowned • Perhaps there's someone in your life who's antagonizing you.

Eruption

A situation or person is about to erupt or explode.

Escalator (See *Climbing*)

Escape

Stop trying to escape the situation; face it head-on and confront the problem. • A need to escape or seek refuge

Exam/Examination

Feeling that you're being tested in life • Need for self-examination • Feeling that you need to prove yourself to others • A fear of failure

Excrement
Needing to release or expel the waste products of your life, such as guilt, resentment, and shame • Something poisoning you from within • Is someone treating you poorly? • A sign of something (within yourself or reflected in others) that you disapprove or despise

Exile
A sign that you feel cut off from people, situations, or even yourself

Explosion
Personal crisis, particularly in regard to a relationship

Eyes
Being willing to see; clarity • I; myself

Faces
An unknown face or faces may represent the parts of yourself that you aren't currently experiencing.

Failure
Perhaps you're feeling like a failure. • A turning point in your life

Fairy
A spirit of nature • Bringing to manifestation your inner desires

Falling
Loss of control; feeling out of control • In the process of learning to walk, everyone falls; if you are on unsure ground in a situation or are experiencing a personal growth spurt and are unsure of yourself, you'll likely dream of falling.

Fast
An issue with the current pace of your life (going too fast or needing to speed up) • "Fast" can be a sign that it's time to fast for purification and cleansing.

Fat

Suppression of emotions and feelings • Abundance

Father

The Divine Father; God • Protector; provider • May refer to your father or father image.

Faucet

Water usually represents your emotions; hence, a leaky faucet may mean leaking emotional energy, a "stuck" faucet can mean you can't turn on your emotions, a rusty faucet may mean being out of touch with your emotions.

Fear

If you're fearful of anything in your dreams, face it; it's most likely an unacknowledged part of yourself (imagine going back into your dream and facing the fear). • There is something in your life that is frightening you that perhaps you are unaware of.

Feather

An excellent dream symbol • Connection to the heavens and the Creator

Feet

Putting your best foot forward; understanding • Connection with the earth • Grounding • Being afraid or unwilling to step forward • Having the courage to step forward; movement

Female

The feminine energy; the female within • The receptive energy: yin

Fence

Feeling fenced in • A need for boundaries in life • "Sitting on a fence" in your life; time to make up your mind and take a stand

Fighting
Suppressed emotions; the need to have and enjoy all of your emotions
• It's time to fight back.

Fingers
The details of life • Pointing a finger at something or someone •
Little finger: manipulation; being wrapped or wrapping around the
little finger • Ring finger: union; marriage • Middle finger: sexuality •
Thumb: will; thumbs-up: go ahead; thumbs-down: forget it!

Fire
Kundalini life force within you • Potency; psychic energy • Opening
to spiritual communication and energy • Initiation • Sexual passion
• Purification by fire • Anger

Fish
Spiritual food • A symbol of Christianity • May be a desire for
acknowledgment or compliments • Misrepresentation; something
seems "fishy"

Flame (See also *Fire*)
Your eternal bright flame • The light of Spirit

Floating
You are in harmony with your intuition and your emotions; there's
great spiritual alignment as you move toward feeling at one with all
things. • Being disconnected

Flood
Overwhelming emotions

Floor
Your foundation or your support

Flowers
A happy omen of beauty and unfoldment

Flying

Flying through the air: astral travel (See Chapter 13) • Moving beyond the bounds of physical limitation • A very significant sign

Fog

An obstacle • An area of your life that you can't see clearly

Food

Nourishment that can be spiritual, mental, physical, or emotional • Different foods have different meanings. For example, a rare steak has a much different meaning than a red, shiny apple. Different memories are associated with different foods. If your mother forced you to eat liver as a child, liver may represent revulsion to you. But if you wanted to become a football player when you were in school, and you ate liver thinking that it would make you stronger, then it would represent strength to you.

Forest

Abundance; growth; strength • Protection • Feeling overwhelmed; you can't see the "forest" for the trees

Forgot/Forgetting

You're preoccupied with something else. • Feeling forgotten and/or left out

Fork

A fork in the road may mean that you'll have to make a decision.

Fountain

Spiritual rejuvenation • Excellent sign of intuition • Spiritual wellspring • Listen to what you're being told.

Four (See also *Numbers*)

Wholeness • In many ancient cultures, the number four represents the entire universe. The Native American medicine wheel is based on the four elements (Air, Water, Fire, and Earth) and the four cardinal directions. • A cross with four directions is a pre-Christian symbol of totality. • Sign of the four quadrants of your being: mental, emotional, physical, and spiritual • If four continues to appear to you, it's a sign that you're balancing all aspects of yourself.

Fox
Slyness; sneakiness; manipulation • May indicate physical attraction

Frog
The beauty behind surface ugliness • Inconsistency; hopping from one thing to another

Frozen
Emotionally closed off

Fruit
Reaping the rewards of your labor • A fruitful harvest; bearing fruit

Galaxy
Unlimited possibilities

Gallbladder
Anger; "He had a lot of gall!" • Maybe a sign to limit your intake of oils

Garbage
Things you no longer need in your life • Things you need to release

Garden
Creative activity • Peace • If the garden is well tended, you can harvest the results of your labor. • If the garden has weeds, there are things in your life that you need to weed out.

Gas
You're running out of fuel in your life and are feeling tired. • A change in your eating habits may be in order.

Gate/Gateway
An entrance between one realm and another • New opportunities •
The Gates of Heaven

Genitals
Potency; power; sexuality • Impotence

Germ
A germ is the earliest form of an organism whether it's a seed, bud, or
spore. • The basis of an idea, or of further growth or development • A
sign that it's time to boost your immune system

Geyser (See also *Water*)
A great release of emotional energy

Ghost
Some part of your feelings about a particular person hasn't solidified.
• This may signify undelivered communication from someone who
has died.

Gift
Acknowledgment of the growth you've made • Good news is coming

Giraffe
Stretching for what you want • Someone above the crowd • Stiff-
necked or unbending

Glacier
Frozen emotions

Glass/Glasses
Seeing from one realm to another • If the glass is broken, it's signaling
a shattered illusion. • Perhaps you need glasses.

Glider
If you're soaring in a glider, you may be having an out-of-body experience (see Chapter 13). • Riding on the winds of change in life; going with the flow

Glue
The connector between separate ideas or objects • A sign of your stick-to-itiveness; stick to your guns • "Coming unglued" is losing your composure.

Gnawing
Something gnawing away at you

Goat
Lecherous; old and cranky • Feeling blamed or made the scapegoat for something you didn't do

God/Goddess
Incredible unity and oneness; universal love; total self-acceptance in the moment • Power to create and manifest • A most powerful symbol

Gold
Great inner treasure • The golden light of inner peace • Heart of gold

Goose
A prod in the rear; you want someone or something to get going • Acting foolishly

Grain/Grains
The potential for life, as grain is a one-seeded fruit of a cereal grass and has the potential for the entire plant within its walls • A sign of abundance • A relatively small particulate or crystalline mass • Grain is also direction or pattern, as in the fibrous tissue of wood; "going with the grain." • Something you should have reservations about, or "take with a grain of salt"

Grandfather
The wise old man; the mature aspect of yourself; the part of you that knows • May refer to your own grandfather

Grandmother
The wise old woman; the mature aspect of yourself • May refer to your own grandmother

Grasshopper
Living for the moment with disregard for the future

Grave
Serious, self-imposed limitations; making your own grave

Gray
Usually a sign that you're feeling lifeless and tired, and have an unclear state of mind • The color of neutrality

Green
Universally represents the fertility and abundance of nature • New growth in your personal development • The color of healing

Greyhound
Speed; swiftness

Guilt
Denying responsibility for something in life

Gun
Feeling a need for protection or self-defense • Traditional therapists equate the gun as a sexual symbol representing the penis.

Guru
Guidance; the guru within • Listen to this dream

Hair
If you're brushing your hair, you're getting the tangles out of a situation. • Cutting your hair may signify new beginnings. • Braiding your hair may indicate forging new links. • Putting gel or mousse on your hair may mean smoothing out a situation. • Hair falling out may mean that you're worried. • Thick, luxurious hair indicates good health. • Energy streams out of the crown chakra, at the top of the head; thick hair can symbolize great spiritual power flowing out of this energy center to connect you to Spirit.

Halo
A blessing

Ham
"Ham it up" • Enjoy life fully • Being a "ham," possibly out of discomfort with yourself or a situation

Hands
Positive: You can handle it • Negative: You can't get a handle on it; can't handle it; can't grasp it • A backhanded compliment

Hare
Overconfidence; in the fable *The Tortoise and the Hare,* the hare lost the race because of overconfidence

Hatred
An emotion that you aren't fully allowing yourself to experience in waking life • Hatred in dreams helps release that emotion so it doesn't damage you physically or emotionally. Often, the hatred you feel in a dream isn't directed toward the person or object seemingly hated; it generally reflects self-anger, and the person or thing represents the part of yourself that you're angry with.

Hawk
View your life from a higher perspective. • Be swift and powerful in pursuit of your goals. • In ancient Egypt, the hawk was the symbol of

the soul. • Symbolizes victory in many ancient traditions, because the hawk swoops down on its prey with ferocity and power

Head
Getting ahead; headway; thinking; analyzing

Heal/Healer
You are being healed. • Access the healing energy within yourself.

Heart
Love; bliss • The center of being • Can mean physical heart

Heat
Passion; intensity • Desires can be awakened by the stirring of the Kundalini fire. • Anger

Heaven
Enlightenment; bliss; oneness; peace

Heels
A contemptible person; "He was a real heel" • To heel, or be commanded to walk in a certain way

Hell
Personal difficulties in your life

Hen
Domestic; nesting instinct • Plump; satisfied

Hide/Hiding
Hiding from a person/situation in life • Keeping a secret • A feeling that a person is hiding something from you • An animal's hide can be a homophone for hiding in your life.

Hills

Rounded hills can signify female sensuality and the breastlike mounds of Mother Earth; this could be a sign to step into your sensuality. • Some small issue in your life seems big; you're making a mountain out of a of molehill.

Hippopotamus

Weighty; ponderous • In ancient Egypt, this animal represented the goddess Taueret, who attended all births.

Hips

Positive: support; power; throwing your hip into it • Negative: fear of moving forward

Hog

Overindulgence • Feeling that you're not getting or giving your share • Selfishness

Hole

Something that you aren't acknowledging or facing • A "hole" in your argument • Could be a symbol for "wholeness"

Holy

That which is holy, sacred, or divine within you and life • The God Force within you

Home/House

Approximately one-third of all dreams take place inside a building, usually a house or home. The most common association for this is your physical or spiritual self—or both. Whatever is happening to the house is what you're experiencing happening to you. For example, if the plumbing is clogged, it may be that your emotions (symbolized by the water in the pipes) are blocked. Being in a dark room represents exploring unknown parts of ourselves, and clutter in the house indicates areas of your life that you need to clean up or things that you need to discard (note which room is cluttered). Different rooms in the house symbolize different aspects of yourself:

- Kitchen: nourishment, sustenance, and creativity (as in "cooking up" ideas)
- Hallway: transition
- Bathroom: elimination of the old
- Basement: your subconscious
- Attic: high ideals and aspirations

Honey

In mythology, honey was the food of the gods and thus came to symbolize the life force in all things: the "land of milk and honey." • Pertaining to the sweetness in life or someone or something you love

Hook

A sign of getting hooked by someone or something • Someone who is feared or dishonest—for example, Captain Hook; be cautious • A hook for hanging things can indicate organization; hang it up; get organized.

Horn/Horns

Musical horns can represent the power of music and the celestial horns of heaven. • Jung stated that the horn was a symbol with two meanings. Although horned animals and horns are often associated with virility and male sexuality, the horn itself is shaped like a receptacle and therefore can also be feminine in nature. • In ancient times, the horn was carved into a cup and represented abundance; the cornucopia, the "horn of plenty," symbolizes this. • Ancient Gnostics said the horn represented the "principle which bestows maturity and beauty on all things." • In some cultures, horned animals symbolized evil—as in the "horned one." Horns can represent the destructive forces within one's psyche. • Horns were used as a warning by many cultures. They were also used to call the forces for the Holy War. This sign might be cautioning you to take care. Be alert.

Horse
Expanded sense of self • Freedom; movement • Questioning another's motives; "Don't look a gift horse in the mouth"

Hospital
Center of healing

Hummingbird
Absolute energy and joy in delving into the nectar in life • Hummingbirds can fly upward, downward, and even backward; expand your joyous energy in all directions. • Being too busy and frantic in life

Hunt
To look for unknown parts of yourself or something in life • Feeling hunted • Something you desire to kill in yourself or in others

Hyena
Noisy; merriment not appropriate to the situation

Ice
Frozen emotions • To be on thin ice refers to a dubious circumstance. • Slipping on ice means being in a circumstance where you don't feel on stable ground or are unsure of yourself.

Iceberg
The tip of the iceberg signals blocked emotions beginning to surface. • Drifting without emotional direction

Icicles
Whatever emotions have been blocked are beginning to release; there will be much more flow in your life.

Ignition
Represents your power switch; you're having trouble getting started in life • Things are about to start.

Illness
Can indicate that your body needs attention

Impotence
Insecurity; fear

Incest
Integrating parts of yourself, such as the adult part with the child part or the male part with the female part • Remember, most often the different people in a dream represent different aspects of yourself. • Can refer to very deep, unsolved issues from your life

Indian
A deep, primordial connection to nature • A part of your basic nature that's still foreign to you • Higher self-guidance

Initiation
Awakening to a new level of consciousness

Injury (See also *Illness*)
You injured someone emotionally or someone injured you. • You're going too fast and if you don't slow down, there might be an injury.

Insect
Something is bugging you. • Maggots represent decay; butterflies are transformational; flies are small annoyances; ants are industrious.

Iron
Pressing out problems • Too many irons in the fire

Island
Self-contained • Feeling isolated • Needing refuge

Ivory
Purity; strength

Ivy
Stability; wealth • Clinging; dependence; attachment

Jack
Diversification; jack-of-all-trades • A car's jack may indicate the relief of a heavy burden, or an easier trip. • Jacking up one's spirits • Jacked up • Being carjacked can result in loss of respect and independence.

Jackal
A part of you that feels like a scavenger, or someone is scavenging you • A sign telling you to be watchful and aware; the jackal has a mournful cry and yap that some associate with a warning • Trust your senses. In Egypt, Anubis was the jackal god, the guardian of the underworld and the one who prepared the way after death. This was perhaps because no matter how well the Egyptians sealed their tombs, the jackals always found them due to their finely-tuned senses.

Jail
Feeling confined; feeling that events are happening to you rather than having the ability to effect change • A lack of freedom

Jam
The sweetness of life • Feeling you're in a "jam" • Traffic jams or logjams signify delays, confusion, and frustration; feeling stuck with no way to turn • Take time to be still and reassess your situation.

Jar (See also *Bottle*)
A "jarring" experience

Jaw
Communication; to "jaw" or talk comfortably with friends • If tightly closed, there's a need for more open communication • Scolding; boring; long-winded • A square jaw connotes strength and toughness

Jealousy

Not feeling included; feeling left out • Work on knowing that you're complete and whole exactly the way you are now; your presence is enough; there isn't anything more that you need to be, do, or have in order to be whole. • Others are jealous of you.

Jelly (See also *Jam*)

Being afraid; feeling unstable

Jellyfish

Floating; drifting along • No backbone

Jesus (See *Christ*)

Jewel

Wealth; abundance; brilliance • Inner treasures

Jog

A reminder; "jogging" the memory • Movement; self-betterment • Jogging in place without getting anywhere

Journey

Self-exploration and growth

Judas

A betrayal—usually, self-betrayal; not being true to yourself

Judge

Self-judgment • It may be directed at another, but it's probably something you've judged within yourself—remember, everything that you've done to others was necessary for your growth and to get to where you are now; holding this viewpoint helps you release judgment and guilt. • May be a guide or your higher self giving you information.

Juggler

Trying to juggle many things at once • If the juggler is doing a good job, so are you. • If the juggler is somewhat out of control, eliminate some things from your life; take time to assess what's really important in your life.

Juice

"Juice up" or give life and energy • Virile strength; vigor • Provocative or racy • Drunk

Jump

Leaping to a new venture; getting ahead • Look before you leap.

Jungle

The wild instinctual part of you • Confusion • Not being able to see clearly

Junk

That which you no longer need, such as ideas, feelings, habits, relationships, and so forth • To get rid of junk in your emotions, get rid of junk in your life. (The symbolic act of cleaning cupboards and drawers and getting rid of things that you don't use or don't love contributes to getting rid of emotional states that aren't contributing to who you really are.)

Jury (See also *Judge*)

Self-criticism • Note the judgments that you feel the jury is making. • Feeling criticized by others

Kangaroo

Restless energy • Mobility

Key

A powerful symbol of opening doors for yourself on both the spiritual and the physical plane

Keyhole

Being close to a solution or a new direction in life, but not quite there. (Go back into your dream and imagine that you're taking a key and opening the door. Notice what is behind the door.)

Kidnapping

Self-sabotage • Feeling out of control or being the victim of a situation • If a child is kidnapped, it may reflect a taking away of your inner child.

Kidneys

Fear • Disappointment • Criticism

Killing

This may indicate that you're releasing parts of yourself that aren't necessary in your present evolution: killing off beliefs or behaviors that are no longer needed by you. • Killing a child most likely refers to killing off your own inappropriate childish behaviors, or it can be the death of your inner child. • Killing a parent may indicate getting rid of the way you've related to your parents or to your own parenting style • Don't feel guilty if you have a killing dream; it usually signifies the beginning of a great spurt of self-growth. This is usually a positive symbol. • If you're being killed, it's likely that you need to take control in your life so that you feel empowered rather than powerless. (Go back into your dream and do battle with your antagonist and *win!* This will help you in waking life.)

King

Power and majesty; God • Self-responsibility; taking charge of your own life

Kiss

Deep communication with self • Warmth; affection; love • Aligning with the masculine and feminine aspects within ourselves

Kite

Incredible spiritual soaring, yet grounded and anchored • Childlike freedom

Knees

Flexibility • Fear (when people are afraid, their knees lock up) • Inflexibility; not wanting to give in • Being in awe; kneeling in worship

Knife

A powerful symbol either creatively or destructively • The cutting away of that which isn't needed anymore—cutting the thorns from a rose or cutting away old patterns of thinking and being • If someone is chasing you with a knife or knifing you, you may be in fear of being penetrated emotionally, physically, or sexually.

Knitting

Tying ideas and life themes together; unifying • Domestic peace • Mending; repairing; the broken bone was "knitting"

Knock

An awareness is trying to make itself known to you. • Opportunity knocking

Knot

Tension; tied up in "knots"; a stomach in "knots" • Making a commitment; tying the "knot" • Untying a knot signifies finding a solution or relaxation in a certain area of your life.

Label

A symbol for separating and organizing • Stereotyping someone or something; pigeonholing • Expand your horizons; move toward perceptions of unity, oneness, and wholeness. • Feeling like someone is labeling you

Laboratory

Finding solutions through experimentation

Labyrinth

Winding through intricate passageways may signify your feeling that there's no way out. The solution to being in a labyrinth is to stop and still your mind. Let your intuition come through, and the way out of your difficulty will become clear.

Ladder

Attaining a higher awareness or reaching new heights in life • Jacob's ladder to heaven and ascending to the realm of the angels • If the ladder is going upward, you're climbing the ladder of success. • Descending a ladder might symbolize going down into the subconscious mind, or it might be that your fortunes are diminishing.

Ladybug

A great symbol of good luck • A sign that you need to tend to your personal home affairs, as in the old nursery rhyme: "Ladybug, ladybug, fly away home, your house is on fire . . ."

Lake

A still, clear lake refers to intuition and deep inner wisdom. • Choppy water indicates emotional turmoil. • Cloudy water signifies stagnant emotions. • To the ancient Egyptians, lakes symbolized the occult and mysterious inner realms. At certain times during the year, priests would cross the lake in ceremonial procession. Celtic symbolism held that the Land of the Dead was at the bottom of the lake. Water can symbolize your subconscious and your deep unknown places. The inner mysterious realms are within you.

Lamb

Sacrifice; martyrdom • Easily led • Purity; innocence

Lamp/Lantern (See also *Light*)
Inner light

Land
Solid grounding; your foundation

Large Intestine
Release of toxic matter; release of that which you don't use or need •
Freedom of movement • Assimilation • Courage; having the guts to
go forward

Laser
Pinpointed consciousness; intense focus and concentration

Laughter
This is a great healer; don't take life so seriously.

Launching
Beginning a new venture

Laundry
Personal cleansing • Cleaning up your "act" • Airing your dirty
laundry

Lava
Something that has been suppressed for a long time, usually anger

Lawn
Nurturing; grounding

Leaping (See *Jump*)

Leather
Strength; "tough as leather"

Leaves

Green leaves symbolize abundance, growth, life. • Yellowing leaves or leaves on the ground symbolize completion, letting go, releasing. • Leaving something or someone

Leech

Something or someone is taking your strength or property. • You're taking advantage of someone else.

Left

Your left side is usually thought to symbolize the receptive forces of the universe, and your right represents the projecting forces. • Feeling left behind or left out

Legs

Feeling that you don't have a leg to stand on • Your stability

Lemon

Cleansing and purifying • Poorly constructed

Lens

A need to focus your attention or take time to focus the direction of your life

Leopard

Prowess; cunning; stealth • Ferocity; valor; power

Leprosy

Wasting away; deteriorating • Note which part of the body is affected.

Letter

Information; news • Indirect communication

Library
Knowledge; inner knowing • A powerful symbol

Lifeguard
Often, this represents a dream guardian or your higher self leading you through an emotional crisis.

Light
The spiritual light within • The quality of the light signifies what you're aware of in life.

Lightning
A potent symbol of great power; a breakthrough ahead • Speed; strength • Awakening of life force

Lily
Life, death, and rebirth; transformation

Lion/Lioness
King of the jungle; majesty; power; bravery; leadership • Test of courage (In some African tribes, part of the rite of manhood concerned pitting one's strength against a lion's.)

Little Finger
Manipulation; feeling like you're "being wrapped around someone's little finger"

Liver
Anger • Can refer to someone who "lives"—hence, is a "liver" • The only organ that can regenerate; can refer to regenerating a part of your life

Lizard
Important messages will come in your dreams. The lizard stays in the shadows during the heat of the day and is thus considered the

keeper of the shadowlands as well as the keeper of dreams. • Your subconscious mind and your inner shadowlands • Earthy; primordial; steady • Considered guardians of the inner worlds by the Australian aborigines

Locking
You may be giving out too much energy and not keeping enough for yourself, so it's time to lock up your energy. • Locking up something indicates a need for more self-acceptance. • Locking something up within yourself that you find undesirable • Being in a house or other structure and locking others out means shutting yourself away from the realities of the world; locking out other people

Lost
Uncertainty about who you are or where you're headed

Lotus
Spiritual awakening • Coming up out of the mud into the light

Luggage
The desire or need to travel • A sign of old habits, patterns, and conditioning that you need to get rid of

Lungs
Grief • Taking in life; the breath of life; taking charge of your life • Needing breathing space

Machinery
Feeling out of touch with the organic process of life • Use of natural forces for power and strength

Magic
A sign that there's a mystical power beyond your normal reality • A desire to listen to your inner magic • Believe!

Magician

Illusion; not real • The tarot meaning is realizing aspirations by reaching inner resources; the magician is the transformer and the one who manifests. • Magic comes from the ancient word *magh,* meaning "power"; the magician symbolizes channeling power from the inner realms to the outer realms.

Magnet

Irresistible attraction

Mail (See also *Letter*)

An obvious sign for messages • A homophone for *male*

Male

The male part of the self; the yang energy within; projecting energy

Man

The male part of yourself; the linear, rational, practical part of yourself; focused conscious awareness

Mandala

A circle or a mandala signifies harmony, beauty, and balance. • A very powerful symbol; often used as a visual aid in meditation and religious worship

Map

Planning your journeys—inner and outer

Marriage

Uniting the male and female sides of yourself; integrating various aspects of self • A uniting or coming together of ideas or people

Mars

Small disharmonies in your life • A sign to use your focused and directed power for achieving prosperity • Mars was originally the god of farming, fertility, and prosperity of the harvest. Later, after the Romans came in contact with Greek culture, Mars became the Roman god of war.

Marsh
Emotionally stagnating; unsure of yourself emotionally

Martyr
Lack of personal power; feeling that you're a victim of life's circumstances • Giving to others and feeling resentful when you don't get sufficient appreciation • A need to work on self-acceptance; accept responsibility for the circumstances in your life

Mask
Different aspects of yourself • Dishonesty • Protection; concealment; nonbeing • Masks were traditionally used in native cultures during initiations. The metamorphoses that initiates experienced during these rituals were so completely mysterious and awesome that these transformations needed to be hidden beneath a mask. Depending on the kind of mask, this can be a powerful sign that you're indeed in the midst of a personal transformation.

Massage
Personal integration • Release of tension

Match
Unlit: potential not yet revealed • Lit: your inner light is beginning to shine forth

Maze (See *Labyrinth*)

Meadow
A place of spiritual harmony and balance • Rejuvenation; nurturance

Mean

People are being mean to you. • You are being mean to others or to yourself. • Caught in the illusion of victimhood • Seeing the true *mean*ing of a situation

Meat

The essence or "meat" of the matter • A homophone for *meet*

Medicine

Healing • Getting some of your own "medicine"

Meditation

May be a sign that your guide desires to speak with you, but your mind is too busy to listen • Be quiet and listen to your heart.

Melons

Wholeness • Something full of opportunity

Melt/Melting

A dramatic inner change through letting go of personal form and structure • Emotions are being freed and opening the way for love, self-esteem, and forgiveness (see also *Water*). • Melting down the barriers between yourself and other people, or within parts of yourself • Melting the old structures to create new dimensional understanding • Metal melting by fire can symbolize form being transformed into spirit.

Menstruation

Releasing the old; new beginnings • If blood is evident, feeling loss of life energy

Mercury

Messenger of the gods; the bearer of messages • God of trade, commerce, gain, luck, travel, and good gifts • Eloquence • Rapid changing of moods

Mermaid
Your intuitive, emotional self • Unobtainable lover • Temptation • Connection with deep emotions and the subconscious

Merry-Go-Round
Feeling as if you're going around and around without making any progress

Metal
Strength; hardness • Immobility

Microscope
Intense self-examination

Middle Finger
An obvious sign of anger or sexuality

Middle Path
Take the middle path in life, and don't go to one extreme or another. Follow the Buddha's course of moderation in all things.

Milk
Mother's milk; nurturance; sustenance • "Milk" of human kindness

Mine
Inner treasures undiscovered

Mirror
A step away from reality; a reflection of what is • Truth; self-realization • A powerful sign with a duplicity of meanings: A mirror can mean your imagination and your conscious thought in the way that it reflects the world around you, or a sign of self-contemplation and the need for you to turn your thoughts inward. Some psychologists associate mirrors with hidden or unconscious memories. • In China, mirrors are used to reflect or dispel unfavorable influences. • In folklore and in

fairy tales, mirrors have a magical association. A mirror is an entrance point or a mythic door between this world and other realms.

Miscarriage
A miscarriage of justice • Plans aborted or unfulfilled (see also *Abortion/ Abort*)

Missing the Boat/Plane/Train
Feeling a lack of progress in your life; feeling left out because of life's circumstances • Lost opportunity • Not making enough of an effort; take time to reassess your goals

Mist (See also *Fog*)
The mystical inner realms • Your subconscious mind and something that you aren't coming to terms with in your life

Mole
Burrowing • Something beneath the surface; something not willing to be seen

Monastery
Inward spiritual retreat • May refer to a withdrawal from the world

Money
Coins signify a change coming in your life • Wealth of experience, finances, and so forth

Monster
An unacknowledged part of yourself that you fear; your hidden fears made manifest • Your fear is of the unknown. • Someone in your life is acting like a monster. • You are acting like a monster. • Confront a threatening monster: instead of being victimized, imagine yourself going back into your dream and doing battle. Emerge victorious.

Moon

The feminine aspect of yourself • Inner emotional peace • Full moon: wholeness and creativity from an intuitive base • New moon or a crescent moon: a time of feeling at one with your internal spiritual self; a time for deep inner reflection

Moth

Perseverance beyond reason • Something being eaten away without your awareness

Mother

May reflect the part of yourself that your mother represents • Nurturance; Mother Earth; the wiser, female part of yourself • Divine Mother • Your birth mother • Your mothering skills

Mountain

An attainable goal or opportunity • Going up the mountain: you're progressing toward your goal; going down the mountain: you're moving away from your goal • A spiritually uplifting experience; monasteries and lamaseries are in the mountains because mountains are a place of spiritual retreat • Don't make a mountain out of a molehill. • Can be viewed as an obstacle or an opportunity

Mourning

Letting go of habits, attitudes, and relationships that no longer serve you in order to make way for more appropriate ways of being • Releasing • A sign that there is something in your life that makes you very sad

Mouse

Feeling insignificant • Temerity; fear • A need for quiet; a concern about being quiet

Mouth

Communication; expressing yourself

Movies
Observing life • Becoming caught up in the drama of life • The different roles in your life

Mud
Feeling stuck; not moving or growing • Things seem "muddy" in your life, not clean • "Mud, mud, glorious mud" that a child enjoys; childlike joy

Mule
Stubbornness • Ability to carry heavy burdens

Murder (See *Killing*)

Museum (See also *Home/House*)
Knowledge; bringing wisdom from the past and assimilating it into the present

Music
Beautiful, harmonious music signifies uplifting spiritual alignment and inner harmony. • Music out of tune: feeling out of tune with your life • In ancient times, individual notes were thought to be intimately connected to the different celestial planets. One ancient philosopher assigned different notes to different animals and gave each note an associated meaning. Another philosopher thought that the shape of the instrument that created the music signified the meaning of the music. • The lyrics in the music will have different meanings.

Musical Instruments
Piano: the keys of life • Flute: nature; freedom; the child within • Drums: primitive nature or primordial instincts; staying with the beat; marching to a different drum • Harp: celestial alignment; angels • Harmonica: the wandering minstrel; time with friends; enjoyment; contentment • Bagpipes: cultural fellowship • Violin or other string instrument: dedication; the sitar reflects Eastern culture; mysticism; internal peace

Nail

Carpenter's nail: support for larger structures; binding together • Getting to the essence of the problem; "hitting the nail on the head" • Getting "nailed"; getting caught • Chewing fingernails represents anxiety.

Nakedness

Total freedom • Vulnerability; feeling exposed • Exposing a situation; baring your soul • Sensuality

Names

In some esoteric traditions, there's great power in one's name. In ancient Egypt, it was believed that personal names were a reflection of one's soul and helped determine one's destiny.

Narrow

Feeling limited and restricted • Need to focus attention and be disciplined in order to reach a goal

Nausea

Something is making you sick to your stomach. • Getting rid of what isn't wanted

Navel

The silver cord that connects your astral body to your physical body • In the East, the center of the universe

Neck

Positive: flexibility; being willing to see both sides of a situation • Negative: a pain in the neck • Being stiff-necked or immovable

Nest

Incubating ideas or projects • Nesting; home and family life; domestic life • Pulling inward for rejuvenation

Net
Feeling caught in a web or net of your own perception of reality (take time to still your mind and allow other realities to be made available to you so that you can choose one that's more in alignment with who you truly are) • Fishing net or butterfly net: help in catching things that are needed • Safety net: catches you when you feel out of balance

Night
Obstacles; delays; not seeing things clearly; not being in touch with your inner knowing • Clear night with visible stars or moonlight: a symbol of your intuition and your inner realms

Nightmare
Nightmares should be viewed as positive experiences. They allow you to deal with unresolved issues in daily life that you aren't allowing into your consciousness. These unresolved issues affect every aspect of life, including your health and relationships. The nightmare is your subconscious way of healing these unresolved issues. Celebrate your nightmares! • Imagine going back into your nightmare and playing it through a few times. Change the circumstances so that there's a positive outcome from your dream. This will assist in healing the unresolved area of your life that was the source of the nightmare.

North
If you live in the Northern Hemisphere, the north represents cold and darkness. • If you live in the Southern Hemisphere, north can represent warmth and light. • To the Native Americans of North America, the north was the realm of the ancestors, spiritual elders, and the realm of death and rebirth.

Nose
Nosy • Self-recognition

Nudity (See *Nakedness*)

Numb

Most often there's some external, physical cause of numbness, such as sleeping in an awkward position. • May signify that you're cut off from your feelings or are suppressing something that you fear

Numbers

Since the beginning of time, numbers have been viewed as signs that have held mystic significance. The following interpretations are based on the ancient Pythagorean system (on which modern-day numerology is founded). If a number keeps appearing to you in various forms, pay attention to its associated meanings.

- **1:** Independence, new beginnings, oneness with life, self-development, individuality, progress, and creativity

- **2:** Balance of the yin and yang energies (the polarities) of the universe; it is self-surrender, putting others before yourself; dynamic attraction to one another; knowledge comes from the balance and marriage of the two opposites

- **3:** The trinity: mind, body, and spirit; it's the threefold nature of Divinity; expansion, expression, communication, fun, and self-expression; also relates to giving outwardly, to openness and optimism: "Third time's the charm"

- **4:** Security and foundations; it's the four elements and the four sacred directions; self-discipline through work and service; represents productivity, organization, wholeness, and unity

- **5:** Feeling free; five is self-emancipating, active, physical, impulsive, energetic, adventuresome, and resourceful; associated with travel and curiosity; it's the number of the free soul, of excitement, and change

- **6:** Self-harmony, compassion, love, service, social responsibility, beauty, the arts, generosity, concern, and caring; it relates to children, balance, and community service

- **7:** The inner life and inner wisdom; it's a mystical number symbolizing wisdom, the seven chakras, and the seven heavens; a symbol of birth and rebirth, religious strength, sacred vows, the path of solitude, analysis, and contemplation

- **8:** Symbolizes infinity, material prosperity, self-power, abundance, cosmic consciousness, reward, authority, and leadership

- **9:** Humanitarianism, selflessness, and dedicating your life to others; a number of completion and of endings; symbolizing universal compassion, tolerance, and wisdom

- Master Numbers in Pythagorean tradition were thought to have a special power and significance of their own: **11** is developing intuition, clairvoyance, spiritual healing, and other metaphysical faculties; **22** is unlimited potential of mastery in any area—not only spiritual, but also physical, emotional, and mental; **33** is all things are possible.

Nun
Pulling your energies inward • Celibacy; spiritual attunement • Can mean *none*

Nurse
Healing; caring; nurturing

Nuts
New life; potential yet to unfold • Abundance; gathering nuts for the winter • A difficult situation or person—a hard nut to crack

Nymph
Minor divinity of nature in mythology; mystical maiden who dwells in the mountains, waters, and trees • Joyous sexuality • Immature insects; incomplete development or incomplete metamorphosis

Oak
Tremendous strength; solidarity; steady progress

Oar
A boat without an oar may indicate that you feel adrift in an emotional dilemma • Oars can mean feeling in control amid emotional imbalance

Oasis
Refuge; place of rejuvenation

Obituary
Release of old ideas, thought forms, and beliefs • Something is nearing completion

Observatory
Getting the bigger picture; seeing the deeper meaning in life

Obstacles/Obstructions
Constant physical obstacles (such as brick walls, locked doors, traffic jams, fences, or even bad weather) that block your way, or personal or business obstacles (such as contracts that don't go through and phones that are out of order) are all strong messages that it's time to withdraw into yourself and reevaluate your life. Or alternatively, gather your inner resources and push through the blockage.

Ocean
Calm ocean: great inner power and emotional and spiritual balance • Rough or choppy ocean: the need for courage to allow you to move to calmer waters amid emotional upheaval • Sea of life: tremendous intuitive power

Octopus
Doing many things at once • Tenacious; grasping • Shy and retiring

Office
Production • Linear thought processes; organization

Officer
Authority • Protection or guidance • Conscience; punishment; self-righteousness • May indicate guilt; you want to be punished or kept out of trouble • An affirmation for accepting authority over your life

Oil
Lubrication; smoothing out difficulties; pouring oil on troubled waters • Anointing with oil is a blessing • A greasy or oily personality

Olive
Peace; the olive branch of peace

One (See also *Numbers*)
Being #1 is a sign of success; being first; being ahead of the pack • Homophone for *won*

Onion
Layers of consciousness • Potential sadness

Open
Be open to life and new possibilities; the way will open for you. • Being too open with others

Orange
You're entering an outward, social time in your life. • Orange is warm and stimulating, and is lighter and higher in vibration than red. It's a happy, social color used by clowns the world over. Orange stimulates optimism, expansiveness, emotional balance, confidence, change, striving, self-motivation, changeability, enthusiasm, and a sense of community. Orange is flamboyant and warmhearted.

Orchard (See also *Garden*)
A great sign for bearing the fruits of your labor and being fruitful in your life

Orchestra
Synthesis; harmony; synergy

Orgasm
Depends on the feelings associated with orgasm and whether you reached the orgasm • Powerful alignment with your inner male and female energies; connection to your Kundalini energy • For a male to reach orgasm in sleep, it may indicate a need to strengthen the prostate gland.

Orgy
Your creative force may be dissipating; focus on your life goals • Allowing your sexual energy freedom of expression

Orphan (See *Abandoned*)

Ostrich
Avoidance of looking at something in life

Otter
Capricious; playful; fun-loving

Oven
An idea or project is incubating

Owl
A powerful symbol of transformation • Wisdom • Most cultures with an esoteric background honor the owl as a revered (and sometimes feared) sign. The owl was feared because it was the sign of darkness and the unknown. Owls were also thought to be associated with death as well as rebirth. Some Native American tribes thought that

owls housed the spirits of the dead. In Egyptian hieroglyphs, the owl symbolized death, night, cold, and passivity. • Seeing clearly where things may seem dark; the owl sees in the darkness what others cannot see • A symbol of ancient wisdom born from the inner realms; Athena, the Greek goddess of wisdom, was depicted as having an owl on her shoulder that revealed inner truths to her. Merlin, the old Celtic magician, used an owl to gain entrance into the unseen dimensions.

Oyster
Guarded energy • Hidden beauty; beauty developing unseen

Pacing
If you're pacing back and forth, you're uncertain about your life's direction; take time to be still. Thinking about the situation isn't always the best solution. As you take time to quiet your mind, the correct solution will gently rise to the surface.

Pack
Carrying a pack: something, someone, or even an idea that you're carrying around with you isn't necessary; let it go • Packing: preparation for a change in your life • Running with the pack • Going it alone; leaving the pack

Package
Sending a package: you're letting go of something • Receiving a package: you're acknowledging an unrecognized part of yourself

Pain
Pain isn't necessarily a bad sign. Usually, it's a message sent by your body, letting you know that there's a problem you need to attend to.

Paint
Note the color, then see Chapter 25. • Redoing; making new • Invoking your inner artist

Palace (See also *Home/House*)
Your sense of your true magnificence

Pan
Greek god of shepherds and hunters who originated panpipes; symbolizes the joy in nature • Panning with a movie camera: getting the bigger picture • Panning for gold: looking for the true essence of something • Pan or cooking pot: incubating an idea

Panda
Tranquility • Lovable; cuddly

Panic
A feeling that you don't have the resources to deal with a situation, or when you feel out of control

Parachute
You are protected

Parade
Being willing to be recognized, particularly for your community efforts • Each of the participants in the parade is an aspect of yourself

Paradise
A place of perfect peace and love; the kingdom of paradise is within you • Innocence, or the fall from innocence; the Garden of Eden represents paradise—however, it was fraught with temptation

Paralyze
Feeling completely immobilized in an area of your life • Conflicting feelings or impulses

Parasite
Something or someone draining or eating away your energy • A sign that you actually have parasites

Parents
Although family members' roles are changing dramatically, your soul memory holds stereotypical images of parents. Fathers represent authority; linear, rational thought processes; projecting force; and yang energy. Mothers represent the yin principle of nurturance, and the inner realms of intuition and magic. • May pertain to your experience of your parents or your own parenting skills • May represent the mother/father energy that dwells within you

Parrot
Insincerity • Copying; imitating; speaking another's words without thinking • Symbol of the exotic; the jungle

Party
Celebration

Passenger
If you are the passenger, you're "along for the ride"; someone else is deciding the direction.

Passport
Represents your ticket for change and creating what you want in your life

Path
Straight and narrow path going upward: you're making progress; you're in alignment with your life's goals and purpose; you're staying on the path • Crooked path: you're wandering off course; you aren't quite sure what direction to go

Pattern
A sewing or an embroidery pattern may symbolize your usual reality system, the one in which you are comfortable • Changing patterns may indicate breaking out of old patterns

Pavement
New pavement is a new direction. • To pave is to make your way easier or smoother.

Peach
Uplifting; vitality

Peacock
Pride; vanity • Confidence taken to the extreme

Pearl
Beauty may come out of the irritating situations in your life, just as a grain of sand that began as an irritation becomes great beauty. • Femininity; associated with the moon, water, and the shell, which are all symbols of the feminine principle in life • Pregnancy or a future pregnancy • In China, the pearl represented "genius in obscurity" because the beautiful pearl was hidden in the course oyster shell. Muslims referred to the pearl as a symbol of heaven; in some mystic traditions, the pearl represented the true center of life.

Pedestal
Putting someone or yourself in a position of elevation or seeing that one as "above you" • This detracts from your inner power because when you experience yourself as a part of all things, nothing becomes higher or lower.

Pegasus
Freedom; inner magic • Winged inspiration • Soaring strength

Pen
Expressing yourself fluidly; communication • Feeling "penned" up and restricted

Pencil
Ability to express yourself; less restrictive than a pen

Pendulum
Uncertainty; weighing several choices • Needing to find a balance in your life

Penis
Yang; projecting energy; the male principle; power; potency

Penny (See also *Money*)
A "small change" is happening or is ahead

Pepper
Spicy emotions • Stimulating

Perfume
If you can actually smell perfume in your dream, it may represent sensuality.

Periscope
Subconscious observation of conscious reality • Objective observation • If the periscope is in water, it means that you're observing your conscious reality from your emotional, intuitive self.

Perspire
A sign that you're afraid or nervous • Exertion

Petal
Petals falling from the flower: sadness • Pulling petals off a flower: "He loves me, he loves me not"

Photography
Objective observation of a situation • Memories

Physician
A sign that perhaps it's time to see the doctor for a checkup • Your inner healer

Piano (See also *Musical Instruments*)
If a piano is out of tune, you're not in tune with yourself.

Pie
An opportunity; "getting a piece of the pie" • The round shape suggests wholeness combined with nourishment. • A whole with the possibility of being divided up into shares

Pig
Overindulgence • Selfish; grasping • Prosperity • Joy

Pill
Something unpleasant or repugnant that must be endured • Someone disagreeable or tiresome; a real "pill" • Healing

Pillar
Strength

Pillow
Intuition; inner realms • Relaxation; letting go

Pimple
Bringing things to a head

Pin
Solid material that fastens separate articles together; a support that allows one article to be suspended from another • A petty annoyance • Getting "pinned down"; held fast or immobile

Pine
Cleanser and purifier • To "pine away" for someone or something

Pioneer
Entering new areas within yourself and in your daily life

Pipe

As a musical instrument: joy and freedom • As a solid structure that conducts liquids or gases: the flow of energy within yourself and the universe • The peace pipe of the Native American: an object of holiness and reverence, symbolizing unity with Spirit

Pirate

Unauthorized use of another's product, conception, or creativity • You need to be your own authority in your life.

Pit (See *Abyss*)

Planets

Heavenly bodies; illumination • Earth: grounding; nurturance • Jupiter: expansiveness; vastness; a huge, imposing connotation • Mars: aggressiveness; passion; a warlike connotation • Mercury: the Greek messenger of the gods; communication and speed; swift change of mood • Neptune: the god of the sea; psychic awareness; mysticism • Pluto: small; concentrated; a spiritual unfolding; capricious joy as found in the Disney character Pluto • Saturn: sardonic; slow to act; a feeling of coldness • Uranus: hidden abilities; changes • Venus: beauty; harmony; femininity; gentleness • You should make plans—that is, *plan it.*

Plastic

Flexibility; capacity to be molded or shaped; pliable • Artificial; bogus

Platform

Taking a stand • Stating your beliefs; a declaration of your principles

Play

Children at play reflect joy and spontaneity • "All the world's a stage . . ."; your life is your script, and *you* can choose to become involved in the drama or not; you can choose the script—it's your play.

Plumbing

Emotions • Backed up; feeling emotionally backed up in your life • Overflowing; emotions overflowing • Frozen pipes; emotions are frozen • Can apply to your urinary tract

Pocket

A place of safekeeping • A cavity containing something of value; a receptacle or container

Poison

Something destructive or harmful—most often, an attitude about yourself; a fear or judgment

Poker

Gambling (perhaps with something that you can't afford to lose)

Police (See also *Officer*)

Protection and guidance • Guilt • Some areas in your own life that you need to police

Pollution

Inner stagnation • May be time for a cleanse

Pond

Any area of water represents emotions and intuition: a calm, clear pond suggests calm, clear emotions; troubled water suggests problems. • The boundaries of a pond are smaller than those of an ocean or a lake, indicating less of an emotional concern.

Pool

More suggestive of intuition and the deep inner realms of self than other bodies of water

Popcorn

Lots of creativity and new ideas moving into manifestation; the kernels (ideas) are expanding • Stale popcorn indicates an unsatisfactory ending.

Porch

An added-on part of yourself; an extension of yourself • That which isn't a part of your basic nature, yet is something you consider in relation to yourself

Porcupine

Something prickly; a prickly situation • Something you want to stay away from

Port

Safety • Depending on the condition of the water nearby, it concerns various emotions. • Good wine; enjoyment with friends

Portrait

How you see yourself or think others see you • Not necessarily your true nature

Postman

Messages; news • Information from an outside source; guidance

Pot

Something you're cooking; may relate to nurturing • Something you're creating • Marijuana; a different level of consciousness; dependence on outer stimulation rather than inner resources

Pottery

Molding your life, attitudes, and beliefs • Things are contained.

Praise

Congratulations! You have done well. • You've earned something.

Pregnancy

You're about to give birth to an idea, feeling, or emotion. • A new, creative project; going in a new direction • A desire to be pregnant • A powerful symbol

Premonition

Note: Most dreams that appear to be premonitions usually point to aspects of growth of the inner self; very rarely are they true enactments of the future. • As upsetting as dreaming of the death of a child may be, it most likely signifies the "death" or putting away of childish things in your life. The dream isn't necessarily a premonition. • It takes practice to recognize a premonition dream from a symbolic, self-growth dream, but there are specific things that you can look for: usually, the colors are quite a bit brighter in a premonition dream; and very often, there's a rounded or round object, which symbolizes the energy of prophecy. In a premonition dream, the symbol will often repeat itself three times. If you aren't sure, ask for clarification in another dream. The more comfortable you become with having premonitions in your dreams, the easier it will be for you to have this type of dream in the future.

President

You are your own authority • Control; leadership • Priest; spiritual authority • Guidance; showing the way

Prince

The most divine masculine part of yourself • The masculine force in the universe: yang

Princess

The most divine feminine part of yourself • The feminine force in the universe: yin

Print Shop

Communication • A solution to the current problem • Repeating the situation many times

Prison
Self-imposed bars; self-imposed confinement (you always have the key to let yourself out; the only person who can imprison you is *you*)

Prisoner
Limiting your own potential; self-confinement • Fear • Feeling imprisoned in life

Profanity
Unexperienced emotions within normal daily life

Prop
Something supporting you temporarily until you step into your own wisdom, judgment, or strength

Prophet
Guidance; teaching; divine direction • The mystic; the visionary; the master • Listen to what the prophet says to you. • A powerful symbol of guidance

Prostitute
Prostituting yourself; using your energy inappropriately; misusing your creativity • Draining of latent sexual energy • Revealing sensuality

Prune
Shriveled; dried up • Old; an older person • Prune what isn't needed

Puddle
Nuisance; small emotional difficulty that's bothering you

Pump
Getting the life-affirming energies going; awakening of life-force energy • Sexuality; power; strength; potency • Free-flowing water from a pump: easy, free-flowing emotion • Pumping without result: emotional constriction or restriction; priming the pump indicates opportunity ahead

Puppet

Manipulation; feeling manipulated or that you're manipulating others
• Giving away your power; not remembering that you're in control

Purse

Tied to another's purse strings • Abundance (if full)

Puzzle

Not seeing the whole picture • Each part of your life is a different part of the puzzle; a completed puzzle indicates unification. • Feeling puzzled; unsure; lacking clarity • Take time to concentrate or focus your energy; the answer will be forthcoming.

Pyramid

A powerful symbol of inner unification and alignment • A symbol of initiation; you've moved to a new level of awareness and understanding of yourself • You're open to guidance from the higher energies around you and from your higher self.

Python

A significant symbol (See also *Snake*) • Kundalini energy: the life force within you

Quail

Fear; to recoil in dread

Quaker

These people are viewed as generally very balanced; they can represent balance and a peaceful life. • Family, unity, and harmony • Can mean an earthquake

Quarantine

Feeling isolated or in a state of isolation • Feeling separate from your true nature

Quarrel

Different aspects of yourself are at war. Visualize the quarreling parties in your dream discussing each other's position with an attitude of understanding and peace. This will allow you to put at rest the parts of yourself that are fighting.

Quartz

Transmitter; energy conductor • Spirituality • Clarity

Queen

The powerful female energy within you; it has more strength and power than a princess • The wisdom of womanliness rather than the purity of girlhood • The goddess within

Quest

A spiritual journey • Spiritual yearning

Quicksand

Fear; feeling as if you're being pulled under

Quilt

Domestic happiness • Protection • Patchwork quilt: different parts of yourself coming together to make a whole

Rabbi

Guidance; showing the way • Teacher

Rabbit

May indicate prosperity • Temerity; fear • Fertility; children • Gentleness; softness • Going fast with no organization; hopping from one thing to another • Look before you leap.

Race

The only person you're competing with is yourself. Slow down, enjoy the run, and smell the flowers.

Radar

Being able to see beneath the surface • Attunement; intuition

Radio

Communication; guidance from another source

Rage

Allow the anger that has been held in for so long to be expressed. Rage expressed in a dream will allow you to release the rage that's being suppressed in your daily life.

Rags

Feeling of poverty of spirit

Railings

Feeling your boundaries; being aware of your boundaries • Holding on to railings for support

Rain

Cleansing; purifying; emotionally refreshing • May indicate that you're going through an emotional time and a cleansing process

Rainbow

A very powerful symbol of joy, celebration, and completion; you've made it through the emotional difficulty

Ram

Masculine strength • Pioneering spirit • Symbolizes initiation or initiating energy; a new beginning

Rape

Accepting someone else's reality as your own • Feeling penetrated • Loss of power and self-esteem; feeling "ripped off"

Rat
Betrayer; wrongdoer • Letting things gnaw at you • Judging yourself through others' perceptions • A mess; a "rat's nest"

Raven
The unknown; death • Flying into unknown parts of yourself • Fear of the unknown • A messenger from the other side

Razor
Cutting through • Separation; release • A safety razor can signify mental clarity

Recipe
Combining the ingredients of your life so there is unity

Record
Feeling like you're going around and around; stuck in a rut or a groove; same old attitudes or feelings; it's time to step off the treadmill

Red
A powerful color that symbolizes passion, physical strength, anger, sexuality, sensuality, aggression, and danger • Life and creation • Blood • The Chinese looked favorably upon this color and painted their banners red as talismans, and the Mother Goddess in India is painted red because she's associated with creation. Even in prehistoric times, individuals associated red with life. They would stain with blood any object they wished to bring to life.

Red Cross
The sign of healing; self-healing

Redwood Tree
Strength; wisdom; grounded yet with spiritual aspirations

Refrigerator
Feeling emotionally closed off; frozen emotions; lack of warmth

Repair
Something in your life needs mending or repairing. In your daytime hours, repair whatever you were trying to fix in the dream. This symbolic act can help "repair" your life.

Rescue
You need to be rescued; not feeling in control of your life • You feel that others are in control, which comes from the viewpoint of a victim. Remember, there are no victims, there are only volunteers. Begin to move to a place of responsibility for your life and your environment. • Rescuing others; you feel that someone needs help

Restaurant
Sustenance; nourishment • Fellowship

Revolution
Different aspects of yourself are at war; it usually suggests a time of change. When awake, move to a resolution of the rebellion or the revolt.

Revolving Door
Opportunities are being missed or passed. • Feeling like you're moving around and around with old attitudes and ideas

Rhinoceros
A sexual symbol • Powerful; forceful; charging ahead without stopping

Rice
Domestic happiness; wedding; joy; celebration • Good harvest

Riding

Riding an animal represents feelings of alignment with nature, mastery, or conquest. • Riding in a vehicle while someone else is driving; you feel that you're not in charge of your life; someone else is guiding you. • You're being taken for a ride; being deceived.

Ring

Long friendship; marriage; engagement • Promise • Eternal love • Completion; wholeness; unity

River

The river of life; the flowing waters of life • "Don't push the river, it flows by itself." • Trying to swim upstream; allow the river to carry you and don't fight the current • You're trying to get across the river but can't find the way. The river usually represents an emotional barrier you're having trouble crossing. When awake, imagine a bridge across the river and walk to the other side. Make yourself a new route in order to resolve the situation.

Road

Your direction in life • Look carefully at the road. Is it rocky, crooked, or straight? Does it go uphill or downhill? Is the way clear? This represents your destiny, your direction in life. Look for forks in the road, which represent major decisions that need to be made. The condition of the road suggests the way that you're running your life at this moment.

Robber

Tremendous fear and insecurity • Feeling like a victim of life (Remember that the other side of *what is so* is, *so what!* There are no victims.) • Begin to take responsibility for your life; accept responsibility for it. • Go back into your dream and defeat the robber. Become the hero or heroine of your dream, and you'll move toward greater strength and security within yourself.

Robin
A very fortunate omen • Harbinger of good things • New beginnings

Robot
Mechanical feelings • Being shut off from your feelings; unfeeling

Rock
Grounding; strength; personal power • The Rock of Gibraltar

Rocket
Soaring to spiritual heights; unlimited potential and power

Roof (See also *Home/House*)
Your protection; this corresponds to your crown chakra • The condition of your roof suggests the condition of your spiritual connection.

Room (See also *Home/House*)
An aspect of yourself

Rope
An attachment to a person, place, or thing • A lifeline • Neatly coiled rope represents organization and balance of mind, body, and soul. • Frayed or knotted rope: dissociation • Feeling tied up in knots; restricted

Rose
Love; beauty; innocence

Row
A fight; an argument • May represent organization; soldiers in a row

Rowing
Moving through an emotional situation

Royalty
Depending on whether the royal is male or female, this relates to the divine aspects of self; the divine feminine; the divine masculine • Feeling a sense of your own royalty, your own divinity

Running
Stop! Turn around and face the truth. • Running from a situation you aren't ready to face; feeling unsure of yourself; fear of a situation or experience that you're not willing to acknowledge (Turn around and face what you're running from—whether in your dream or when awake—and as you confront your adversary, you'll begin to dissolve the barrier in your daily life.) • Running in slow motion signifies that the time is coming soon when you'll have to face that difficulty. • Running toward something: you're in a time of great acceleration within your spiritual life; celebrate

Rust
Talents or abilities aren't being used. • You are a bit rusty in your skills; polish up those talents and abilities.

Sack
Future events yet to be revealed • Hiding or self-concealment • Getting "sacked"; losing your power

Sacrifice
Someone or something being sacrificed refers to an area of your life where you feel that you're making a sacrifice. (This is martyrdom. See *Martyr.*) • Feeling at the mercy of life rather than in control of it

Saddle
Feeling bound; feeling saddled to a situation that you wish to be free of

Sailboat
Navigating through emotional change • Moving quickly and easily: soaring through emotional change with ease

Saint

Your guardian angel or protector; your higher self • Listen very carefully to the messages, and notice the symbols that occurred in this dream.

Salmon

The sacred fish of the Celts • Moving ahead against all odds

Salt

The salt of the earth • The element earth • Strength and stability • Purification and dispersing negativity • It's reported that Kabbalistic tradition considers salt a sacred word because its numerical value is the same as God's name of power, Yahweh, multiplied three times. • In ancient times, salt was thought to be a substitute for the Mother Goddess's regenerative blood. In both Jewish and Christian religion, salt was considered a substitute for blood on the altar as it came from the womb of the sea and had the savor of blood. • Salt has remarkable purifying properties. In the ocean, it acts as an antiseptic to destroy bacteria.

Sand

The sands of time; nothing is permanent; everything is an illusion • A house built on sand, not on a permanent foundation • Change • Irritations; small, temporary annoyances

Saw

Cutting one down to size • Construction; building; creating; making; doing • Pruning

Scar

An emotional wound from the past is healing but is still not forgotten. Check the other symbols, people, and situations to identify the emotional scarring that still needs to be healed.

Scarecrow
Not real; false • Being afraid; scared • As in *The Wizard of Oz,* not much intellectual ability • Scaring people off with a false front or false appearance

School
The school of life; the lessons you've chosen for yourself in this lifetime • Allow life to be your teacher; let each circumstance and person be your guide to show you the way.

Scientist
Left-brained; analytical; thinking; rational; intelligent; let the heart rule as well as the head

Scissors
Cutting away; releasing that which is unnecessary in your life • Feeling cut off from others or from yourself

Sea (See *Ocean*)

Seam
Coming apart at the seams • That which binds things together

Seasons (See Chapter 22)

Seeds
Great things grow from small beginnings, provided they have all the right ingredients. • A new beginning • "As you sow, so shall you reap."

Seesaw
Feeling that you're going up and down but not getting anywhere

Semen
Power; potency; strength; the creative potential

Sex (See also Chapter 15)
A subconscious sexual energy brooding within you

Shadow
The latent potential of an individual • Fear; illusion • The unknown part of yourself

Shapes
If there are undefined shapes in a dream, when you're awake say, "What does that shape remind me of? What feeling do I have about this shape?" Allow the shape to take form. It can be something unformed or not quite solidified within your life. If you allow the shape to take form in your imagination, soon that project, idea, or feeling will begin to take shape in your life.

Shark
Omen of danger • Hidden fear • Cruel misuse of power

Shave
A close shave; a close call • Grooming; bolstering self-confidence • Monks will shave their heads to show humility and renunciation of the worldly path.

Sheep
Following without using your judgment • Nonthinking trust • Being taken advantage of monetarily; being "fleeced"

Shell
Emptiness; an empty shell • Pulling into your shell; closing off from the outer world • Inactive; nongrowth

Shepherd
Guardian of the spirit; guardian of the inner way

Shield
Your protection that allows you to stay balanced and centered amid change • May symbolize a defense mechanism

Ship (See also *Boat*)
Yourself; your whole self • A time when life is uncertain, particularly in regard to emotions

Shoes
Steps to be taken in life • Grounded; connecting to the earth • Don't judge others until you walk in their shoes. • Filling too many shoes; filling too many roles

Shooting
Shooting at a target: focusing energy for a particular goal • Shooting someone: killing off an aspect of self • Being shot: feeling penetrated; the victim

Shopping
Decisions; choices

Shoulders
Strength • Accepting responsibility • Putting your "shoulder to the wheel"

Shower
Emotional cleansing; cleaning up your act

Signs
Messages hidden in the words of the sign that catch your consciousness

Silk
Luxuries; riches; wealth • Sensuality; ability to flow

Silver
Second best • May be the silver cord; spiritual connection • Inner light

Singing
Celebration; joy; uplifting of spirit; spiritual light • Troubles are over; harmony

Sister
Female aspect of self • Religious aspect; nun • Relatedness; sisterhood

Skeleton
Things unacknowledged; a skeleton in the closet • Doesn't necessarily mean physical death; can mean emptiness; devoid of content

Skiing
Exhilaration • If you're going too fast, may be a sign that you're speeding through life; feeling out of control • Using your skills to master the difficulties in your life

Skunk
Social disapproval • Something "smells" • Inner power of protection

Sky
The heavens; no limitation to success; the sky is the limit • Freedom; expansion

Slave
Being a slave to old habits, ideas, or beliefs • A slave to other people or situations

Sleeping
Dreaming that you're sleeping may mean that you are astral-traveling and are observing yourself from outside your body. • Unwillingness to change; stagnation

Slide
Feeling out of control

Smoke
"Where there's smoke, there's fire"; a warning of danger • Lack of clarity; things are confused • To Native Americans, smoke was the vehicle on which prayers could travel to the Creator, and through which the Creator's blessings could journey back to Earth.

Snail
Things are moving slowly; going at a "snail's pace" • Break out of your shell; get going!

Snake
A very significant symbol that isn't to be feared • Healing; life potency; the power within; Kundalini power • Spiritual awakening; spiritual healing (The two intertwined snakes on Hermes' staff are used as the symbol of the medical profession.) • Feeling tempted or wanting to tempt someone • "Snake in the grass" • Transformation and resurrection

Snow
Cleansing • Purity; a fresh start; a new look at the world; a new beginning • Frozen, blocked emotions

Soap
Cleansing; purification

Soldiers
War within and without • Organization; discipline

Sole
A homophone for *soul,* which is the true heart of the matter

Speedometer
Going too fast; going too slow • Look at the numbers on the meter, then see Chapter 26

Sperm (See *Semen*)

Sphinx
Spiritual understanding • May signify past-life recognition from Egypt

Spider
Industry • The eight legs of the spider signify material wealth; wealth through industry • Trap; entrapment; getting caught in your own web

Spiral
The image of evolution • The intricate component of all of life, the DNA and RNA helix • A very powerful transformational symbol

Spirit
A ghost from the past; a haunting memory • Spirit world trying to contact you

Sponge
Soaking up everything; learning indiscriminately • Sponging off other people; feeling others are sponging off you

Spring (See also Chapter 22)
New growth, new possibilities, and new life

Spy
Feeling unsafe • Being intruded on or intruding on others • Involvement with another person rather than with your development

Square
Stability • Old-fashioned; not in touch with the times; out of step • Boxed in; controlled

Squirrel
Frugality; comfort through patience

Stag
Sexual vigor • Powerful; potent

Stage
The stage of life • The role you play in life • How you think others see you

Stairs
Ascending: a rise in status; success • Descending: loss of recognition; loss of confidence

Star
A significant symbol of light, guidance, and insight • You are your own star; you are your own light.

Statue
Frozen feelings and emotions • Feeling immobile; you can't move • Lifeless • Not coming from your own strength or energy • Needing to work on self-confidence

Steel
Strength; immobility; inflexibility • Determination • A homophone for *steal*

Stomach
You just can't stomach it • Stomach holds nourishment; helps you digest attitudes, ideas, feelings • May indicate an inability to assimilate that which is new; fear of the new

Stones (See also *Rock*)
Leave no stone unturned • Solid • Strong

Stork

New beginnings; new arrival • Conception; birth of a new idea • May be an omen of domestic happiness and contentment

Storm

Internal conflict • The air is clearing in regards to a situation in your life.

Straw

"This is the last straw." • Insubstantial, as in a "house of straw" • "The straw that broke the camel's back"

Sucking

Nursing; nurturing; sustenance • If you're nursing a baby, you're nurturing new ideas, a new way of being. • Something is sucking you dry.

Suicide

Self-guilt; self-persecution • Killing off aspects of yourself • Giving up • A warning not to give up; know that you're never given anything in life that you can't handle, do, or accomplish • A sign to reach out for help from those around you; pray

Summer (See also Chapter 22)

Maximum fulfillment; confidence; happiness; contentment

Sun

God; Great Spirit; Christ; the god within • The Source from which all flows • Power; strength; clarity • Your inner light

Sunflower

Joy • Embracing life

Swamp

Feeling completely bogged down with absolutely no clarity or way to get out; feeling overwhelmed or swamped with work

Swan

The sign of the white goddess • Beauty • Strength • Gliding to new heights; freedom • A black swan may be a sign of the inner mysteries of life and intuition. • The balance of male and female energies • Apollo, the god of music, was aligned with the swan because of the mythic belief that the swan would sing with exquisite beauty at the point of death—the swan song.

Swastika

A symbol that far predates Hitler's abuse of it, the swastika is found in almost every ancient culture in both its clockwise and counterclockwise forms, including Indonesian, Asian, Celtic, Viking, Native American, pre-Columbian, and Germanic cultures. It has been discovered in Christian catacombs in Ireland, Britain, Mycenae, Gascony, and among the Etruscans. • The masculine and feminine aspects of God: clockwise represents the masculine, and counterclockwise symbolizes the feminine aspects of divinity • The creation of the universe in motion because of the rotating arms

Sweets

The sweetness of life • Lovers • Honoring oneself

Swimming

Don't swim against the current • Stay afloat amid emotional changes. • Swimming through a situation

Sword

Defense • Attack • Power; truth; honor • Slaying the ego, inner demons, or illusions

Syrup

Overly sentimental or emotional to the point of insincerity • Stickiness

Table
Putting off a decision; "tabling" a decision or emotion; beliefs that are clearly seen by others • Putting your cards on the table

Tape
Playing the same problems over and over again; stuck in the same pattern • Taping things together may represent unity or unification

Tapestry
The tapestry of life; each part of the tapestry represents a different part of you

Target
Your direction or goal • Self-focus and self-discipline are needed.

Tax
Burden • Being taxed to your limit; the taxing of your strength

Tea
Friendship • Relaxation • Can represent the initial "T"

Teacher
The guru within • Self-reliance • Each person in your life is your teacher; each aspect within a dream is your teacher during the night.

Tears
Releasing; cleansing; balancing

Teeth
Chewing; preparing for digestion • Biting into a problem • Chewing the fat; talking; discussing • If teeth are falling out, it may mean talking too much, scattering your energy, or not understanding a problem or situation. • Loss of teeth may reflect losing "face," a spoiling of the appearance in some way, or a loss of power. According to Edgar Cayce, tooth loss meant careless speech, and false teeth signified

falsehoods. • An infected tooth signifies foul language. • Teeth stand for decisiveness; loss of teeth symbolizes loss of the power of decisive action. • Loss of teeth may symbolize growing up—moving to a new stage of development, just as baby teeth are replaced by permanent teeth. • Loss of teeth may indicate dental problems; check with your dentist.

Telegram
Staying in touch with the world around you • A message from afar or from an estranged part of yourself

Telephone
Listen to others • May indicate a guide who's trying to get your attention; listen carefully to the message • Telephone dreams are important

Telescope
Farseeing, but not all is revealed

Temple
Private retreat; inner sanctuary

Tent
Impermanence; temporary • The image of self isn't solidified

Thread
Karma; fate • A thread of truth • Hanging by a thread

Throat
Positive: being willing to speak your own truth • Negative: feeling strangled • Can't swallow it

Thumb
Thumbs-up means go ahead • Thumbs-down, forget it!

Thunder

Release of suppressed emotions and feelings • The warning voice of the gods • Anger; hostility; rage; the aftermath of a powerful, emotional psychic release • Along with the accompanying lightning, it's the fire from the heavens. It has the power of illumination and contains the creative forces of the universe. Connected with Aries, which is the first sign in the Zodiac, lightning is associated with springtime, initiation, and the initial stages of any project. It's a sign of bringing the fire of creative energy to any project. • Jupiter, the Roman God, used three thunderbolts containing the energies of chance, providence, and destiny to mold future destinies. • Thunder and lightning pierce the darkness like a flash of illumination, revealing truth and giving clarity. In Tibet, the *vajra* is the symbol for both thunderbolt and diamond.

Tidal Wave

A huge emotional upheaval

Tide

The ebbing and flowing of your emotions • The ebb and flow of life

Tiger

Cunning; prowess • Power; energy

Tightrope

Feeling tense; feeling as if you have to walk a tightrope; great pressure and stress

Tires

Mobility; movement • A flat tire means you aren't balanced

Toad (See also *Frog*)

Grounded, fertile energies of the earth

Toilet

Elimination of what isn't needed in your life

Tomb
Transformation, death, and resurrection • Restriction

Tower
Isolation; being locked in an ivory tower; cut off from different aspects of yourself • May represent a spiritual point of clarity; spiritual vision • Freudian therapists suggest that a tower is a phallic symbol.

Toy
Joy; life is play • Feeling that you're being toyed with

Train
The collective and individual journey through stages and events of your life • Power • Perseverance, as in *The Little Engine That Could* • Missing the train can mean missing opportunities in life. • A freight train carrying a heavy load can indicate that you're carrying too heavy of a load in life.

Trash
Junk; emotional junk that you're carrying around; letting go of it; eliminating it; releasing it

Treadmill
Feeling that you're getting nowhere; you're stuck with the same beliefs, attitudes, and thoughts

Treasure
Original ideas; personal wealth • Inner wealth; gifts from Spirit

Trees
Life and knowledge • Family matters; a family tree • Life's development • Feeling rooted and grounded on the Earth plane, yet soaring to spiritual heights • Old, gnarled tree: wisdom and strength • Slender willow tree: being able to bond with circumstances • Aspen: fear; quaking with fear • Oak: strength • Pine: spiritual clarity; purification

• Cedar: clarity; spirituality • Apple: see *Apple* • Other fruit trees: bearing fruit in life • Palm: warmth; freedom • The meaning can depend on whether the tree is just beginning to leaf, is full with leaves, losing its leaves, or has no leaves (see Chapter 22). • Is the tree straight or crooked? As the tree bends, so it grows.

Triangle
Trinity; protection; body, mind, and spirit • Integration • Power of the pyramids

Tunnel
Light at the end of the tunnel • Inner passageway to the self • Tunnel vision; close-mindedness • An out-of-body experience (often you'll have a dream of moving through a tunnel) • May signify a near-death experience; changing realities or levels of consciousness

Turtle
A powerful symbol • Slow but steady progress toward the goal • Completion through diligence • May signify a wish or a need to withdraw from a problem and go inward to gather forces

UFO
Personal integration; psychic potential; higher intelligence • Fear of the unknown; fear of unknown aspects of yourself

Umbrella
Protection; being sheltered from life's storms

Uncle
Crying "uncle"; giving up • Feeling foolish; being a "monkey's uncle" • May refer to your uncles

Underground
Your unconscious; your subconscious

Undertaker
Undertaking an unpleasant situation or experience

Undressed
Feeling exposed • Personal secrets being revealed; being open

Unicorn
A powerful symbol • Traditionally, the symbol of Christ; spiritual unfoldment; purity; virginity • A symbol of sexuality

Uniform
Rigidity; inflexibility • Authority

University
Center of healing

Upper Lip
Carrying on in spite of difficulties; keeping a stiff upper lip

Urine
Relief from tension • Emotional release; cleansing • A need to relieve yourself

Urn
"Ashes to ashes, dust to dust" • Reincarnation

Vacation
Enjoyment; relaxation • Letting go; release • Take a new look at your ideas and goals.

Vaccination
Emotional protection

Vacuum
Feeling as if you're living in a vacuum; isolated; uncreative • Clean or remove that which isn't needed; eliminate the negativity in your life.

Vagina
Openness; acceptance; receptivity • Womanliness • The inner valley of the spirit • If you've had any negative sexual experiences where the vagina was involved (either your own or someone else's), this sign can be bringing repressed memories to the forefront for release.

Valley
The low point in life; the mountains and valleys in life • A need to pull inward; feel sheltered for a time

Vampire
Exhaustion • Draining of vitality by others

Velvet
Sensuality • Look to see what's beneath the surface.

Ventriloquist
What you hear might be wrong or inaccurate information. • Voicing someone else's opinions rather than your own

Veterinarian
Healing your animal nature

Vine
A spiritual connection

Vineyard
Harvesting the fruits of your labor and experiences

Virgin
Purity; chastity • Mother Mary; the female aspect of God • Newness; a fresh phase in life

Volcano
Explosion of suppressed emotions

Vomit

Getting rid of what you don't need; releasing old ideas, attitudes, and beliefs • A need to express and communicate anything that you're holding back or is making you sick • Getting things out in the open

Vulture

Feeling as if there's something or someone waiting for you to make an error • A need to clean away something that you consider complete or "dead"

Waiter/Waitress

Being of service to others or to yourself • Feeling that you have to wait on others • A sign that you need to have patience and "wait"

Walking

Your goals will be met through a slow but sure pace.

Wall

An obstacle; a blockage • Feeling walled off from others

Wallet

The personal beliefs and thoughts that you hold privately • Your identity; loss of your wallet can be a loss of identity

Wand

Spirituality • You can change things instantly; transformation

War

Conflict; inner aggression • Unresolved issues

Warehouse

Your potential; all that you ever need is within

Washing

Releasing the past; forgiving • Letting go of old attitudes and beliefs

Wasp
Feeling threatened • Stinging thoughts or words

Watch
The passage of time • A sign that says that you need to "watch" for the signs around you • Watch out.

Water
Emotional energy; intuition • Check to see whether the water is clear or murky. • Spiritual alignment and attunement; your unconscious self; the waters of life • The mysterious realms of the archetypal female energy • Fertility, new life, and new creative potential • The Chinese considered water to be the source of all life. • In Christian baptismal rites, water represented life, death, and resurrection. When one was submerged underwater, the former person disappeared and a new one emerged. • The birthing process is accompanied by uterine fluid, providing another analogy between water and life.

Waterfall
Complete healing; emotional release • Emotional recharging

Wave
Waving at someone or someone waving at you; love; connection; acknowledgment • An ocean wave suggests surging forward; great strength and power • Using your emotions creatively • Watching waves symbolizes recharging your inner batteries.

Wax
Easily molded; the situation can be changed • Cleaning; making a surface shiny; making something look new

Weasel
Treachery; betrayal • Feeling someone is pushing you out of the way or "weaseling in" on your territory

Weather
Your emotional state; your health • Clear weather: excellent health • Stormy weather: some area in your body may need alignment

Weaving
The pattern of your life woven in and out; the tapestry of your life • Putting things together; creating wholeness

Web
Feeling caught or entangled • Beware of a trap • The pattern of your life: you are the weaver

Wedding
Union of your conscious and unconscious, of your body and spirit

Well
Inner riches; wisdom accumulated from past experiences

Whale
A significant symbol • Perception; intuition • Tremendous power and strength • May concern the size of something; a "whale" of a job • May indicate a cry for help, as in a "wail"

Wheel
The wheel of life • The wheel of fortune • The wheel of karma; sowing and reaping; endings and beginnings; completion; never-ending change

Whisper
Feeling held back • Being unwilling or unable to communicate what's in your heart and mind

Whistle
A warning; something is trying to get your attention

Willow
Sadness • Being able to bend and move as the situation warrants

Wind
The winds of change • The element of Air, representing thought and intellect • Messages from the realm of Spirit, the celestial breath of God • Changing winds may signify changes coming up for you. • In many native traditions throughout the world, it's believed that the wind carries messages from the realm of Spirit. Each directional wind carries its own meaning, which varies from tribe to tribe. For example, in some traditions, the North Wind brings messages from personal ancestors.

Window
Interdimensional viewing; being able to see different levels of consciousness • Seeing the future or the past

Wine
Prosperity; abundance • Celebration • Relaxation • Spiritual attunement, with wine representing the blood of Christ or the spiritual energy within; God

Wings
Freedom; soaring

Witch
The current implication of being fearsome or ugly • The word *witch* comes from *wicca,* meaning "wise woman"; it may represent the wise female energy within you.

Wolf
Community and social feeling; family support • Fear, especially being pressed for something without having the resources to meet the need; a "wolf" at the door • Inappropriate flirtatious behavior

Womb
Nourishment; safety; protection • Pulling in your energies and regrouping before the next endeavor

Worm
Hidden preparation or work beneath the surface • Lowlife; no backbone • Being intruded on; those who are "worming" their way in

X-ray
Unseen forces • Seeing what's within with more clarity and understanding • Inner depths; inner comprehension

Yawn
Boredom; need for another outlet for creativity

Yo-Yo
Feeling as if you're going up and down; repeating the same patterns

Zero
The zero hour • Feeling that you are nothing; emptiness • Absolute completeness, because the physical representation of zero is a circle, which is a universal symbol of unity, wholeness, and infinity • Ground zero

🐚🐚🐚 🐚🐚🐚

Chapter 29

Starting a Dream Group

A powerful way to connect more deeply with your dreams is to join a dream support group or start one yourself. A dream group consists of individuals who periodically meet to share and discuss their dreams. This provides encouragement and support in your dream journey.

Purpose

To form a dream group, first determine the purpose for the gathering. Perhaps you want to develop individual psychic abilities or process daytime difficulties through examining your theater of the night. Write down your intentions in clear, concise language so that each group member can consciously choose to be in alignment with the group's purpose. This first step is imperative and will enhance the synergy in future meetings. Decide on a time—perhaps once a week—when it's convenient for all members to attend.

Each dream group will have its own dynamics. However, here's a simple format you might consider: for the first meeting, sit in a circle and go around to each person so that all members briefly share something about themselves. Each individual should include personal information, such as goals, purpose in life, and so on. Let the first meeting be a time for clarification of purpose and intent, as well as for developing the beginnings of synergy among all members of the group.

Grounding

Each time you gather, begin the session by devoting a few moments to centering and relaxing. (You may wish to have a leader for this process.) All members should be in a circle, sitting with their spines straight and feeling very relaxed. Form a grounding cord by imagining a silver light moving up, from the earth through the soles of your feet and the base of your spine, and on up and out the top of your head, cascading around you like a waterfall. After all members have completed this, begin breathing in the essence of each individual in the circle. Take a deep breath, breathing each person into your being, and then slowly releasing him or her. As you do so, imagine everyone as strong, healthy, and well balanced. This process weaves a deep spiritual connection among all the dreamers in the group. Next, breathe in the essence of your own being three times. Imagine a brilliant silver white light spinning around the group, creating a whirlpool of energy and light. When everyone has completed this meditation, take just a few moments of silence before proceeding with the dream sharing.

Dream Sharing

In sharing around the circle, it's necessary that each person be given adequate time to relate his or her dreams. If an individual feels that the events of the week are connected to the dream in some way, sharing these events may be valuable. It's important to keep in mind, however, that it's really easy to wander from the point, so others may be denied a chance to share. To prevent this, you might want to create a time limit. Also, before selecting a specific dream to work with, make sure that everyone has had a chance to speak. Not being able to share a dream simply because you've run out of time can be very disappointing. Since every dream is a composite of multitudes of complex images spanning several dimensions, it would be easy to devote several sessions to only one dream. Keep in mind the value of doing some work with each dream shared by those in the group.

When each member has the opportunity to communicate dreams, this begins to build a deep connection with the others in the group. As a result, you'll experience a heightened sense of telepathy among the members and even a similarity of dream symbols.

When sharing your dream, always use the present tense rather than the past—for example, "I am running," rather than "I was running." This enables you to be far more present with the dream as you communicate it to others. Also, speaking in the first person will usually make it easier to discover new insights about yourself. When an individual begins to share a dream using the present tense and then slips back into past tense, it generally indicates a point in the dream where there are difficult emotions. It's valuable to point this out to the dreamer. Occasionally this will enable the person to experience a revelation, an "Aha!"

Listen carefully to the specific words people use in describing their experience, and closely observe the dreamers' body language as they express the dream.

Maintain the attitude that each dreamer in the group is a different reflection of yourself. As a dream's secrets unfold to the others, it will generate a new awakening within you. Pay attention to the manner in which each person discusses the dream. Every dream will have special significance for you, for each person's dream is also about you. You've all been drawn together because of similar energies. All of the others in the dream group are present with you. For each session, appoint a leader who can keep the group on track. One means of doing so is to establish a revolving leadership, with a different member in charge at each new meeting.

Dream Meanings

When a dream is selected to be explored more closely by the entire group, it's valuable for the person sharing the dream to hear everyone's insights. However, it's crucial that the dreamer accept only what "feels right" regarding the others' interpretations.

If your group is an especially expressive one, you might have occasional "theme weeks." One week you may all decide to incubate for prophetic dreams concerning the coming year. Another week you might focus on emotional cleansing of blockages formed during childhood. If you're feeling especially whimsical, you might devote a week to telepathic communication with aliens. More practically, perhaps the theme of the week may be to analyze the actions of the stock market. You might also devote a week to healing—night healing, day healing, or self-healing.

Be creative in your dream groups. In one session, you could all dance your dreams; in another, you may come equipped with crayons and paper to draw your dreams. You might choose to select dream partners and dream for each other during the week, setting aside one specific evening for this purpose. I've discovered this last exercise to be especially powerful for me in gaining insights into myself. Often what is a blind spot for one dreamer is easily perceived by another. Even those with relatively little experience in dream work have been able to dream for another, unwrapping symbols extremely significant for that person.

Bring your dream journals to each session, sharing them freely with one another. You can also set apart a section in your journal where you note some of the insights given by others in the group.

Other creative ways to explore your dreams are to construct a dream mask or dream shield. Also, the group as a whole could take a particularly significant dream and act it out as a play, with each member taking a different role in the dream script.

Set a specific starting and ending time so that members have some idea of how long they may take in sharing their dream. This plan ensures a sense of completion for each one in the group . . . and have fun!

ᗪ ᗪ ᗪ   ᗪ ᗪ ᗪ

THE ENDING

Row, row, row your boat
Gently down the stream,
Merrily, merrily, merrily, merrily
Life is but a dream.

꿈 꿈 꿈

ACKNOWLEDGMENTS

Thank you, Leon Nacson, for having the dream that inspired me to write this book. You are a wonderful friend.

Allison Harter, what an immense blessing it is to have you in our lives. I am so grateful for the depth of your kindness and support.

Ann Sewell, it was your unwavering dedication that took this book to its completion. Your willingness to consistently and undauntedly persevere will always be an inspiration to me. You brought this book to life.

To the Computer Mystic and Agent of Fortune, Karl Bettinger, I give my sincere thanks.

Thanks, Barb Kelly. You made creating this book so much fun. Who would think typing copy could be funny?

To my wonderful editor in chief at Hay House, Jill Kramer, thank you so much for your support and love! To Hay House editor Lisa Mitchell, I can't begin to tell you what a joy it's been working with you on this book.

Jane Bakkan, as your long-awaited child grew within you, your gentle magic helped give birth to this book. Thank you.

Barbara Roper, your quiet wisdom warmed many late nights.

Alice Allen, thank you for guiding us softly down the path of graciousness.

Lydia Christofides, thank you for your remarkable insights.

Anne Sweet, your poems carried us on dream wings of the night.

Thanks, Cheryl Steinle, for your steadfast dedication.

Phillip Crockford, you're always part of our family. Thanks for your help with the Chinese Clock section. I'm deeply grateful.

Thank you, Ken Collbung (Nundjan Djiridjakin), spiritual leader and senior male clan leader of the Australian Aborigine Bibulmun tribe, for your insights and support.

To Glynn Braddy, I'm glad you're in our life.

Much thanks to Dancing Feather, friend and teacher. You are never far from my heart.

𝒟 𝒟 𝒟   𝒟 𝒟 𝒟

ENDNOTES

Chapter 1

1. Sharon Begley, "The Stuff That Dreams Are Made Of," *Newsweek,* August 14, 1989, pp. 41–44.

2. Michael E. Long, "What Is This Thing Called Sleep?" *National Geographic,* December 1987, pp. 790–91.

3. Ibid., pp. 787–88, 802.

4. Ibid., pp. 792, 802, 818.

5. Jill Morris, *The Dream Workbook* (New York: Fawcett Crest, 1985), p. 15.

6. Ibid., p. 16.

7. Ibid.

8. Ibid., p. 13.

9.   Ibid., pp. 16–17.

10. Nerys Dee, *Your Dreams and What They Mean* (New York: Bell Publishing Company, 1984), pp. 43–44. (U.K. edition: Aquarian Press, 1984.)

11. Long, p. 820.

12. Jeremy Taylor, *Dream Work* (Mahwah, NJ: Paulist Press, 1983), p. 6. (U.K. distributor: Fowler Wright.)

13. Ibid., pp. 6–7.

14. Ibid., p. 7.

15. Ibid., pp. 7–8.

Chapter 2

1.   Nerys Dee, *Your Dreams and What They Mean* (New York: Bell Publishing Company, 1984), pp. 56–57. (U.K. edition: Aquarian Press, 1984.)

2.   Ibid., p. 57.

3.   Ibid., pp. 58–59.

4.   Jean Dalby Clift and Wallace B. Clift, *Symbols of Transformation in Dreams* (New York: The Crossroad Publishing Company, 1987), pp. 6–7.

5.   Ibid., p. 7.

6.   Ibid., pp. 11–12.

7.   Ibid., pp. 12–13.

8. Dee, p. 62.

9. Clift and Clift, pp. 9–10; Dee, pp. 62–63.

10. Clift and Clift, p. 14.

11. Ibid., p. 17.

Chapter 3

1. Harmon H. Bro and Hugh Lynn Cayce, ed., *Edgar Cayce on Dreams* (New York: Warner Books, 1968), p. 7.

2. Ibid.

3. Ibid., p. 8.

4. Ibid., pp. 8–9.

5. Ibid., pp. 16–19.

6. Ibid., pp. 11–32.

7. Ibid.

Chapter 4

1. Patricia Garfield, *Creative Dreaming* (New York: Ballantine Books, 1974), p. 215.

2. Ibid., pp. 20–21.

3. Nerys Dee, *Your Dreams and What They Mean* (New York: Bell Publishing Company, 1984), p. 14. (U.K. edition: Aquarian Press, 1984.)

4. Ibid., p. 15.

5. Dee, pp. 15–16; Jean Dalby Clift and Wallace B. Clift, *Symbols of Transformation in Dreams* (New York: The Crossroad Publishing Company, 1987), p. 90; Ann Faraday, *The Dream Game* (New York: Harper & Row, 1974), p. 63.

6. Dee, p. 16; Garfield, p. 24.

7. Garfield, pp. 24–25.

8. Dee, pp. 16–17.

9. Ibid., pp. 17–18.

10. Ibid., p. 18.

11. As quoted in Garfield, p. 26.

12. Garfield, p. 26.

13. Dee, pp. 18, 22.

14. Ibid., p. 23.

15. Ibid., pp. 25–26.

Chapter 5

1. Patricia Garfield, *Creative Dreaming* (New York: Ballantine Books, 1974), pp. 59–60.

2. Jeremy Taylor, *Dream Work* (Mahwah, NJ: Paulist Press, 1983), p. 108. (U.K. distributor: Fowler Wright.)

3. Ibid.

4. Ibid., pp. 108–9.

5. Ibid., p. 109.

6. Garfield, p. 69.

7. Ibid., p. 73.

8. Ibid., pp. 71–72.

Chapter 7

1. George Frederick Kunz, *Curious Lore of Precious Stones* (Philadelphia: J. B. Lippincott Company, 1913), pp. 176–224. (U.K. edition: Dover Publications, 1972.)

Chapter 8

1. Patricia Garfield, *Creative Dreaming* (New York: Ballantine Books, 1974), pp. 20–21.

2. Ibid., pp. 21–23.

Chapter 9

1. Patricia Garfield, *Creative Dreaming* (New York: Ballantine Books, 1974), pp. 151–69; Stephen LaBerge, *Lucid Dreaming* (New York: Ballantine Books, 1985), pp. 23–25, 144–45.

2. Michael E. Long, "What Is This Thing Called Sleep?" *National Geographic,* December 1987, p. 787.

Chapter 10

1. Virginia Bass, ed., *Dreams Can Point the Way: An Anthology* (Sugar Land, TX: Miracle House Books, 1984), p. 145.

Chapter 11

1. Eve Loman, *You Are What You Dream* (Greenwich, CT: Fawcett Publications, 1972), pp. 61–62.

Chapter 12

1. Marcia Moore and Mark Douglas, *Reincarnation, Key to Immortality* (York Cliffs, ME: Arcane Publications, 1968), pp. 17–31.

Chapter 13

1. Carlos Castaneda, *Journey to Ixtlan* (New York: Simon and Schuster, 1972). (U.K. edition: Penguin, 1990.)

2. Oliver Fox, *Astral Projection* (New Hyde Park, NY: University Books, 1962), pp. 32–33.

3. Herbert B. Greenhouse, *The Astral Journey* (New York: Avon Books, 1974), p. 4.

4. Ibid.

5. Ibid.

6. Ibid., pp. 4–8.

7. Ibid., pp. 9, 13.

8.   Ibid., pp. 15–16.

9.   Ibid., pp. 16–18.

Chapter 15

1.   Patricia Garfield, *Creative Dreaming* (New York: Ballantine Books, 1974), p. 104.

2.   Ibid., pp. 104–5.

Chapter 25

1.   G. A. Dudley, *Dreams: Their Mysteries Revealed* (Wellingborough, Northamptonshire, England: Aquarian Press, 1979), p. 78.

2.   Ibid.

3.   Ibid., pp. 78–79.

4.   Ibid., pg. 79.

5.   Ibid., pp. 79–80.

Ð Ð Ð   Ð Ð Ð

INDEX

ABOUT THE AUTHOR

Denise Linn's personal journey began as a result of a near-death experience at age 17. Her life-changing experiences and remarkable recovery set her on a spiritual quest that led her to explore the healing traditions of many cultures, including those of her own Cherokee ancestors, the Aborigines in the Australian bush, and the Zulus in Bophuthatswana. She trained with a Hawaiian kahuna (shaman) and Reiki Master Hawayo Takata. She was also adopted into a New Zealand Maori tribe. In addition, Denise lived in a Zen Buddhist monastery for more than two years.

Denise is an internationally renowned teacher in the field of self-development. She's the author of the bestseller *Sacred Space* and the award-winning *Feng Shui for the Soul,* and has written 16 books, which are available in 24 languages. Denise has appeared in numerous documentaries and television shows worldwide; gives seminars on six continents; and is the founder of the International Institute of Soul Coaching®, which offers professional certification programs in life coaching.

For information about Denise's certification program and other lectures, please visit her Website: **www.DeniseLinn.com**, or write to her at:

Denise Linn Seminars
P.O. Box 759
Paso Robles, California 93447

ॐ ॐ ॐ   ॐ ॐ ॐ

Notes

Notes

Notes

Notes

Notes

Notes

Notes

Notes

Notes

Notes

Notes

Notes

Hay House Titles of Related Interest

YOU CAN HEAL YOUR LIFE, *the movie,*
starring Louise L. Hay & Friends
(available as a 1-DVD program and an expanded 2-DVD set)
Watch the trailer at: **www.LouiseHayMovie.com**

THE SHIFT, *the movie,*
starring Dr. Wayne W. Dyer
(available as a 1-DVD program and an expanded 2-DVD set)
Watch the trailer at: **www.DyerMovie.com**

🕉 🕉 🕉

ANGEL NUMBERS 101: *The Meaning of 111, 123, 444, and Other Number Sequences,* by Doreen Virtue

ANIMAL SPIRIT GUIDES: *An Easy-to-Use Handbook for Identifying and Understanding Your Power Animals and Animal Spirit Helpers,* by Steven D. Farmer, Ph.D.

COURAGEOUS DREAMING: *How Shamans Dream the World into Being,* by Alberto Villoldo, Ph.D.

CRYSTAL THERAPY: *How to Heal and Empower Your Life with Crystal Energy,* by Doreen Virtue, Ph.D., with Judith Lukomski

MESSAGES FROM SPIRIT: *The Extraordinary Power of Oracles, Omens, and Signs,* by Colette Baron-Reid

REPETITION: *Past Lives, Life, and Rebirth,* by Doris Eliana Cohen, Ph.D.

A STREAM OF DREAMS: *The Ultimate Dream Decoder for the 21st Century,* by Leon Nascon

WHAT COLOR IS YOUR PERSONALITY? *Red, Orange, Yellow, Green . . . ,* by Carol Ritberger, Ph.D.

All of the above are available at your local bookstore,
or may be ordered by contacting Hay House (see last page).

🕉 🕉 🕉

🐚 🐚 🐚

We hope you enjoyed this Hay House book.
If you'd like to receive our online catalog featuring additional
information on Hay House books and products, or if you'd like
to find out more about the Hay Foundation, please contact:

Hay House, Inc.
P.O. Box 5100
Carlsbad, CA 92018-5100

(760) 431-7695 or **(800) 654-5126**
(760) 431-6948 (fax) or **(800) 650-5115 (fax)**
www.hayhouse.com® • **www.hayfoundation.org**

🐚 🐚 🐚

Published and distributed in Australia by:
Hay House Australia Pty. Ltd., 18/36 Ralph St., Alexandria NSW 2015
Phone: 612-9669-4299 • *Fax:* 612-9669-4144 • www.hayhouse.com.au

Published and distributed in the United Kingdom by:
Hay House UK, Ltd., 292B Kensal Rd., London W10 5BE
Phone: 44-20-8962-1230 • *Fax:* 44-20-8962-1239 • www.hayhouse.co.uk

Published and distributed in the Republic of South Africa by:
Hay House SA (Pty), Ltd., P.O. Box 990, Witkoppen 2068 • *Phone/Fax:*
27-11-467-8904 info@hayhouse.co.za • www.hayhouse.co.za

Published in India by: Hay House Publishers India,
Muskaan Complex, Plot No. 3, B-2, Vasant Kunj, New Delhi 110 070
Phone: 91-11-4176-1620 • *Fax:* 91-11-4176-1630 • www.hayhouse.co.in

Distributed in Canada by: Raincoast,
9050 Shaughnessy St., Vancouver, B.C. V6P 6E5 • *Phone:*
(604) 323-7100 • *Fax:* (604) 323-2600 • www.raincoast.com

🐚 🐚 🐚

Take Your Soul on a Vacation

Visit **www.HealYourLife.com®** to regroup, recharge,
and reconnect with your own magnificence.
Featuring blogs, mind-body-spirit news, and life-changing
wisdom from Louise Hay and friends.

Visit **www.HealYourLife.com** today!